# SURVIVING CISSY

## Praise for *Surviving Cissy*

"Kathy not only gives us the insider's look at TV's classic, *Family Affair*; she also shares the affairs of her own family with detailed accounts of their influence and guidance through her journey. The result is an uplifting message to guide all of us to get the most out of life."

—PAUL LISNEK, WGN-TV; host, *Broadway in Chicago Backstage*, Comcast Network

"Kathy Garver didn't just survive after Cissy, she thrived! All too often we hear of child stars whose best years were their first years. This was not and is not the case for the talented author of this book. Kathy shines as an all-too-rare exception of how to be a young star and gracefully transition through a life filled with normalcy . . . Hollywood style."

—NEAL SABIN, creator, MeTV Network

"There are very few former child stars lucky enough to continue working in Hollywood in their adult years. Kathy is one of those—but luck had nothing to do with it. This book could have been called *Surviving Cissy: The Art of Reinvention,* because, in it, she proves to be a master of that craft. Kathy is someone who has garnered both experience and friends with each surprising twist and turn her life has taken."

—JON PROVOST, actor, *Lassie*

"If you like a great book, you'll love *Surviving Cissy*. I was producer/production manager of all Don Fedderson's family shows, including *Family Affair*, and can attest that Kathy was the talented and hardworking backbone of that show. She has continued her acting career with films, TV, the stage, and voice-overs. In this book, she has transferred her experiences onto the page so everyone will know where the multitalented Kathy Garver has been!"

—JOHN G. STEPHENS, executive producer and production manager whose work includes *My Three Sons*, *Family Affair*, and *Simon and Simon*; creator and producer of *Major Dad*; author of *From* My Three Sons *to* Major Dad

# SURVIVING CISSY

## My *Family Affair* of Life in Hollywood

KATHY GARVER

Foreword by Patty Duke

LP
LYONS PRESS
Guilford, Connecticut

LYONS PRESS

An imprint of The Rowman & Littlefield Publishing Group, Inc.
4501 Forbes Blvd., Ste. 200
Lanham, MD 20706
www.rowman.com

Distributed by NATIONAL BOOK NETWORK


Lyons Press Paperback Edition 2021



British Library Cataloguing in Publication Information available

**Library of Congress Cataloging-in-Publication Data available**

ISBN 978-1-4930-5932-4 (paper : alk. paper)
ISBN 978-1-63076-116-5 (electronic)

∞™ The paper used in this publication meets the minimum requirements of American National Standard for Information Sciences—Permanence of Paper for Printed Library Materials, ANSI/NISO Z39.48-1992.

*To my Mom and Dad*

# CONTENTS

# FOREWORD

In reading your book, it's not surprising that we had so much in common as child actors.

I confess here that I always envied how pretty you were in *Family Affair*. You've proved then and since your talent and skills as an actress.

Kathy dear, you took my breath away several times as I read of the life challenges you faced.

You inspire me to rededicate myself to my career and use my imagination as you have done to remain vital in your career and, most importantly, in your life and family.

Thank you for writing this book. I needed it.

—Anna Patty Duke

# PROLOGUE

## *A Hair-Raising Audition*

It was my third year as a student at UCLA; I was sharing a room at the Pi Beta Phi sorority with my good friend and the president of the sorority house, Sandy Blue. At 2:00 p.m., the phone suddenly jangled me out of my concentrated study, having reread paragraph one in my Psychology 101 textbook three times. Half-falling out of my single bunk, I stumbled over to the prized private phone, courtesy of my roommate's vaunted political position. I mumbled a hoarse, "Hello?"

Hazel McMillan, my theatrical agent, excitedly told me she had an audition for me. It was for a new television series called *Family Affair.* The show had already been sold to CBS, thirty-two episodes, an interesting anomaly in show business where pilots are first made and then hawked.

Now fully alert, I listened raptly as Hazel explained the setup. It seemed simple: A bachelor uncle and his valet live in a posh penthouse in the sophisticated city of New York. Suddenly they become caretakers of the bachelor's two orphaned nieces and a nephew from the countrified town of Terre Haute, Indiana. The show was cast except for one remaining family member. The front office had to quickly complete the main cast with a blond teenager. The producer wanted to see me that afternoon.

There was a slight problem: I wasn't blond, and I wasn't a teenager. Well, I am blond now, but back then, my hair was a very dark brown. It was panic time. But I was sure my mother had the solution; or rather she had the can. That's right, an aerosol can of Streaks and Tips. Streaks and Tips was the name of a sticky spray in the sixties that, spattered onto the hair, would instantly change its color.

I confidently told Hazel that yes, of course, I would be there for my appointment at 4:00 p.m.

I quickly called my mother and asked her to hurry over with a can to the sorority house from her home twenty minutes away; we had to be across town in two hours. Rushing to the drugstore to buy the aerosol, my mother then sped to the sorority, fully armed. I held my hands like a double salute to my forehead so that the streaky substance would not get into my eyes or dye my eyelashes blond.

Thus protected, I peeked out as my mother then attacked me and my short hair with professional velocity. She quickly moved the spray to and fro, painting glistening, golden streaks onto my brunette locks. The dark curls eventually lightened, but it seemed as if a steel helmet had been plastered to my head; my Vidal Sassoon do was immovable to the touch, and I felt like one of the gilded characters from the James Bond movie *Goldfinger.*

I dressed as young as I could in my best preppy outfit; my character was supposed to be fifteen years old. I had just turned twenty. I felt that I could pass as a teenager, though. I was still going up to Mammoth Mountain in California on weekends, scrunching low at the ticket office and buying a twelve-and-under child's ski-lift ticket. Who can tell one's real age under all those bulky layers? Having a baby face and being five-foot-one also helps.

The producers wanted someone older who could play younger—always a plus for productions, because once a juvenile hit the magical age of eighteen, he or she could work the hours of an adult and not be restricted by the child labor laws. I planned on telling them I was eighteen.

I hurriedly put on my maroon crewneck wool sweater and matching skirt as my mother urged me to "make haste slowly," and we then sped away from the comforting pastel sorority house. Next it was time to fight the traffic from Westwood to Hollywood and meet with Edmund Hartmann, one of the creators and producers of *Family Affair.* Virginia Martindale, the efficient casting director, had hired me for several previous roles and knew my skills; Hazel had confidently coaxed her into having me go "direct to producer." The powers that be were anxious to find a perfect girl quickly for the starring role of the teenage Catherine Patterson Davis.

So, there I was in Mr. Hartmann's office with my resplendent streaked and glistening hair. The pleasant secretary had escorted me in and left with a smile. I sat nervously, and Mr. Hartmann started chatting with me. He then executed an almost comical double take and asked, "What's wrong with your hair?"

"My hair?" I warbled innocently.

"Yes," he said. "It's turning green!"

Realizing that Ed Hartmann was not doing a female remake of *The Boy with Green Hair,* I chuckled a little and then too brightly said, "Oh, it must be the light."

I'm sure I was quite a colorful sight, with my yellow hair and red face. But the rigid golden bouffant broke the ice, and Mr. Hartmann and I started laughing and chatting, and he liked me a lot.

The next day, Hazel called again. She informed me that the producers and casting director had decided to order a screen test for me. Next week, I was to report to Desilu Studios, where they were shooting the pilot episode. In the interim, I was to go to Max Factor (the premier beauty salon and supply store in Hollywood) to be fitted with a hairpiece and then to wardrobe to be fitted with a dress. The hairstylist chose a long blond wig for me. The wardrobe mistress selected a frilly blue cotton dress. I felt and most likely looked like adventurous Alice, about to descend the rabbit hole into Wonderland.

The following week, my mother drove me to Desilu Gower Studios, not Wonderland, for my screen test. On set, I wandered around the fabricated living room looking at the various paintings on the faux walls, much as Alice had examined her new surroundings in the rabbit warren. I admired the expensive furniture that had been chosen to decorate the interior of the luxurious penthouse apartment where Bill Davis would be residing with his manservant.

During a break in the shooting, director James Sheldon, with whom I had previously worked on *The Patty Duke Show* and *The Bing Crosby Show*, interviewed me on camera. I believe the producers basically wanted to see my personality. They had already viewed the TV episode of *Death Valley Days* in which I had starred the year previous. In that show, I had played the young Isadora Duncan opposite June Lockhart. I was eighteen, playing a twelve-year-old. I'm sure the *Family Affair* producers thought that if I could play a twelve-year-old, I could certainly play a believable fifteen-year-old, and they had told Hazel they thought I was an excellent actress, a review with which she heartily concurred. Now, could I follow direction and carry on an intelligible conversation?

Mr. Sheldon had noticed me touring the set and asked me what I had observed. I told him I admired the artwork and we got into a lively discussion about creativity. He then asked what my acting experience was. With over sixty television shows, forty commercials, eight feature films, and several stage plays to my credit

June Lockhart and I starring in an episode of *Death Valley Days*. This show helped seal the deal for me to garner the role of Cissy in *Family Affair.*

The dramatic role of Isadora Duncan showed the *Family Affair* producers my strengths—also how an eighteen-year-old could believably play a twelve-year-old.

since I began as a child in show business, I had lots to talk about. It helped to have had three years of college under my preppy belt and look fifteen.

Now the wait.

Hazel called the next day. I quickly dove for the phone in my room at the Pi Phi house. My agent triumphantly told me that not only had I been cast in my second role on the TV show *This Is the Life* (also cast by Virginia Martindale), but . . . had landed the starring role of the regular part of Cissy in the new CBS television series *Family Affair.* Jumping with a quick leap of joy, I let out a small scream, which brought girls in various states of dress racing and chattering to my door.

"Shh," I told them. Hazel was still talking.

"There is a caveat," my proficient agent interjected.

"What?" I asked nervously.

"The producers love you," Hazel informed me. "But they requested that you never wear that blond wig or that blue dress again!"

I heartily chanted, "No problem!"

All the girls echoed, "No problem!"

It was a very good day. And in my growing spiritual connections, it was interesting to me that a religious show, *This Is the Life*, was coupled with a series that was destined to become a beloved classic and make me a cultural icon.

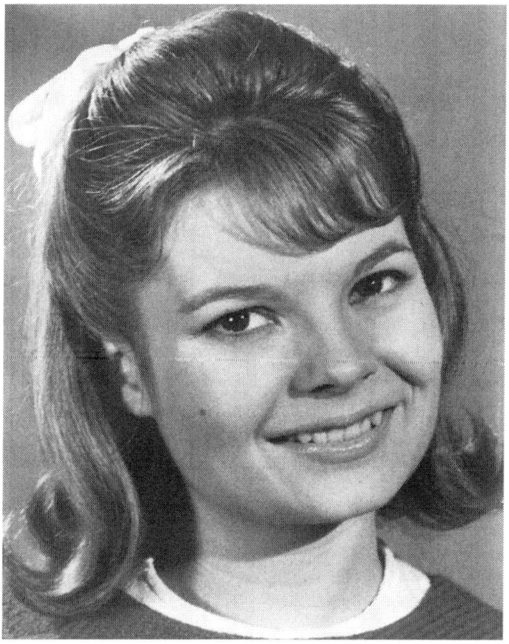

The first year as Cissy on *Family Affair.*

# 1

# Beginning of the Threads

Appearing in successful projects that have become classics has been a joy and a challenge throughout my career in show business. The business hasn't always been a cakewalk or even a cupcake walk. It's hard to be an actress. At any age it's tough, but it's especially difficult when you begin performing at the tender age of three. Many child actors don't survive the grueling work schedules, emotional demands, and unrelenting publicity.

It is also intimidating when your first day of professional work is to cower in a corner on a set at RKO Studios, watching in fright as actor Robert Mitchum hurtles down creaky steps into a faux jelly-jar cellar in a drunken rage. The movie we were shooting is the now classic film noir, *The Night of the Hunter.* I was hired as the stand-in and double for Sally Jane Bruce, who had been cast as Pearl in this haunting film. Because Sally was only six and it was her first movie and in contrast I had reached the mature age of eight with extensive singing and dancing training to my credit, I was filmed as her character in many of the scenes and in all of the long shots.

The first day on set, I was to hide with my reel brother, Billy Chapin, the male child star of the film, behind a coal scuttle in the dark cellar of our mother Shelley Winters's house. When action was called for my inaugural scene, Mitchum's character, the crazed preacher Harry Powell, came raging down the steps of the creepy cellar, fumbling, and then stumbling and falling into wooden breakaway supports. The pine two-by-fours held rickety shelves on which were placed spider-webbed jam jars. The breakaway glasses clattered noisily to the hard floor, shattering when the crazed preacher fell into them. I showed true fear of the intimidating preacher-turned-killer. I held my breath, but my coactor, Billy Chapin, gently took my hand and we raced out of the cellar with the menacing Reverend Harry Powell close behind us. Billy was able to shut the door on the preacher's hand just as he grabbed for us.

The smell of the spray used to create the stringy webs in the cellar was strong, and as I breathed in the heady, sweet stench, I wonder whether I might have been a little "high"—the smell artificially enhancing my experience of that first day of making movie history. Maybe it wasn't just the spray that was making me heady; I was eerily fascinated to be involved with this beckoning, entrancing, and addicting new realm.

I had been happily dancing and singing since the age of three, when my parents had enrolled me in classes at the Meglin Studios in Hollywood, under the tutelage of feisty founder Ethel Meglin. She was the vital, vivacious, and energetic woman who had helped push Shirley Temple onto her successful path to fame. Shirley was an adorable youngster who had been trained by Mrs. Meglin in musical tradition and discovered at her dance academy by Charles Lamont, a director at Educational Pictures. He had visited the "Meglin Kiddies" scouting for one of their new projects and chose Shirley, hiding under the piano, for a part in *Baby Burlesks*, a series of shorts that the studio was about to make. And so the tiny movie-icon-to-be began her road to stardom, as did several of Ethel Meglin's hundreds of other dancing kiddies such as Judy Garland, Mickey Rooney, Gwen Verdon, Gloria Lynn, and . . . me.

My mother was convinced I was to be the next young star to follow in Shirley's magical footsteps. She tootled me up to Western Boulevard, a half-hour drive from our home in Baldwin Hills, to learn the entertainment ropes and to soak up the enchantment that emanated from the simple stucco buildings of the Meglin Studios. Tap-dancing, ballet, and singing lessons led me to perform in the Busby Berkeley–like shows that Mrs. Meglin devised and produced. She had created the Meglin Kiddies variety act, and every year her troupe entertained at the grand Shrine Auditorium in Los Angeles. Her talented "finds" would sing loud, tap louder, and smile until plastered grins began to quiver. As a toddler, I performed on the same immense stage where live elephants had marched and trumpeted to the grand strains of the opera *Aida*.

It was not daunting to me, however. I did what I was told, happily following the grand gestures and encouragements from Mrs. Meglin, who stood valiantly in the wings, energetically miming the movements she had taught her group and pointing to her lips to remind us to "smile, smile, smile!"

The audience enthusiastically received our routines. One number our troupe debuted at the elegant Ebell Theatre on Wilshire Boulevard in Los Angeles was called "The Doll Dance," complete with sparkling horsehair costumes. It was one of my favorite routines, but I remember the difficulty of getting into the wardrobe and the greater difficulty of taking off the scratchy, glittering dress. As a potential hoarder, I still have the "Doll Dance" costume stored in the back of a treasured cedar chest in the basement. My mother, a tried and true hoarder, had used the chest to secure packets of hair cuttings from my first visits to beauty salons to small mementos from fairs and cherished occasions. Some of those riches are still lovingly tucked away.

Performing "The Doll Dance" with the Meglin Kiddies when I was a tot. I'm third from the left—the one looking at my feet.

I usually was the smallest in the performing classes, so I was placed in the front line of dancers, either at the end or in the middle. The night of one of the big shows at the Shrine, stuffed in a small dressing room with other excited tappers, my mother admonished me to stand still as she tried to tie a mottled horsehair bow to my curls, styled like Shirley's. Then her command was to stop talking so that she could apply the bright red lipstick on my Clara Bow–shaped lips. I was eager to tread the boards, but my mother's usual aphorism, "Make haste slowly," stilled my wriggling toes waiting to tap to my music. It was finally time. I waited in the wings, heard my intro music, and confidently pranced onto the grandiose Los Angeles Shrine Auditorium stage.

Lineup for the Meglin Kiddies. I'm the last one on the left.

# 2

# Ties to Oklahoma

My family had not always lived in California. My two older brothers and sister were born in Oklahoma. The eldest sibling, my sister, Beverly, was a prodigy who started reading when she was only three years old, before preschool learning computers taught toddlers. She was featured in many newspaper articles about this unusual feat. When Beverly began elementary school, she skipped the first three grades. Perhaps she got some of her extreme brain cells from my father's side of the family. Hayes Gilbert Webster William Garver (I don't know why he had all those names) graduated from OU—the University of Oklahoma—in Norman with a degree in architecture. My father's aunt, who also had graduated from OU, was the first woman ophthalmologist in Oklahoma. She started her practice in Guthrie, where she met and married Dr. Charles Barker, another renowned ophthalmologist, who pioneered the use of moving pictures to describe the different aspects of the eye, ear, nose, and throat in his lectures, books, and practice.

My mother's side of the family held no academic slouches or dullards, either. My grandmother—my mother's mother—was a real-estate maven who bought vacant property and enlisted her youngest son, John, to help build apartments and homes around the Los Angeles area.

Marie Gertrude Schwenner was an amazing woman and a great model for me with her strength and independence. I was given her name, Marie, as my middle name. She immigrated alone to America from Austria when she was just eighteen years old. Cousins in Ohio welcomed her, and she stayed with them for a short while. The comely lass was soon married to a stalwart fellow, an enterprising barber who hailed from Switzerland. They moved to Oklahoma and bore four children—two girls and two boys. My mother was the second oldest. Then tragedy struck—Grandma's husband died at thirty years old of a heart attack while undergoing a gallbladder operation.

The grieving young widow, Marie, was faced with four children to raise. What to do? First, my resourceful grandmother turned her home into a boarding house. The income from the rentals was meager, however, and she could not support her entire family. She decided to put my mother and my mother's older brother, Oliver, into an orphanage until she could accumulate enough money and emotional stability to raise her family properly. Through hard work, she was able to start a bank account and, after a couple of months, retrieve her beloved children. This experience, though, darkly colored my mother's emotional life. It also created in her, however, a strong sense of survival.

Tragedy struck again in the family when my grandmother and her children were still living in Oklahoma. Grandma Marie's oldest child, Oliver, drowned while testing the icy waters in a pond. After her grief, Grandma trudged on. Time passed, and her remaining children found spouses and began their own families. Marie joined the many who were escaping the Dust Bowl in Oklahoma and moved to California. Land was cheap and my grandmother was strong. She was able to get a loan and build. She built a house, and then she built an apartment building. After Grandma built and sold her apartment building in Redondo Beach, she bought land in Duarte, California, where she and her son, John, built six homes. She lived in one of them until she died at the age of 101, alert, smart, and looking forward to every new day. Grandmother was a self-made woman. She produced my loving mother, Rosemary. These are the two strong, independent women after whom I model my life.

Rosemary graduated from St. Anthony's Academy in Oklahoma as a registered nurse. She was always proud to display her picture of the academy's stellar basketball team for which she was captain, an athletic feat as she was only five foot three. She also appeared successfully in the senior play. Her interest in theater may have been the inspiration for my foray into entertainment.

Rosemary and Hayes met at the Oklahoma City medical center. My father had been admitted to St. Anthony's Hospital to undergo an appendectomy. Rosemary was the nurse assigned to tend him. The assignment was made in heaven. Her gentle care and attentiveness, plus her beautiful brown eyes and curly brunette tresses, stole his heart while the doctors took his appendix. Their marriage and love lasted for more than fifty years.

Rosemary and Hayes wedded in Oklahoma City in 1933, the year my mother graduated from the school of nursing. My parents wanted to get married on December 31, New Year's Eve—a symbolic start of their new life together—but the Catholic priest forbade them marrying on a holiday, so they obediently complied and were duly joined in holy matrimony on December 30. The happy newlyweds moved to Norman, Oklahoma, and delivered an adorable baby whom they named Beverly. The small family next moved to Ponca City, Oklahoma, and added my first brother, Hayes Gilbert Garver, Jr. (they deleted some of those middle names) to their brood. They then all moved to the larger, more urban Oklahoma City, where my brother Lance was born.

Times were rough in the 1930s and early 1940s. The young Garver family was

Family portrait with my mother standing to the right of my father, Hayes. Seated (left to right) are my sister, Beverly, fourteen, brother Lance, seven, brother Bud, eleven, and my grandmother with me on the edge of the couch, age two and a half.

Early photo of my mother, Rosemary.

Photo of my father, Hayes.

Childhood photos of sister, Beverly, and my brother Hayes, Jr. ("Bud").

suffering through the Depression, and my father's degree in architecture could not be utilized. There was no money for people to build new homes or even to renovate old ones. My father did draw the plans and build a church in Norman, but the Dust Bowl was kicking up, and my parents decided it was time to "get out of Dodge."

Childhood photo of my brother Lance.

# 3

# Los Angeles Strings

Exploring the possibility of jobs in California before moving from Oklahoma, my father found there was scant employment in that state, too, but did discover he could be hired for design work at the Naval Shipyard in Long Beach. He packed up the family, and they all migrated to Southern California. My mother was hired as a registered nurse at St. Mary's Hospital in Long Beach, and things began to improve. My father landed a better-paying job at the Federal Housing Administration as a construction inspector. And then I came along.

My mother went to the doctor concerned that her stomach was bulging. She thought she had early menopause or . . . a tumor. The doctor said, "That's no tumor, ma'am, that's a baby!" My mother was flabbergasted. She had thought her nest was full, that she was finished having children. But God had another idea. She welcomed the pregnancy and hoped for a tiny little girl—and there I was, nine months later, a six-pound bundle to care for.

With this new family addition, my parents bought a larger house and moved to an up-and-coming suburb of Los Angeles, Baldwin Hills, in 1946. The new home was on Alsace Avenue. I've always thought that my father was attracted to that street because his father was from Alsace-Lorraine in France. It was a nice middle-class home, complete with an Acrosonic upright piano in the living room which has been passed down and now resides in my family room. My father built an extra bedroom onto our home that was called "the boys' room." A new bathroom was also installed, and the corridor between the original house and the addition became my playroom, much to my brothers' chagrin. I furnished it with my doll's bunk bed, my baby doll's crib, and other feminine, childish paraphernalia. I was prepping for my own family affair in the future. The proximity to my brothers' territory did little to ingratiate me to them, but it provided me the opportunity to play with my toys as well as to visit their room and operate their exciting electric trains and construct imaginary models with their Erector set. It engendered in me a lifelong affection for building, whether the result is families, houses, or careers in entertainment.

My mother, thinking all her children had talent, twice entered me in the Better Baby Contest conducted by the *Los Angeles Herald Examiner*, and each time I was honored with a certificate and a score of 98 percent. I have always been annoyed, overachiever that I am, that I didn't get 100 percent. Aren't all babies perfect? Where was that extra 2 percent? I guess we all can't be perfect, even though my husband says I am. Most of his comments are tinged with sarcasm, however.

It was the belief of my Catholic parents that their children should have a firm foundation in religion and morals. The children should be baptized, confirmed, and learn their catechism. Then they should get a dose of reality and start public school. We all started our free academies in the seventh grade, after six years of Catholic education. And, believe me, Mrs. Meglin had nothing on those nuns when it came to discipline and respect. Sister Virginia Mary (whom I used as a prototype for my role as Sister Augustus in the film *Hercules Saves Christmas* in 2011) made me write "I will not disobey" one hundred times on the chalkboard after school one day at Transfiguration Elementary School in Baldwin Hills. I was in the second grade and was talking too much in class (*moi*?) and not following her instructions. That experience developed in me a lifelong suspicion of authority

Me at the family piano when I was three years old.

and power. And big black gowns. Meanwhile, my brothers went to Audubon Junior High School in Baldwin Hills and, when it was time, my older brother, Bud, followed my sister into Dorsey High, which was just down the street from Audubon.

All her chicks now in school, my mother's incredible energy and intellect demanded further outlets. She started scouting property around the Los Angeles area. Finding a desirable lot in Baldwin Hills on Somerset Drive, she convinced my father that they should buy the vacant land and that he should draw the plans and build a sixteen-unit apartment building. Hello, Lucy Arnaz! My talented father took on the challenge and designed and then constructed the complex. The venture was accomplished and turned out to be a very successful project that even provided me housing twelve years later, when I started filming *Family Affair.* In 1967 my parents moved into the apartment building they had built. They took one unit and gave me another. I felt so grown up having my own apartment at twenty, even though my parents lived right below me. Perhaps my mother inherited her real-estate acumen from my grandmother.

My grandfather on my father's side, Harry Gilbert Garver, was the superintendent of the Oklahoma County School District. But tragedy also befell the Garver household when Grandpa Harry died of a heart attack while only thirty-one years old, near the train tracks while looking at a possible site for a new school. His widow, Susan Quillin Garver, raised her two children, Hayes—my father—and his sister, Pauline, alone, with some help from her sister and brother-in-law, the Doctors Barker.

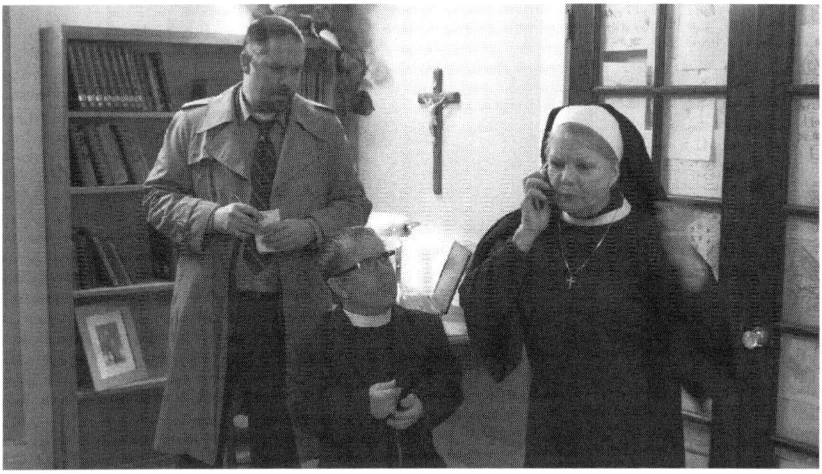

Using the model of my teacher Sister Virginia Mary from Transfiguration Elementary School, I created the role of Sister Augustus for the movie *Hercules Saves Christmas* in 2011. Pictured are Edward Hightower, Shorty Rossi (*Pit Boss*), and me.

It may have been that the early loss of their respective fathers brought my parents close together. They shared a strong emotional and experiential bond because of their early parental deprivations. Perhaps that is the reason my mother decided to be a nurse—so that she could help and nurture people. My parents were each raised by a single mother, but the experience enabled them to help each other move toward a fulfilling, successful, and loving life.

My father expressed most of his artistic and intellectual abilities in architecture and construction. One of the buildings he designed for the General Services Administration is a towering office building, which still stands on the corner of Wilshire and Sepulveda Boulevards in the Westwood section of Los Angeles. It was recently cited as a historic building for its attention to clean lines and modern leanings. My mother expressed herself in her joy of nurturing—her family, her friends, and the wonderful real estate projects she found, which also live on in beauty.

# 4

## Unraveling Theatrical Threads

In 1954, after Mrs. Meglin's training, I climbed onto the professional film stage. My Aunt Florence had engaged a theatrical agent for her two boys, John Tunney and Jim, to represent them in the entertainment business. One day, she called my mother to tell her that her boys had gone on an interview for a new movie being shot close to our home in Baldwin Hills. Even though her boys did not get the parts, she discovered that the production company was looking for a little girl to double for Sally Jane Bruce, one of the child stars of the movie who had already been cast. Sally was only six years old and not very athletic. There were many running scenes and other scenarios that required physical dexterity, so there I was, after five years of dance training, two big brothers, and two years older but the same size as Sally.

It was at RKO in Culver City where I met the great actor Charles Laughton, who was directing his first film, *The Night of the Hunter.* Attending to each aspect of his debut behind the camera, he wanted to make sure that the double hired for the child's role of Pearl would be believable. On one of the side streets at the studio, he asked me to run from where we were standing to the end of the road. Always competitive, I ran as fast as I could.

"Nice run," I heard him grumble, as I finished sprinting the short street. I smiled, then heard, "But do it again, and this time pretend you are six years old."

This time eschewing my eight-year-old athleticism, I ran as I thought a six-year-old might scuttle. I got the job.

When I arrived at RKO that first day at 9:00 a.m. to begin my professional film career on *The Night of the Hunter,* I was escorted to the dank, dim set. The crew had been there hours earlier to set lights and camera. I was asked to crouch in the corner behind some stacked coal, standing in for Sally Jane. I thought, "Hmm, so this is show biz!"

Charles Laughton was directing his first and last film. A stellar cast had been assembled for *The Night of the Hunter*, a film now honored in the annals of movie history. Robert Mitchum, as the monstrous Reverend Powell and star of the film, first gained prominence and an Academy Award nomination for supporting actor for *The Story of GI Joe* in 1945. Western and film noir parts followed before he accepted the role of the reverend. He claimed that his role in *The Night of the Hunter* was his favorite among many strong character parts that he played throughout his sterling career.

Mitchum was an imposing presence on the set and was reputed to retire to his trailer after a scene to "nip a few." He was also known as a prankster. One day, the manikin of Shelley Winters, whom Mitchum murders in the film, was discovered in Shelley's designated chair on set. We all wondered how the damp dummy, the faux body of the character Willa, who had been found in a scummy, wet pond, wound up in Shelley's chair. With Mitchum's reputation for playing practical jokes, it wasn't hard to figure out.

Shelley Winters was also a headliner in the film. She had an abbreviated role as Willa Harper, the love-starved widow of bank robber Ben Harper, who dies shortly into the movie. Ms. Winters, an eminent craftsperson, had created a breakthrough performance in the film *A Place in the Sun*, with Elizabeth Taylor and Montgomery Clift, for which she earned an Academy Award nomination for best actress in a leading role in 1952.

Ms. Winters began her career as a blond bombshell–type actress with Marilyn Monroe as one of her early roommates. Shelley had seen the limitations of the "dumb blond" types of roles and started selecting parts that showed off her depth of talent. After she showed her prowess with her excellent performance in *The Night of the Hunter*, she then went on to win Oscars for her portrayals in *The Diary of Anne Frank* and *A Patch of Blue*.

Peter Graves, James Arness's brother, had a small but important part as Willa's bank-robbing husband, Ben Harper, who met the preacher Powell in jail. Escaping prison, he runs to his family home with the $10,000 he had stolen in the economically depressed times and sets the scene for the fascinating movie. Ben is captured but had told the reverend about the money, and as soon as the preacher was released from jail, he went on the hunt for the lucre and for the widow Harper. Peter was best known for his portrayal in the TV series *Mission: Impossible*. He was a wonderful person with a great sense of humor who was later amiably appreciated for the movies *Airplane!* and *Airplane II: The Sequel*. Peter delighted audiences and worked until his 2010 death of a heart attack. We skied together and got to know each other in the 1970s at celebrity events. The last time I saw him was at the Hollywood Collectors Show in 2009, where we autographed photos, signed memorabilia, and traded anecdotes. He was as gracious and personable as he had been all through the years.

Billy Chapin and Sally Jane Bruce played Willa's children, John and Pearl, also stars of the film. Sally was the little girl for whom I was hired to stand in and then double. This was her first and last movie. Billy Chapin is the brother of Lauren Chapin, who gained fame as "Kathy" on the long-running TV series *Father Knows Best.* Their brother, Michael Chapin, played one of the minor characters in *The Night of the Hunter.* Billy had amassed many theatrical credits before being cast in the film and continued working in episodic TV until he quit the business in 1959.

Other stars included Lillian Gish, the armed savior figure who appears toward the end of the film. In her long and esteemed seventy-five-year career in show business, Ms. Gish was noted for many fine performances, and her excellent portrayal of Rachel Cooper in *The Night of the Hunter* was high on the list. She persevered in a tough business, and to quote her, "I think the things that are necessary in my profession are these: taste, talent and tenacity. I think I have had a little of all three." In my opinion, she certainly did, and it was an honor to work with her and soak up her talent and graciousness.

*The Night of the Hunter* was cinematically years ahead and was built on a German expressionistic mode in black and white with stylized dialogue, odd camera angles, and dark shadows. It was not well received, and Charles Laughton became so disturbed over the reviews that he vowed never to direct another film. He stuck to his vow. In future years, *The Night of the Hunter* would be heralded for its quality

Group photo from *The Night of the Hunter.* Laughing Lillian Gish is standing between Charles Laughton to her left and Robert Mitchum to her right. I am in in the front row sixth from the left, next to Gloria Castillo, who played the role of Mary. Our great prop person, Joe La Bella, is next to Gloria, and then Mike Chapin, Billy and Lauren's older brother, is next to him.

and creativity and become a cult classic. Some have named it one of the most wonderfully horrifying movies ever made, and the simplicity and starkness of the settings further magnified its style.

*The Night of the Hunter* was rated number thirty-four on the American Film Institute's *100 Years . . . 100 Thrills*, number ninety on Bravo's *100 Scariest Movie Moments*, and number two in *Cahiers du Cinema* in their listing of the one hundred most beautiful films. When the DVD of the movie came out, I gave it to my son, Reid, who was eleven years old at the time, to watch. The next day he excitedly appeared with "L-O-V-E" and "H-A-T-E" written in black ink on his knuckles, in the same fashion that the killer preacher had tattooed the motto onto his hands. I discovered that this impressive film might not be appropriate for children.

But a child I was when I spent three months filming the movie. I ran in the dark and sneezed in haylofts. I cut faux paper money into dolls, and my screen brother stuffed the bills back into a rag doll. It's my hands you see doing those dexterous cutting moves in the film and my legs scurrying up stairs to escape the raging, angling hands of the preacher.

I traveled with the cast to Lee Ranch in Canoga Park (near Los Angeles), where some of the film was being shot, to toss balls in the background, and then to RKO's "Forty Acres." An old riverbank shanty had been erected on the grounds, and in the story John pleads with "old Birdie," who lives in the shack, to help him and Pearl, but Birdie Steptoe is drunk and rambling and of no assistance. To escape the pursuing crazed preacher, the children, with me as Pearl, rush out of the shanty and run through the marshes. I ran in the day and I ran in the night, with the mosquitoes flitting and the frogs croaking. In the outtakes of the movie, you can hear Laughton barking directions to me and Billy as we get into a creaky wooden skiff. Billy follows instructions as he gently puts me into the boat and then shields my face. We then float down imitative murky waters. The river scenes were exciting to film, but I had a lot of mosquito bites to scratch and mud to be rinsed.

The river scenes were an intriguing learning experience. As I look back, it was like a Disneyland ride—a jungle cruise without the lions, tigers, and crocs (Oh my!). In the skiff with Billy Chapin, Sally only did a couple of scenes and close-ups. During this part of the film, I enjoyed lazily looking at the water as it swirled by. Laughton and the cinematographer paid special attention to the look and cries of various creatures they had carefully placed on the shore. Even as a child, I could sense the haunting tone that the sounds evoked in the stillness as our characters continued the frightening and lonely journey, not knowing where we were going, drifting along the gray river with the eerie notes of the crazed preacher echoing through the darkness. I learned that attention to style and tone was elemental to the creation of a film.

Stanley Cortez was the talented and brilliant cinematographer. In one of the scenes toward the end of the movie, John and Pearl hide in a hayloft. Because the style was expressionistic and he wanted to give a sense of distance, Stanley devised a way to photograph the preacher riding his horse by using a midget on a donkey to give the correct perspective. The hymn Reverend Powell sang in that scene was *Leaning on the Everlasting Arms*. Robert Mitchum recorded the evocative verses in postproduction, and when I hear even one refrain from that haunting song, I am back on the river, in the moment, listing on the edge of the splintered boat, languidly dangling my hand in the muddy swirls and hearing in my mind the doleful melody.

There was always an abundance of food on the set of *The Night of the Hunter*, even when we were on location at Lee Ranch. The caterers set up tables for the cast and crew with red and white checked vinyl tablecloths and brought fried chicken and coleslaw and lots of cookies. When it was time to shoot the scenes with Rachel Cooper (Lillian Gish) at her film home, which had been built at the RKO set in Culver City, more food was offered as Ms. Gish generously provided snacks at 3:00 p.m. every day when energy started to wane. Salami, cheese, and all sorts of goodies were offered. I went from being a tiny little girl to a chubby little darling at the end of the filming. I also ate many sugary and delicious doughnuts supplied each morning by Joe La Bella, the fabulous prop person. Maybe those early experiences are why I am so into food and my first book was *The Family Affair Cookbook*!

Charles Laughton teaching us children how to cut out patterns with Lillian Gish looking on, having provided the array of salami, cheese, and crackers for an afternoon snack. Left to right are Billy Chapin, myself, Mary Ellen Clemons, Charles Laughton, Cheryl Callaway, and Lillian Gish.

The loft scenes that we picked up toward the end of the shoot were truly a roll in the hay. Sally couldn't climb up the ladder to the second level of the barn; she wasn't in those scenes at all. So Billy and I hid in the wooden silo, snuggling deeply into the prickly straw to hide away from the deranged preacher. That introduction to odoriferous dried grass is when I first realized I was allergic to hay. I had such a bout that when I went to *The Night of the Hunter*'s wrap party at Visconti's restaurant on La Cienega Boulevard, my nose ran and my eyes watered throughout the entire occasion. But I bravely signed my name to the souvenir flyer that Hilyard Brown, the art director, had created as a present for Mr. Laughton. All the cast and crew signed that memento, and Laughton displayed a hearty smile when it was presented to him. I traipsed around the restaurant sniffling and watering but still managed to collect autograph treasures written in my now cherished *The Night of the Hunter* novel.

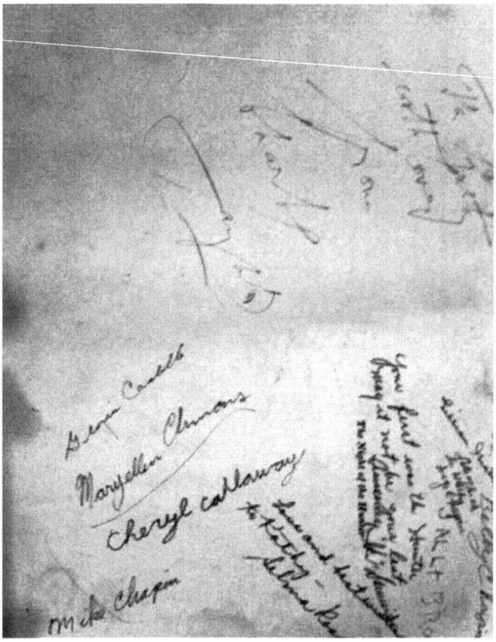


Autographs from the cast of *The Night of the Hunter*, including Charles Laughton and Lillian Gish. Hilyard Brown busied himself by drawing a rendition of the barn we had used in those loft scenes in my book, decorating it for history with his artistry.

Previously unpublished drawing of the barn that the Academy Award–winning art director Hilyard Brown drew inside my copy of the book *The Night of the Hunter.*

# 5

# Biblical Cords

When *The Night of the Hunter* was completed, another interesting movie awaited. I now had an agent. My sister, Beverly—remember the prodigy?—began Mount St. Mary's College in Westwood, California, at just fifteen. I was four. Not only was Beverly smart, she was also talented. She was cast in her college play, *Everyman*, and the director needed two children to complete the ensemble. I think to gain "Brownie points" my ambitious sister eagerly volunteered my brother Lance and me to round out the cast. In the audience the night of our performance was the agent, Hazel McMillan, the mother of one of Beverly's classmates, Gloria. Gloria had gained fame as a child by creating the role of Harriet Conklin in the excellent *Our Miss Brooks* radio series starring Eve Arden. The audio sitcom was about a spinster English teacher, Constance Brooks, who battled with her principal, Osgood Conklin, played by Gale Gordon to great comical effect. Robert Rockwell played her love interest, Mr. Boynton, and Richard Crenna played the very funny Walter Denton, a high-pitched, voice-cracking teenager who drove Miss Brooks to school every day and nearly crazy. The radio show enjoyed a ten-year run from 1948 to 1958. *Our Miss Brooks* was such a success that a televised adaptation began and ran concurrently with the radio version from 1952 to 1956. Gloria, as Principal Conklin's daughter, appeared in both the radio and TV series for the entire runs. As many mothers of actors who manage their children's careers, Hazel McMillan learned the business quickly and became a successful entertainment agent who guided not only her daughter but many young stars in their theatrical pursuits. We were fortunate to meet Hazel at the *Everyman* presentation. I have always believed that God or a special spirit guides us; we just have to listen and follow. Situations are presented to us and we must act on them.

When my alert mother met Hazel at *Everyman,* she wrote down her number and, when she returned home, placed the contact information in a special place in her mahogany slant-front desk. After *The Night of the Hunter* experience in 1954 and with her two boys old enough to be left on their own, my mother called Hazel and arranged a meeting. She then signed a contract for Mrs. McMillan to represent me.

The first job Hazel secured for me was epic, literally. She sent me to Hollywood to appear in one of the greatest biblical films ever made, directed by one of the most famous directors of epics, Cecil B. DeMille, *The Ten Commandments*. Some scenes of the grand movie were being shot at Paramount Studios on Western Boulevard in the heart of Tinseltown. Many extras would be needed to fill the grandeur of DeMille's dream to bring his movie to current and vocal light. DeMille had produced a silent version of *The Ten Commandments* in 1923.

My mother and I arrived at Paramount Studios, and I was issued a rough hopsacking shift with a long, striped scarf from the wardrobe department and then sent to the next stop. The makeup room was filled with lanolin's sweet smells and background actors. I tried to stand still as the harried cosmetic artists prepared all of us for camera. There were large mustard-colored sponges with jagged holes in them to absorb dark makeup to then be applied to our skin. I stood in front of a small heater as a sponge was dipped in cool water, then onto the round of makeup base, and then onto my skin. The water evaporating on my arms from the mushy damp sponge gave me the shivers.

Then it was time to go on set. And what a set it was! There were large wagons and braying donkeys and masses of people. Henry Wilcoxon, the assistant director, brought me over from my mother's protective arms on the edge of the set and placed me onto a wobbly splintered wagon. Then an unforgettable and novel experience for a city girl—I was to hold a baby lamb in my lap. I have a fondness for animals and they seem to relate to me rather well; to be able to hold one of the soft curly lambkins in my arms would be a special treat. It was. Until she peed. Being the dedicated, disciplined trooper that I was, I didn't utter a peep or a baa—Ethel Meglin would have been proud.

However, I'm sure I had a startled and stunned expression on my face. I started to cry out, but I heard a great voice overpowering me from above, shouting, "Don't let that little girl's face get in the camera!"

"Who was that?" I wondered in amazement. "Was that God?" We were, after all, doing *The Ten Commandments*. The voice was coming from far above me.

The assistant director, Mr. Wilcoxon, rushed over to me breaking my heavenly thoughts into realistic notes and gently placed a rough, scratchy blanket over my body, partially covering my head. He instructed, "Stay under the blanket and hold the lamb. After the shot I'll come and get you."

"After the shot?" I thought. "Hold the lamb? What about my damp costume and the lamb squiggling to get down?"

The booming command of "Action!" arrested my thoughts, and the wagon began to roll. Bumpily, the flimsy cart joggled over ruts in the newly wrought dirt road as extras dressed as slaves bustled all round. It was the start of one of the Exodus scenes of *The Ten Commandments*.

"Cut!" a looming voice bellowed. "Print!"

As promised, Henry Wilcoxon came over and lifted me and the drying lamb gently from the wagon. Then God came down. It wasn't really God. It was Cecil B. DeMille. But then again, DeMille is a cinema deity. He descended from a tall yellow crane on which he had been seated, directing from above. When the heavenly transport reached ground level, DeMille slid off and came over to me. He asked my name and how I liked working on the movie. I enthusiastically said, "I love it," but wisely did not tell him about the lamb who peed. He left, and after a few minutes Mr. Wilcoxon reappeared and said, "Well, looks like you're going to be working on the film a lot longer." I didn't know quite what that meant, but my mother seemed very happy about the idea when I told her.

Cecil B. DeMille's skill in making excellent epics was to be able to incorporate scenes of human warmth to ameliorate and make more accessible the splendor and majesty of the large story he was telling. For instance, Moses saves an old lady who was in certain danger of being crushed when two unfinished block walls move her slowly toward her doom. A small slave girl, played by my friend Mimi Gibson, and her slave brother describe details of the massive exodus of the bustling slaves to their blind grandfather—another example of DeMille's human touches depicted in the film. And now I joined DeMille's stable of warm, relatable characters as Rachel, the slave girl.

Mr. DeMille personally wrote special scenes into the movie for me after we met. The first one occurs in the middle of the movie, when the slaves are beginning preparations for the exodus. My part begins when I appear on the stone staircase of my rough-hewn home, in search of my doll, Rebecca. The camera focuses on me at the top of the stair as I chime, "Do you have the pumpkin?" and then anxiously declare, "Where's Rebecca?" Quickly slipping down a step, I then ask, "Grandfather, do you have Rebecca?" I further descend the steps as a disembodied hand appears and a curt voice replies, "Here's Rebecca."

"Thank you," I say, gratefully grabbing my prized possession. The camera follows me as I wind my way through throngs of people over to the town well, where young women are chattering. I try and fill a clay vessel with some of the splashing water, but the girls have claimed their territory and I am too small to get any purchase. Preparations continue to be made at the well for the exciting move to a new life, but I continue my disappointment at not being able to fill my water jug.

Another scene DeMille wrote for me takes place on a large papier-mâché mountain, where I am stranded during the closing of the Red Sea depicted on set at Paramount. Originally, there was to be a boy sitting next to me. But Mr. DeMille changed his mind and the boy was replaced with blankets and belongings. Charlton Heston, as Moses, approaches me on his trek through the sandy soil of the Red Sea during the Exodus and asks, "Are you afraid?"

I claim, "No, but Rebecca is!" I thrust out my alter ego Rebecca so that he can see how afraid she is. He then lifts us both off the great mountain.

Charlton Heston was a large and imposing figure, and with his great robes and

As Rachel with Charlton Heston as Moses at Paramount Studios shooting the epic film *The Ten Commandments*. © 1956 Paramount Pictures Corporation

beard, somewhat intimidating to a tiny eight-year-old. The warmth in his eyes and the kindness in his demeanor allayed my fear. After he gently lifted me and Rebecca off our ledge, we continued our route on the sandy path through the parted sea.

I appeared in additional Exodus segments. One of the most memorable scenes to me was a part of the final dramatic closing of the roiling Red Sea. I had been situated on another of the faux mountains at Paramount. My direction was to climb up a few feet into the waiting arms of Bithiah (Nina Foch) when I hear the megaphone-shouted call of "Action!" Large vats of water had been set around the periphery of the set on towering catwalks. The waters were to be poured forth and released to simulate the closing of the sea. The scene involved the intricate timing of the descending waters, camels and mules being rushed through the temporary gritty trail, and hordes of actors hurriedly stumbling to the shore of safety and freedom.

Mr. DeMille liked to use more than one camera to record these grandiose events. This time, he had situated one cameraman to capture the master scene, one to focus on another angle, and, for good measure, one operator with his camera placed high up in the catwalks, where the vats of water were to be turned and emptied on cue. After many hours, everything was in place and I anxiously waited in my roughed-out faux stone nest. Then I heard the shouted command of "Action!" I shot out of my space and felt the chilly water splash around me as I slipped up into Nina Foch's protective arms. The camels lumbered by, urged on by eager extras, and masses of people and wagons hurriedly scuffled down the trail to escape the tail end of the waves of the closing sea.

"Cut! Great!" DeMille's voice boomed, "Camera number 1, how was it for you?"

The cameraman sheepishly replied, "I'm sorry, Mr. DeMille, water splashed on the lens and I missed the shot."

Astounded, DeMille shouted, "Camera number 2, how was it for you?"

"I'm sorry, Mr. DeMille, a camel walked in front of the camera and I didn't get it!" Thoroughly aggravated, DeMille then remembered the cameraman way up on the catwalk. He thundered, "Camera number 3, how was it for you?'

The cameraman excitedly shouted back, "Ready when you are, C.B.!"

The above story has been termed an urban myth, but I was there and it is totally true.

There was a holding stable for the animals used on *The Ten Commandments*, and the other children and I would scurry down to the dusty enclosures to visit them every chance we could, but were warned to stay away from the spitting camels. The lambs and burros were more kid friendly, and we would dash to the pens to see whether the pregnant donkey had given birth to her new foal. I never saw the baby. Three months after my original two-week assignment on the movie, my filming was completed and I was off to another role, and the little donkey was taken away to a different stable. The experience was actually priceless, but due to the generosity of Paramount and Hazel's negotiations, even when I was not scheduled to work, I was put on hold and was paid—nice income for an eight-year-old.

Sometimes audiences are not aware of the breadth of an actor's talents. I had appreciated Charlton Heston's acting abilities on-screen and onstage, but I did not fathom the depth of his talent until he delivered a eulogy for our dear friend and my mentor, impresario James Doolittle of the James A. Doolittle Theatre, nee the Huntington Hartford Theatre. Jimmy, ever the theatrical promoter, had arranged for Charlton to travel to China to direct a Chinese theater company in the play *The Caine Mutiny*. Mr. Heston had originally starred in the show at the Hartford, and Jimmy thought Charlton would be the ideal candidate to direct this historic performance of East meets West. Jimmy plays an important part on my life's stage and will emerge later in this book right after my debut of *Family Affair*.

Although Jimmy and Charlton had been friends and business acquaintances, the directorial assignment tightened their bond. When Jimmy died, the family asked me to speak at his funeral service in the Grand Hall of the Dorothy Chandler

Pavilion at the LA Music Center. I agreed and wrote and delivered the eulogy to honor my dear friend. After the memorial, our funeral procession took us to the Forest Lawn Cemetery in the Hollywood Hills, where Jimmy was to be buried. There, on a small, grassy hill, Charlton presented the most touching monologue from Shakespeare I have ever heard. He stood in the open meadow with no lights, camera, or editing and gave a stirring, heartfelt, and moving paean to our dear friend. I know Jimmy was smiling at us all from his special place in heaven.

Charlton and I continued our friendship when I dated the actor Michael Dante (*Winterhawk*) in the 1970s. Michael was a tennis and acting friend of Charlton's, and Michael and I would wind up curvy Mulholland Drive in Los Angeles to Charlton's grand home, where competitive sets of tennis were played as I sat, watched, and drank lemonade on the veranda. After matches, we would gather and chat. Later in Charlton's life, when Alzheimer's disease had robbed him of some of his strength and memory, he was, as ever, kind and generous. I wrote him a letter asking him to autograph ten copies of a picture that featured him and me from *The Ten Commandments* during the "Rebecca on the mountain" scene. I signed one to him and then requested he autograph the rest of the photos and send them back in the SASE. The signed photos were sent back promptly with a lovely letter.

# 6

# Sewing Together a Resume

Now that I had an agent and professional headshots and after my experience on *The Ten Commandments*, my mother and I were set to commandeer the Los Angeles audition scene for TV, film, radio, and theater. Because of Hazel McMillan's "in" with *Our Miss Brooks*, my next job and first television exposure was on that Emmy Award–winning comedy series, which starred Eve Arden, Gale Gordon, Richard Crenna, and, of course, Mrs. McMillan's daughter, Gloria. I played a little Italian girl who gets a big close-up when I mimic my father's hand gesture. I was chosen from my photo, which helped secure many jobs for me in commercials, TV, and film. Photos were taken by one of the best photographers in Hollywood at the time, John E. Reed, at the suggestion of Hazel, who claimed he took the best headshots of glamour queens, celebrities and the "up and coming."

I now had three great credits under my belt and the disciplined instruction of Mrs. Meglin. I could be called a contender, not a "backyard kid," as my mother would despairingly name the competition who had no training. However, I had lots of competition from kids who were trained, like sweet Cheryl Callaway, whom I had met on the set of *The Night of the Hunter*. Cheryl played one of Lillian Gish's rescued orphans at the end of the film and then went on to play the role of Kathy Hudson in the TV series *Dr. Hudson's Secret Journal*. Her mother and my mother became great friends, and they would talk on the phone for hours about their precious, talented daughters.

Then there was beautiful Anna Marie Nanasi. She later changed her name to Ahna Capri and filled out to become the buxom lead in *Enter the Dragon* with Bruce Lee and John Saxon. There was cutie Sherry Alberoni, who became Mouseketeer Sherry on TV's *The Mickey Mouse Club*. Sherry became my best friend, Sharon, on the *Family Affair* TV series, and we are still good friends. And there was freckle-faced Patty Ann Gerrity.

Patty and Sherry were my main competitors to secure the starring part of Alice

My first professional photograph for show business by John E. Reed.

in a new series to be filmed in 1956, *This Is Alice.* The three of us had won the first and second rounds of interviews over many other hopefuls, and we were to have our final screen test at the studio. After we performed the selected scenes on the set, we were to sing a song. I don't remember what the other girls sang, but I remember mine vividly. My parents and my singing teacher, William Lockwood from the Meglin Studios, selected the melodious "A Sweet Old-Fashioned Girl," originally recorded by Teresa Brewer, for me to perform. They all decided it would show off the two distinct sides of my personality—sweet and strong. There was also a little bit of choreography included to demonstrate my dancing ability.

The final audition day arrived, and we were given "Brownie" uniforms to don as our costumes. There were Sherry and Patty looking cute as the proverbial buttons in their freshly pressed outfits. I thought I looked okay, but I would wow them with my great song and dance routine. I believed my main rival was Sherry—she was so adorable and had such a great personality. I didn't consider Patty as a contender.

It was time for me to appear on camera. I took a deep breath and approached the set. I performed my scene, and then I began to sing my song. The tune began very softly with doo-wop words: *Doo-be-doo-be-doo-be-doo-be-doo-be.* Then I got into the first verse, sweetly delivered in dulcet tones:

*Wouldn't anybody care to meet*
*A sweet old-fashioned girl*
*Scoobley-dah-doo-bee-dum*
*Doesn't anybody care about*
*A sweet old-fashioned pearl*
*Scoobley-doo-bee-dum*

Then the speed, tenor, and volume increased exponentially. And, remembering Ethel Meglin's dictum, I smiled and heartily released my belting voice for the entire world to hear:

*Who's a frantic little bopper*
*In some sloppy socks*
*Just a crazy rock'n'roller*
*Little Goldilocks*

My voice then returned quietly to the dulcet tones of the first verses.

*Wouldn't anybody care to meet*
*A sweet old-fashioned girl?*

I accompanied the boisterous lyrics with the gyrations of a female Elvis Presley impersonator. Now this technique may have been ideal for the immense Shrine Auditorium, where elephants trod, but it definitely wasn't a good idea on a sound stage with delicate recording equipment. Especially when the technician was not prepared for the loud pitch and screaming sound change. Over my rocker's belt, I heard a piercing, "Cut!!"

"What?" I replied.

Sidney Salkow, the director, shouted, "Too loud!"

"Oh," I disappointedly shot back.

"Not to worry. We just have to be prepared when you are going to switch volume. Let's start again."

"Okay," I said, in my sweet old-fashioned voice.

So I resumed with the winsome lyrics:

*Doesn't anybody care to hear*
*Some sweet old-fashioned talk*
*A-scoobley-doo-bee-dum*
*Wouldn't anybody like to take*
*A nice old-fashioned walk*
*Scoobley-doo-bee-dum*

I then ramped up to my roaring rock and roll voice:

*Take a walk around the corner*
*Where the cats all stop*

*Where you dig the juicy ribs*
*And then you'll dance that bop*
*Wouldn't anybody like to take*
*A nice old-fashioned walk?*

This time the crew was still startled but more prepared technically for the loud sound change. They even applauded when I was finished with my raucous song and dance routine.

I still didn't get the job. The starring role of Alice went to Patty Gerrity—I was quite surprised that Sherry didn't get it. I guess God had it designed so that Sherry would be free to accept her large-eared role on *The Mickey Mouse Club.*

Phyllis Coates as Alice's mother, Clarissa Holliday, and Tommy Farrell as Chet Holliday, Alice's father, filled the other starring parts in *This Is Alice*, the situation comedy about nine-year-old Alice and her misadventures. Phyllis Coates had gained fame as TV's first Lois Lane in *The Adventures of Superman* in 1952, which also starred George Reeves. Noel Neill replaced Phyllis in the second year of the series as Lois. Later, Phyllis would play Lois Lane's mother on an episode of *Lois and Clark: The New Adventures of Superman* in 1993, which starred Dean Cain. Ah, it's a small world.

Comparing the wardrobe Phyllis wore playing Lois Lane in *The Adventures of Superman* (1952) with Teri Hatcher as Lois in *Lois and Clark* (1993), Phyllis said, "I saw Teri in this beautiful dress with her boobs pushed up and I thought, 'That's Lois Lane?!?!' I had a suit up to my collarbone. I felt like a horse with a bit in my mouth." Tell it like it is, Phyllis!

Tommy Farrell essayed many roles in Hollywood after the one-season run of *This Is Alice.* He played the role of Riff Ryan in the *Dobie Gillis* TV series in 1959 and Jack O'Hallohan in *Bourbon Street Beat* in 1960. He also had roles in Elvis Presley's film *Kissin' Cousins* and in *A Guide for the Married Man*, which starred Walter Matthau, Robert Morse, and a host of celebrities, including Jack Benny, Lucille Ball, Terry-Thomas, and the inimitable Jayne Mansfield. It was Jayne's last role before her untimely death six months after the film was released in 1967.

After *This Is Alice*, Patty Gerrity went on to play roles in *The Loretta Young Show*, *Lassie*, and *Leave It to Beaver* and in movies such as *Cat on a Hot Tin Roof* and *The Trouble with Angels*, which starred Rosalind Russell. I was also in *Angels* but in a small part at the end, and Patty and I had no scenes together. *The Trouble with Angels* was Patty's last show-business role, and she sadly died an untimely death at forty-two years old.

Patty was an adorable child and very natural looking. I believe the producers opted for a younger and more "realistic" look than Sherry or me. Sherry and I were pretty slick for eleven-year-olds. Also, I recently watched some of the episodes on DVD provided by my friend Bob O'Brien from Palm Springs, and I, for the first time, saw that I was taller than the other girls. I realized, then, that I was two years older than Patty and more "mature."

Although the main role went to Patty, the director and producers liked me immensely and installed me as a semiregular in *This Is Alice*, as Alice's best friend, Sally. An incident on set I will never forget occurred in one episode when Sally was going to have to move out of town. My character was very upset about the whole situation. I was supposed to cry. To make sure I would shed copious tears, Sidney Salkow, the director, kept saying, right before I started and while doing my scene, "You can't cry. You're not a good actress. You are a horrible actress." Well, he certainly got me to cry buckets! He yelled, "Cut!" and then said, "That was brilliant!" After the scene, he came up to me and said, "I was just kidding; I think you are a terrific actress. It's the way I direct." Well, the damage had already been done, just as if a parent spanked you and then came in later to apologize and ask forgiveness. It may have been Mr. Salkow's method of working with child actors, but I certainly did not appreciate it. But from then on, I could cry in a scene at the drop of a hat, pin, or ego.

I've actually never taken criticism very well. Maybe it harks back to the second grade and Sister Virginia Mary at Transfiguration Elementary School—the same school where I wantonly left my blue Popsicle.

I took piano lessons at Transfiguration in addition to attending classes while not working onstage. The only available slot to take music for me was during the lunch break. One day, I was quickly finishing my homemade peanut butter sandwich and noticed there were special Popsicles for sale—blue raspberry. I had never seen a blue Popsicle, much less eaten one, and was totally fascinated. I quickly bought one of the luscious icy desserts with part of my coveted allowance. I was sitting on the stone steps at the side of the main building where I was to take my piano lesson upstairs, savoring every lick of the tasty treat. I suddenly remembered my lesson. I was going to be late! What to do? I had to trounce up the stairs immediately or face the wrath of Sister Mary Catherine. I did the only thing I could do. I gathered my music books and left the blue raspberry Popsicle on the stairs. It extended its slowly melting tentacle arms, painting the gray stone a bright purple. I made it to my lesson on time. But . . . the next day, the principal came to our class and in front of all the students proclaimed in a stentorian way that SOMEONE had offensively left a Popsicle to melt on the side steps of the main building. Who had laid waste to this perfectly good edible treat? Who had defiled the clean stairs? Who was so lazy as to not properly dispose of the blue mess? I ashamedly averted my eyes and cautiously looked down at my navy blue and white saddle shoes. I was sure the principal knew it was I—the perpetrator of this vile act. I could feel her eyes bore into me. After an interminable silence without anyone confessing or raising his or her hand—*I* certainly wasn't going to—our principal (why can't I remember her name? Hmm.) emphatically straightened her black robes and swept away. I've never eaten a blue Popsicle since.

# 7

# Nice Threads, or the Good Girl

I had a great introduction to movie making with *The Ten Commandments*, but I became typecast and branded as the "good little girl." And that would be the story of much of my life in film and television. I was destined to be in wholesome "family fare." One of the shows in which I was cast in the 1950s was entitled *This Is the Life*. It was a half-hour series dealing with moral dilemmas and offered parables. As with much of TV at that time, the show had good intentions. But in one of the episodes, instead of my usual casting as the good little girl, frightened and in trouble, I was cast as the mischief-maker, Molly. Robert Rockwell played my father. He had played Mr. Boynton in the TV series *Our Miss Brooks*; it's a small entertainment world. *This Is the Life* was recently released on DVD, repackaged as *Christian Scare Films*. I showed the video to my son when he was ten years old. He was amazed that I was ever so young. I'm sure he had never considered me as a little girl. He wasn't scared, either. But I thought it was rather ironic that this innocent show had to be marketed as a series of "scare" films.

There were many financial benefits to doing television as a youngster. Because of a scandal in the 1920s with child actor Jackie Coogan, California enacted the "Coogan Law" to protect the income children accrue in the entertainment business. Mr. Coogan had starred in many movies, including working with such famous actors as Charlie Chaplin, who had headlined with the young Coogan in the movie *The Kid*. Unfortunately for Jackie, his parents spent all of his money. As an adult, he was broke. He eventually regained fame as Uncle Fester in the 1960s television series *The Addams Family*. My good friend Lisa Loring played Wednesday on that black comedy and has related what a good cast it had and how wonderful it was to work with the experienced and talented Mr. Coogan. I recently received an invitation in 2015 from his grandson Keith Coogan to attend the celebration of what would have been Jackie's one hundredth birthday, where there was to be a tribute and a showing of his first film, *The Kid*.

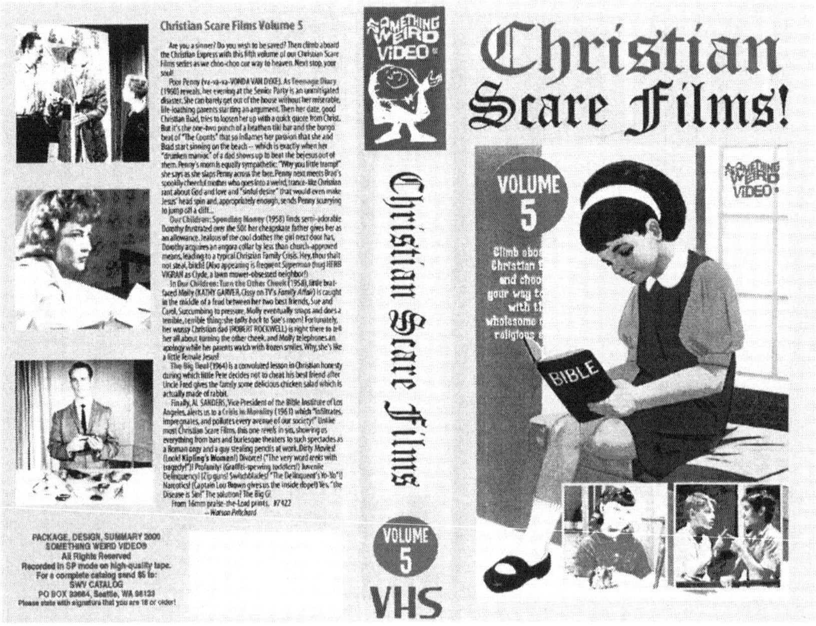


Starring in Christian "scare" films. I'm on the cover, first frame on the left.

At the time I started in the business, the Coogan Law applied only to steady players—children who had long-term contracts with movie studios. An actor friend of mine, Paul Petersen, who gained fame as Jeff in the classic TV series *The Donna Reed Show*, worked long and hard with the Screen Actors Guild, the SAG Young Performers Committee, on which I sat for a short while, and state lawmakers in Sacramento to change the law to include every child who worked under a contract in Hollywood. In 2000, the revised bill was put into effect to include all children who work even one day in film, television, or commercials and to have their earned money put into a special account for them to access when they turn eighteen. Their Coogan account must be preserved at an approved bank to which the production company sends 15 percent of the child actor's gross earnings. Currently, the law applies only to California and New York. However, there is renewed effort with Scott Schwartz taking over the reins of A Minor Consideration from Paul to enact this law nationwide. Progress is being made.

One of the main reasons I believe I survived the child actors' plague was because of my parents. Supportive and not using me as their personal bank, they saved the money I earned even before the Coogan Law. And saved all of it—not just a percentage to be put away. They did not use it to pay their bills or to support other members of my family. Many times, the parents of child actors use what their child has earned to overpay for business and family expenses and install themselves as managers so that they can collect a salary. Without control, sometimes all the monies that the child has earned disappear. This leaves child actors not only penniless when they are adults, but bitter.

I also had as normal an upbringing as parents of a child actor could muster. I believe that their handling of my career was another reason I survived the potentially debilitating entertainment whirl. With the first job I did, I had to miss regular school and be tutored on the set. To keep my child-acting boat on an even keel, my mother admonished me to not tell my friends at school where I had been, just simply that I had missed class. I followed her dictate. When people meet me, they are apt to say that I am very "down to earth." The attitude comes from my strong foundation, the way I was raised, and it is why I was able to survive Hollywood, if not a megastar, a happy megasurvivor.

Being a child actor comes with many benefits. First, an accredited teacher/welfare worker is hired to ensure minors are never overworked. There are specific time limits for each age of a child. Under the age of six, a youngster can work only a six-hour day. From ages six to eight, seven hours, from ages nine to fifteen, eight hours, and from ages sixteen to seventeen, ten hours. No overtime permitted. The union and the state in which an actor works have codified other regulations.

The studio teacher also sees to the child actor's schooling. Guess how many hours a day a minor actor must to go to school? Three. My son would like that schedule. The school time is recorded in twenty-minute blocks. Small amounts of time don't count; at least twenty minutes must pass in each session. Even though the time is short, it is like homeschooling with a professional tutor. I recently read a quotation by Frankie Muniz, the youthful headliner in the TV series *Malcolm in the Middle*. Frankie was a very successful child star. In the article, he was asked whether he missed anything about his childhood and growing up. Sitting back in his shiny black Porsche, a turbo my son tells me is one of only eighty-five made in the world, Frankie said, "I don't think so—what am I missing?" He has since gone on to become a triumphant and very happy open-wheel race-car competitor.

I had two big advantages when I entered show business going for me (besides my natural talent and training!). I looked younger than my age and I was small. I know I still don't look my age. It seems that everyone wants to be tall, but in Hollywood, being short is considered an advantage. Look at Mickey Rooney, Barry Gordon, or Sally Field. Being older and looking younger means you can play more youthful parts; you are more mature and are able to work longer hours.

My dear friend John Stephens, who was the production manager on *Family Affair* and who went on to produce Brian Keith's TV series *The Brian Keith Show* (née *The Little People*) as well as *Simon and Simon* and *Major Dad*, both starring Gerald McRaney, told me that producers look at the parents before they hire any child to headline a series. Looking to future episodes and the longevity of a show, the creators don't want their new little stars growing out of their roles. If the parents were short—the kids were in!

Not only petite, I also have always been very limber and could do the splits, both side and front, and wrap my ankles under my chin while on my stomach. I would be what is called a contortionist these days, but my father hated that word and said that's what circus performers do, and his precious little "Snooky" was definitely *not* going to be a circus performer! Snooky at that time was not an allusion to the infamous New Jersey performer of the 2000s and was definitely not in the lexicon of my white-collar father. He said I could continue with my dance classes as long as it was dance and acrobatics and had nothing to do with contortions (or New Jersey).

Gymnastics was not well known as an area of expertise at the time I was growing up or I would have certainly taken some training in that sport and perhaps have had aspirations for the Olympics or other athletic competitions. I have the body type of Cathy Rigby and have always been small, lean, and limber, although I must admit I was leaner younger. I settled for dancing, acrobatics, and cheerleading. Tennis and golf would come later. Gymnastics was not in the heavenly cards. But starring in wholesome fare definitely was.

# 8

# The Thread Theory

Threads! The fabric of my life is sewn in many different colors. Threads that continue to be gathered are those which God has set forth for me. Many times the threads are wound around guideposts. Sometimes they unravel quickly from tightly held spools and sometimes they are held taut, teasing to be cut. Sometimes they are like wisps of cotton left in a dense forest, swirling and tantalizing me to pick them up, perhaps to rub them together and form new threads. Sometimes hanging strings tantalize me to question where to put them in my coverlet of life. I am amazed how brightly some of these dazzling threads can shine and what they signify. Sometimes there are invisible threads and some black ones along the way. Sometimes small swatches are formed and laid before me; they amass at different times to add to the whole. The "thread theory" is the way I view some of the coincidences in life, or the series of fortunate events that happen, or harbingers to which God is beckoning me. Interwoven, they become my multicolored quilt of life.

One of the early guest spots I did on TV was for a 1950s series called *The Crusader*. I was cast in the part of a homeless waif. The show starred an excellent and virile actor who played Matt Anders, a seeker of justice. His character's goal was to free captives from Communist countries. Guess whom it starred? My future "reel" uncle, Brian Keith. It was one of the first coincidences and one thread that would be added to my *Family Affair* garment.

Then there was *The Millionaire*, not the reality show where Regis Philbin gave away buckets full of money, but the filmed TV series with Paul Frees, who played the part of John Beresford Tipton, millionaire, who indulged himself by giving money to those he deemed worthy of his largesse. A million dollars in those days was equivalent to about $8 million today. The amount would be quite a windfall and challenge to anyone. The show was very successful and was produced by Don Fedderson Productions, the same company that would later produce *Family Affair*.

As I looked at the cast and crew of *The Millionaire* on IMDb, the Internet Movie Database, I saw many people cataloged who later worked on *Family Affair.* For instance, Fred Henry was Don Fedderson's assistant producer in 1955, and he later filled the same position for *Family Affair* in 1966. Show business colleagues can be a loyal family. Once you have proved your worth as a reliable, responsible, and talented person, you can expect to be rehired. There is also a large amount of nepotism. And why not? Family members grow up and soak in the world of the relatives with whom they live. Film family members get firsthand experience of what, how, and whether things work in the business. Tido Fedderson, wife of Don, acted in ninety-three episodes of *The Millionaire* in 1956, playing the part of a nurse. Later, she played the part of a nanny in the first season of *Family Affair* and she hosted the premiere party of the new series at the Fedderson home in Encino Hills, California. The hairstylist Florence Bush and the makeup artist Jack Barron started our first year on *Family Affair* and also worked years before on *The Millionaire.*

As Annabelle in "The Mildred Milkin Story" episode of *The Millionaire,* I learned a big lesson. I was always quick to memorize my lines. When I was cast in this episode of *The Millionaire,* I was busy going to school, interviews, and dance classes. I recall that I learned my lines around 9:00 p.m. the night before the shoot. I had an early call but I was pleased to have memorized my lines perfectly and get a good night's sleep. Except, as I found out to my dismay the next day, I didn't learn the cues. If you gave me the first word of my line, I could easily complete it with dramatic feeling, but when was I supposed to *say* it? When it was realized on set that I didn't know the cues, I went to the side with the script supervisor and this time got the gist of the entire scene and when I was to contribute. This was another lesson learned on camera, never to be forgotten.

Born blond, my hair darkened as I grew older, and by the time I was eight years old, my locks had taken on the dark sheen of my French heritage. It seemed a natural for me to be cast as the little girl, Simone de Lannes, in the 1953 television series *The Adventures of Jim Bowie,* complete with an authentic Gallic accent. My sister, the reading prodigy, is also a wizard at languages and was the head of the language department at Scarsdale High School in New York. As a side note, she taught and also directed Peter Scolari in plays at Scarsdale High. Peter was the star of the TV series *Bosom Buddies* with Tom Hanks. He also starred in the TV series *Newhart* and in *Honey, I Shrunk the Kids* and is one terrific guy. I booked him in 2009 for a "Dine with the Celebrities" event I produced, which was assembled by my good and generous friend, Bill Gruber, from Chicago. Both Bill and Peter are warm, intelligent, and wonderfully personable. I'd love to perform the play *Love Letters* with Peter sometime—what a wonderful actor. More about Bill Gruber later in the book.

So . . . my sister . . . she could speak seven languages and taught with enthusiasm and aplomb. She devised the National French Exit Test for all US high school seniors. She was my dialect coach when I was a child, and under her tutelage, I emerged with a realistic accent for my role as Simone in *Jim Bowie.* She has also helped with other dialects that I needed for specific projects. Merci beaucoup, Beverly!

Westerns were big in the 1950s and 1960s, and I loved them! I could ride horses, jump on wagons, and cavort outdoors. I remember one weekend when my family treated my agent, Hazel McMillan, to a stay at the Smoke Tree Ranch in Palm Springs. My parents, Hazel, and I all had a grand time riding the galloping horses in the arroyos. In the 1990s, my brother Lance used different horsepower and kick-started a campaign for me to have a star on the Walk of Fame in Palm Springs on Palm Canyon Boulevard. More about the star later.

Because there was not as much political correctness in the 1950s and 1960s, and because of my dark hair and eyes, I played many Indian, Mexican, and French girls. In a turquoise squaw dress with a silver trinket belt, I costarred as the Indian child in a 1956 TV series entitled *Sheriff of Cochise*. John Bromfield, who had been characterized as a cross between Rory Calhoun and Steve Cochran—other 1950s "hunks"—starred as Sheriff Frank Morgan. Desilu, the company that I would revisit when I began filming the first year of *Family Affair*, produced the series. More threads unraveled, western and turquoise in hue.

# 9

# Taking the Reins

*Fury* was another western TV series I embraced with joy. I had a small crush on Bobby Diamond, who starred as Joey Newton in the show, so I was excited to be cast in an episode. Being a little shy, I masked my admiration of him with too many giggles and boisterous behavior. Fifty years later, I appeared with him and other stars at the Western Film Festival, and I was still shy around him!

My scenes on *Fury* were shot on location at Iverson Movie Ranch in Chatsworth, California. The set included corrals and a small house plus other outbuildings—it looked very realistic. I was always happy to shoot outdoors, especially on a beautiful day. With the wind blowing my hair and the sun warming my cheeks, I was in my favorite environment.

Also starring in *Fury* was Peter Graves, and even though we didn't have scenes together, he was on the set, emanating his pleasing presence. We had first worked together on *The Night of the Hunter.* There was the wonderful horse, Fury—what a grand animal! At a salary of $5,000 per week, this stallion was one of the most successful and highest-paid actors in the 1950s and 1960s. A gentle giant, he poked his head through the white rail fence, nudging for a carrot when I was doing one of my scenes. I happily complied. What a good time.

The western sets usually corralled my favorite animals, horses and . . . dogs.

I have always loved canine companions, from my first remembrance of our family mongrel named Blackie to my present-day ebony cocker spaniel, Coco. Hugging them and teaching them tricks gives me a sense of comfort and accomplishment. Coco can "stay," "come," and "roll" with a simple nod of a head or wiggle of a finger. She will shake with her paw and jump for a treat out of my hand—anything for a cookie. Unfortunately, she fell recently and had to have a very expensive back operation. I'm still making payments to the vet. Before her accident, she was a star, though, and appeared in the series *Trauma* and in an unsold pilot for a new TV show. We put everybody to work in our household.

My dog Coco after a Memorial Day parade.

I was very happy to be cast in the TV series *The Adventures of Rin Tin Tin* and *Sergeant Preston of the Yukon* when I was eleven and looking like an eight-year-old. *Rin Tin Tin* starred child actor Lee Aaker. It was fun on the set, but Lee seemed a little distant. *Sergeant Preston of the Yukon* was much more enjoyable. It starred Dick Simmons as the sergeant. He was supported by Yukon King, his trusty Alaskan husky (which was played by a malamute) and Rex, his stalwart horse. The TV series was an adaptation of the original radio show, *Challenge of the Yukon*, which began in 1938 and lasted until 1951 under that name. The TV series was titled *Sergeant Preston of the Yukon* but gained followers when the basic story of the *Challenge of the Yukon* remained the same and was then enhanced by the visual venue. Viewers observed the vital team slide across icy terrain in pursuit of evildoers.

The experience of *Sergeant Preston* developed in me a lifelong wish to experience the thrill of riding on a sled pulled by a dog team. My dream was fulfilled when my son, Reid, who was fourteen at the time, and I took a trip with Crystal Cruise Lines to Alaska. One of our ports was in the town of Skagway. Even though the wind was howling and snow swirled tiny, sharp icicles through the air when we docked, I was determined to go on a dogsled ride. Reid and I found the only company in the small hamlet that would operate on that frosty day. We took a harrowing trip in an aged helicopter up the steep side of a snow-laden mountain and were then deposited at an icy musher camp on the Denver Glacier. Donning additional layers of thick, water-repellent coats and gloves, my son and I firmly grasped the handles of our wooden sled and were thrillingly towed by the strong huskies at a fast clip through the crunchy ice as turbulent snow whirled around us. Cheeks pink and eyes watering, the speed was exhilarating, and even though I had waited over thirty years for this exciting ride, it was well worth it. It is no wonder that Disney's *Eight Below,* about brave huskies who survived six months on their own in Antarctica, is one of my favorite movies. I love survivors, canine or human. "Victim" is not in my lexicon.

# 10

# Foam Warp

Falsies. I was cast in an episode of *My Favorite Husband* in 1955. This TV series, like *Sergeant Preston*, had its start as a radio show. It starred Lucille Ball and Richard Denning and ran from 1948 to 1951. The main sponsor was Jell-O from General Foods. The 1948 radio version opened with announcer Bob LeMond proclaiming, "It's time for *My Favorite Husband* starring Lucille Ball!" followed by Lucy greeting the audience with, "Jell-O, everybody!"

CBS, which was producing radio and television, wanted to install *My Favorite Husband* on the new visual medium. The producers made an offer to Lucy and Richard to re-create their original roles for the TV version. Lucy refused to do the show unless her real-life husband, Desi Arnaz, played opposite her. After many conversations, CBS agreed to cast Desi, but not in the original form of *My Favorite Husband*. They reworked the show, used some story ideas from the original radio show, and introduced this version to the television audiences in what was to become the classic and beloved show *I Love Lucy*. CBS still wanted to do the *My Favorite Husband* concept on television, however.

Finally, in 1956, *My Favorite Husband* debuted on TV following the original radio concept. The series starred Joan Caulfield and Barry Nelson in the lead roles. When the time came for me to do my appearance on the show, the wife's role had been recast, and Vanessa Brown had taken over Joan Caulfield's part. A continuing thread in my garment of coincidences appeared when I realized that Edmund Hartmann, who was to become very important in my life on *Family Affair*, wrote some of the stories for *My Favorite Husband*. My episode was titled "The Child" and revolved around a youngster in some compromising situations. It was revealed at the end of the story that my character was not a child but a midget. I guess the producers thought it would be more convincing to have an actual child (me) aged instead of having an authentic midget dressed down, so I played the part of the little person. I was in the canvas dressing room on the stage of Desilu. My mother had been asked to help me dress. She entered with some strange-looking foam cones in her hand.

"What are those?" I asked innocently.

"You don't know?" my mother said, surprised.

"No," I said. "Do you put them under your arms?" They would seem to fit shape wise, I thought.

"No," she laughed. "You're supposed to be a grownup in this show . . . ?"

"Oh," I said, the light dawning and pink creeping into my cheeks. "I get it!"

And, indeed, I did get it, and I emerged on the set with quite a convincing and stunning figure for a ten-year-old!

Falsies again played a part in my life when I was cast in the movie *Monkey on My Back*, the true story of Barney Ross, championship boxer and ex-marine hero who became a drug addict. I costarred as the daughter of the actress Dianne Foster, who was playing Barney's girlfriend. Dianne's career in 1957 was on the upswing. Besides starring in *Monkey on My Back*, she essayed the part of Charlotte Drew, in the Western film *Night Passage*, which headlined James Stewart, Audie Murphy, and the handsome Dan Duryea. Dan's son, Peter, later played my boyfriend on *Family Affair.* Dianne also starred in *The Brothers Rico* with Richard Conte. Kathryn Grant, who later married Bing Crosby and was a friend of my sister from the UCLA days, was in this mafioso film too—another thread gathered.

In *Monkey on My Back*, Cameron Mitchell stars as Barney Ross. The real Mr. Ross had won the Silver Star and Purple Heart serving as a US Marine at Guadalcanal. As a former World War II bombardier, Cameron could accurately portray that aspect of Barney Ross's life. Barney had also won a Life Star as an unbeatable boxer: he was never knocked out as a pro and was the world lightweight boxing champion from 1933 to 1935. Cameron was in great shape. He received excellent reviews for his portrayal of Barney Ross, but there was some controversy at the end of the film. Barney claimed that the production company had not correctly depicted his life. Also, he was upset that the title of the movie had been changed from *No Man Stands Alone*, the name of the book he had authored, to the working title of the movie, *The Barney Ross Story*, finally to *Monkey on My Back*, an allusion to addicts who cannot extricate themselves from their drug problems. Ross was proud of the fact that he had been a hero and a renowned boxer. He had overcome his addiction and wanted the emphasis in the movie to be more on the things that he had accomplished rather than the addiction phase of his life. However, the film noir genre was strong in the fifties, and the producers thought they could get more play by exploiting the dark side of the story. The movie posters exhibit the shock element they were pursuing in their marketing campaign. Ross was on the set almost every day while we shot, so even though he instituted a lawsuit against the company, his claim was soon dropped. My mother told me she thought he had involved the attorneys to draw attention and publicity to the film. However, I now believe he was genuinely concerned about a true depiction of his life.

The wonderful André de Toth, who was an incredibly intriguing character to

Poster from the movie *Monkey on My Back*, in which I costarred with Cameron Mitchell and Dianne Foster.

me with the black patch he wore over his eye, directed the movie. Another thread that tightened my packet of life was that he was the director on Brian Keith's TV series *The Westerner*, which was filmed in 1960.

Oh, the falsies. Well, since *Monkey on My Back* covered a good bit of time, I had to age from playing a seven-year-old to a thirteen-year-old. I was eleven at the time and thought it would be difficult for people to believe me as a seven-year-old. I was much more confident that I could essay the part of an older woman of thirteen. After all, I could wear my foam falsies. Watching the film recently, I saw that my baby face and stature made me much more believable as the child of seven. I also was very surprised to hear my Oklahoma accent. Even though I had never lived in Oklahoma, I decided I must have picked up my parents' and siblings' dialect, surprising to me because my father was very insistent about the way his children spoke. We could not say "tin"—the number was "ten." We could not say "thang"—the correct pronunciation was "thing." Hmm, I wonder, is that why I have had a lifelong fascination with words and how one pronounces them? And why I majored in speech at UCLA?

From the film *Monkey on My Back*, where I aged from seven to thirteen. Sitting between Dianne Foster and Cameron Mitchell. © 1957, United Artists Corporation

From *Monkey on My Back*, where I am depicting a thirteen-year-old. With Cameron Mitchell, Dianne Foster, and Lisa Golm. © 1957, United Artists Corporation

A new garment is being sewn as I recently talked with Yaron Zilberstein, who is writing, directing, and producing a new film about Barney Ross to be released in 2016. Yaron had been deeply affected by the death of one his close actor friends who had died from an overdose and wanted to create a film which would show that no matter how difficult, one can overcome the tightening ropes of drug addiction. I will be playing a part in this film, sure to be a winning excursion into the inspiring life of the brave Barney Ross.

# 11

# Spinning Cotton

Creating more threads for my entertainment garment, in 1955 I tried out for and won a spot in the Oscar-winning film *I'll Cry Tomorrow*, starring Susan Hayward. The drama was based on the life of Lillian Roth, a Broadway star who rebelled against her domineering mother and became an alcoholic. The movie was nominated for several Academy Awards and garnered one for best costume design by Helen Rose. Directed by Daniel Mann (*Come Back, Little Sheba, Five Finger Exercise, The Teahouse of the August Moon*, and more), the film was an education, even though I only worked on the movie a few days. On the set, I gained experiences to tuck into my growing theatrical file. I could follow direction, find my marks, and smile on cue.

I auditioned and then secured a part in the suspense movie *The Bad Seed*, starring Patty McCormack, directed by the great Mervyn LeRoy (*No Time for Sergeants, Mister Roberts*, and more). *The Bad Seed* was nominated for four Academy Awards—Best Actress in a Leading Role (Nancy Kelly), Best Actress in a Supporting Role (Eileen Heckart and Patty McCormack), and Best Cinematography, Black and White. My big scene took place by a lake near Los Angeles. Shelley Fabares and I confront Patty in her role as Rhoda Penmark, who is suspected of being a murderer. I chastise Rhoda for her bad behavior toward a classmate, who is later found dead. It was quite a nice scene. The movie has become a cult classic, and I recently appeared with Patty when the film was exhibited at the Castro Theatre in San Francisco. We did a Q and A and signed autographed photos after the showing. The movie was adapted from its successful Broadway stage run and is very theatrical and at times overwrought, but makes for great drama and is great fodder for parody.

*The Bad Seed* cast rode on a studio bus to the location site for the 1956 film. My mother had bought me a new outfit to wear for the movie, gray and white polka-dot shorts and a contrasting white and gray polka-dot top. I was a little younger than Patty and Shelley, and there were some older extras that had been hired to fill out the scene. They had rolled up the pant legs to their shorts and jeans, the style of the day, but my mother said I couldn't do that, and the wardrobe lady agreed. I felt uncomfortable, and the scratchy new fabric of the shorts chafed my thighs. But I overlooked the wardrobe and continued to berate Rhoda for her unseemly behavior. Unfortunately, my scenes were "left on the cutting room floor." My mother said it was because I was so good that I showed up Patty. I thought it was because my shorts were too long.

Many guest spots on episodic TV followed, and I loved acting in two of the most-heralded series in the 1950s: *Matinee Theater* and *Climax*. These were repertory series, taped live, which showcased a complete story each week presented like a stage show. Acting without retakes had its positive and negative aspects: what was done was done, no stopping. In one *Climax* episode, "The Heat Wave," I played a Chicago girl suffering through the summertime weather. To get relief, my friends and I were to cavort in the cooling stream of a fire hydrant. On live TV, we put our heads near the sprays of water, but the hydrant didn't turn off

Patty McCormack, Shelley Fabares, and I shooting *The Bad Seed*, with Tony Award–winning actress Nancy Kelly looking on.

when it should. There we were, frolicking in the watery bursts, and frolicking, and frolicking. The show was finally over and we had a flooded set.

Another anthology series I enjoyed doing was *Telephone Time*. This show had a future *Family Affair* connection, which I will explain later. The show's writer, host, and narrator was John Nesbitt. On the series, Mr. Nesbitt covered topics that exposed the good and bad qualities of people. My episode, "Parents of a Stranger," concerned the John Tracy Clinic, which was founded by actor Spencer Tracy and his wife, Louise Treadwell Tracy. The Tracys had discovered that their son, John, was deaf and so opened a Los Angeles hearing clinic in 1924 to help others in need. John Nesbitt thought their clinic would be a good basis for a meaningful story. I was cast as Carol Wallace, the older sister of a little girl (played by twin six-year-olds Debra and Diane Wayne) whom my screen parents discover is deaf. In

From the TV series *Telephone Time*, where I am throwing a tantrum (as my character) in the episode "Parents of a Stranger."

the episode, my jealousy rages as I see my little sister getting far more attention than I get. In a memorable scene, which was filmed in one take, I explode and in a rampage grab the family photo from the bedside table in my parents' bedroom, smashing it again and again on the edge of a wooden table. I then start to cry hysterically and, spent, throw myself on the bed. It was a wonderful cathartic moment for me personally as well as for the character. After the dramatic scene, my reel parents come in and offer me solace. With their comfort, I realize that my parents love me, too. They see I have needs that also must be met. The experience softened my character's temperament. In one of the later scenes, I am quietly and sweetly reading to my little sister in cozy new blue flannel pajamas that I got to keep. It was important to Mr. Nesbitt that this lesson of remembering and attending to the emotional needs of others in the family, when dealing with ones that seemingly need the most care, be learned. At the end of the show, John Nesbitt interviews the real child on whom the story was based—a client of the John Tracy Clinic. The *Family Affair* connection? Paul Ivano was the brilliant cinematographer on this *Telephone Time* episode and later became the director of photography on the first season of *Family Affair*. And as a straggling thread, Sebastian Cabot also appeared in a *Telephone Time* episode entitled "The Prince of Wales."

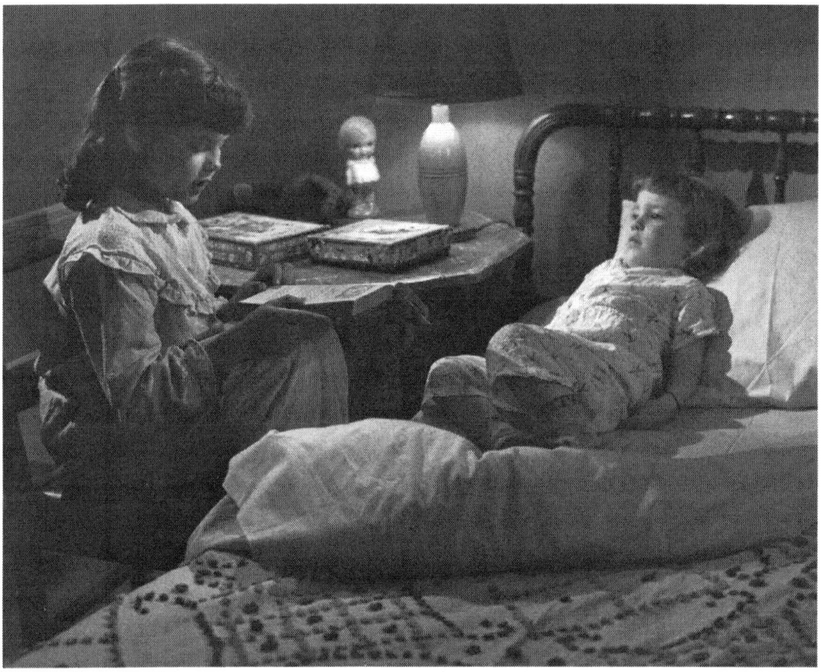

Reading to my pretend sister in an episode of *Telephone Time*.

As Hamlet proclaimed, "the play's the thing," and I enjoyed acting in classic plays as a child at the Los Angeles Shakespeare Center off Melrose Avenue in Hollywood. I played in *The Comedy of Errors* as Luciana and then as Helena in *A Midsummer Night's Dream*. The roles were great preparation when I tackled the role of Juliet in *Romeo and Juliet* in London years later. These bases of theatrical portrayals which extended to film, radio, and voice-overs as I gained more experience and this early training helped me develop credible characters throughout my career.

# 12

# Selling Threads

Commercials were strong threads strung throughout my career. Landing a national commercial just when the bank account was starting to thin was always a cause to celebrate. One of the first commercials I secured was almost my last. I was cast in a national Sugar Jets cereal commercial. The scenario is that my reel brother and I are hiking when we get stranded on a papier-mâché mountain—shades of *The Ten Commandments*. We find ourselves on the high ledge of a rocky mountain cliff that had been built on the concrete studio floor. Below us wolves bay and clamor to jump up and make us their next meal. We siblings, not to be deterred, gobble a bit of mighty Sugar Jets cereal and fly off the ledge, spirited away by the sugary sweet energy. I was wearing a harness over a leotard hidden under my short, red-checked dress. During a break, instead of being escorted off the plastic mountain by the crew and then removing the fly-rigging and paraphernalia like my brother, I chose to remain on the precipitous ledge. I was enjoying the excitement of looking down on everything below and also didn't want to take the time to take everything off and put it back on again. The rigging handler was below to watch me. He pledged to protect me. Peering farther over the edge, I inched closer to the precipice, looking to see where the wolves had gone. Then my foot slipped on the glazed surface and I started to fall off the faux mountain. It was about thirty feet down. The quick-thinking rigger immediately sprang to action pulling the strings, literally, and guided me, as if I were a marionette doll, back to my spot on the ledge. Another "Whew." I told you it's hard to be an actress. And sometimes perilous. But I was able to survive this precipitous experience.

New technology has saved many early films, TV shows, and commercials. I watch with fascination as I see how young I was and the adventures I experienced in these early shows and advertisements. I recently was sent a DVD titled *Kid's Commercials from the Golden Age of Television*. In one, I am shown peddling the wonderful qualities of Scotch tape. I could hardly remember doing the commercial. But I recognized the dress. It was the same red-checked one I wore for the Sugar Jets commercial.

# 13

# Radio Connections

Besides television, radio played a large role in my early and later career. Even before auditioning for the film *The Night of the Hunter*, my first interview was for the radio show *Baby Snooks*. Fanny Brice had originated the character of Baby Snooks in 1944. The radio program did very well, even though Fanny, a forty-year-old woman, played the part of the child, Baby Snooks. Unfortunately, Ms. Brice suffered a cerebral hemorrhage in 1951 and the show had to be canceled. The Baby Snooks character was so beloved that CBS wanted to revive the show—this time with a real child in the title role. My mother heard about their quest and dressed me like a frilly little doll in a pastel green dress, replete with dainty contrasting stiches, to go on the interview—even though it was for radio. I had never heard of *Baby Snooks* and wondered why I would go on an interview for a baby when I was a big girl of six. But go I did, with a big pink and green bow in my curly hair to complement my crisp hand-smocked dress. I didn't get the job, and evidently CBS could find no one to replace the wonderful Fanny Brice. She died in 1959.

A milestone and a learning experience came when I was cast in the anthology radio series *Whispering Streets*. I was so excited. It starred the one and only Bette Davis. My mother and I were going to meet and I was going to get to work with the great star. Miss Davis was the semiregular host of this romantic soap opera–style drama. Mom and I dressed in our nicest outfits to meet her at the recording studio. I carried a new, clear plastic, lunch box–type purse. I could put different colored scarves in it to match my dress. I thought Bette would be quite impressed. I was attending Emerson Junior High in Westwood at the time. My mother picked me up from school and we honked our way through traffic to Hollywood. Climbing the steps to the ABC Building on Highland Avenue, our excitement grew as we prepared to meet the luminous actress. Flinging open the door, we expected to see the star already there, as we were a little late. Breathlessly we asked, "Where is Miss Davis?"

"Oh, she's not here," the engineer said.

"Where is she?" we asked expectantly.

"She's in New York."

"Well, how she is going to record her part?"

"At the studio in New York."

I was getting a little confused at this point and somewhat frustrated. It was finally explained that Bette taped her narration part in New York—the radio play was recorded in LA with the cast and then the engineer and director spliced the whole mishmash together.

"Oh," we sighed with disappointment.

"You'll still hear your voices together," he said consolingly.

It was little solace, and I never carried my plastic bag again, somehow blaming it for my bad luck.

I recorded more episodes of *Whispering Streets*, but I never did get to meet Bette Davis. I did discover something from that experience, however—the excitement of acting primarily with one's voice. This experience would serve me later in life, and to this day, in the wonderful world of voice-over work. I also learned that some things never change.

Not long ago, I was hired to record episodes of *The Twilight Zone Radio Drama*, inspired by the classic Rod Serling TV series. My friend, Carl Amari, who had owned the company Radio Spirits, is a radio enthusiast. He worked long and hard with the owners of *The Twilight Zone* teleplays to obtain the rights to adapt the original television stories to radio shows. Carl was quite successful in his endeavors, and *The Twilight Zone* radio plays now appear on CD and at www .TwilightZoneradio.com.

The first episode I recorded for the *TZ* radio shows is called "The Fever." This story is about my character's husband, who becomes obsessed with a slot machine in Las Vegas. Stacy Keach played the part of my husband. I've always admired his work, and I have to admit I have a little crush on him. I couldn't wait to meet Stacy. I'm still waiting. He recorded his part at a studio in LA. Ah well, at least our voices intertwined!

In November 2011, I attended the final convention in New Jersey of Friends of Old Time Radio, which had been founded by Jay Hickerson. Sometimes life goes full circle as Gloria McMillan, my long-time agent's daughter, and I participated by re-creating some of the roles in the great radio shows of the forties, fifties, and sixties. Other legendary voices added their talent to panels and to the radio re-creations of the original shows *Gunsmoke*, *Ethel and Albert*, *My Favorite Husband* (remember the falsies?), and others. Ben Ohmart, author of over ten books on classic radio, TV, film, and voice-over as well as publisher of the same genres, conducted a one-on-one interview with Arthur Anderson, author of *Let's Pretend and The Golden Age of Radio* and *An Actors Odyssey: From Orson Welles to Lucky the Leprechaun*. Arthur performed the voice of the Irish character for Lucky Charms cereal for twenty-nine years. Ben is another one of the threads that winds interestingly around my spool of life. He published my first book, *The Family Affair Cookbook*, through his Bear Manor Media publishing company.

Joe Franklin, who had previously interviewed me and who hosted *The Joe Franklin Show* for forty consecutive years, is considered to be one of television and radio's most durable personalities. For a time, Joe hired Bette Midler with her accompanist Barry Manilow as his in-house singer when he hosted his long-running TV talk show. Woody Allen, Dustin Hoffman, Barbra Streisand, Bill Cosby, and Liza Minnelli are among the world's great talents who got their first exposure on *The Joe Franklin Show*. This Friends of Old Time Radio event was a grand good-bye to Joe and the thirty-six-year-old convention, which brought radio enthusiasts, classic radio stars, and fans together to relive and delight in the wonderful feelings those radio memories elicit.

The clamor for old-time radio however, could not be stilled. In May 2015 I went to Cincinnati to appear at the Nostalgia Expo and Old Time Radio Convention. Radio enthusiasts again heard the sounds of yore on the wonderful equipment of today. The sound effects and music that were presented enhanced our live re-creations. So another event was planned. You can't keep a good radio event down.

My *Family Affair Cookbook*, which I penned in 2009.

# 14

# Silken Cords

After my dad's stint with the government as a Federal Housing Inspector, Ross Cortese, land developer extraordinaire, hired my talented father in the 1950s. Mr. Cortese was most well known for having created Leisure World for retirees in Orange County, California. Before Cortese created those complexes, however, he developed a successful walled community near Los Alamitos, California, named Rossmoor. One of the reasons Rossmoor flourished was because of Cortese's innovative way to lure potential buyers by building a completed, decorated model home that prospects could view while the rest of the housing community was still under construction. Cortese sold 3,800 homes in Los Alamitos in three years. And my talented father was the one who brought Cortese's dreams of a beautiful tract of homes to fruition as architect/contractor of Rossmoor.

My father bought some of the fancy furniture from one of those Los Alamitos model homes to furnish my mother's next project—a custom-built home on the outskirts of prestigious Beverly Hills. Mom had found a lot off Benedict Canyon in 1956. Dad drew the plans, this time for our single-family dwelling. I was delighted to design my own room. Benedict Canyon was home to many stellar actors, and Mary Pickford's mansion sat regally on the hill above our house. My friend Karen Jacobson lived at the end of our street, Shadybrook Drive, and we would go on grand adventures to explore our surroundings. At the time, Shadybrook dead-ended at an enormous vacant piece of land. Karen and I would clamber over a low wooden fence and investigate the terrain and pick wild kumquats from the laden trees. It struck my guilt-ridden Catholic heart that we were trespassing and perhaps we should ask permission to go on our illicit quests. Karen decided that I should be the one to venture up to the big estate on Benedict Canyon, which oversaw the verdant lands, to get sanction. One day, I anxiously squeezed through the large iron gate that was built to keep out intruders like me and then cautiously ambled up the long drive, gathering my courage. Finally reaching the mansion's stone entryway, I timidly knocked on the massive wooden door. A large man in an impeccable butler's uniform slowly opened it. I softly gave him my request and he emphatically bellowed, "No!"

"No?" I timidly replied.

"NO!" he roared louder.

I slinked away and never again traipsed up to the grandiose estate of the famous silent film star Harold Lloyd. However, just because our request was not granted to amble on the large grassy vacant lands, Karen and I did not stop our covert pursuits. We had exercised our due diligence and had asked politely. Adventures were more important at age twelve than stolidly following the law, so we continued to surreptitiously gambol over the fence, march around the meadows, and gather forbidden fruit.

Every November, land to the right of Lloyd's property served as a palette to the spray-painting of mammoth green fir Christmas trees. The newly tinted timber was then placed in the Beverly Hills parks, which lined Santa Monica Boulevard. I don't know why they were painted blue, but I thought they were quite pretty, if not classic, and I retrieved some of the anomalous colored branches that were left behind after the spraying was completed. I displayed them with pride in my gaily decorated bedroom at home during Christmas, alongside my traditional baubles and bangles of bright red and green.

One holiday, all I wanted from Santa was a chimpanzee. A real chimpanzee. My parents usually tried to fulfill their children's wishes, and I was adamant that I would not be a happy child on Christmas morning if I did not have a live, furry monkey to feed, dress, and love. The special December morning arrived, and I scampered to our living room with our traditional green tree with its silver icicles, assorted ornaments, and multicolored bubble lights, hoping to see my chimpanzee jumping about. There, on the floor in the center of the tree on the fake snow was a gigantic, woolly, black chimpanzee. Stuffed. It wasn't a chimpanzee that had ever lived in a real, green jungle. I think my father bought it at the Beverly Hills Drugstore—but it was big, plush, and snuggly. I lugged that winsome toy beast around with me for three years.

When my family and I migrated from Baldwin Hills to Beverly Hills, I started Beverly Hills Catholic School. I was eleven and in the sixth grade. My friend Jon Provost (Timmy from the TV series *Lassie*) was just a couple of years behind me. Another classmate with ties to celebrity was in my grade. Gail Stone Darley is Rosemary Clooney's half-sister, George Clooney's kin. She recently became my Facebook pal and we relived some memories. Love that technology. As Gail Stone, she starred with Eve Arden in the delightful 1957 series *The Eve Arden Show*. Laura Montalban, Ricardo Montalban's daughter and Loretta Young's niece, was also in my class. These stars and the children of stars had been rumored first to be at the school and then proclaimed in whispered awe to belong to our church. It was as if they were saints. We found out later they weren't saints, just situated in an august position. They became names that were conversation starters, as everyone wanted to know all about them because, after all, hadn't they been introduced on TV or the films? They were practically friends already (as well as having star power).

Gail, Laura, and I were confirmed together at the Catholic Church of the Good Shepherd on Santa Monica Boulevard in Beverly Hills. Loretta Young, Frank Lovejoy, and a spattering of other stars were all at the ceremony. It was quite a stellar affair!

There is a part during the Confirmation Sacrament where the confirmands are to stand and take a vow to refrain from drinking until the age of twenty-one. I am embarrassed to report that all the class stood except my older brother Lance, who was being confirmed alongside me. Four years my senior, I suspected he had already had a little "experience" in the drinking realm and he knew he wouldn't be able to keep the vow legitimately. I shouldn't be too hard on him. When I was seventeen and enrolled in UCLA, I immediately got my fake ID and scampered to the students' favorite pub, "Mom's" in Westwood, and participated in and won many beer-chugging contests.

More embarrassment came my way on Confirmation Day when I discovered I had left my name card in the pew. As I slowly walked, as rehearsed, up the aisle to the altar, I shockingly remembered I had left this important card, with my confirmation name for the cleric to read, on the church bench. Recalling the shades of horror on the faces of Mrs. Meglin and Sister Virginia Mary when I had committed other equally heinous faux pas, my hands began shaking and my throat went dry. In addition to that anxiety, I realized that our confirmation class had been selected to have the revered Cardinal McIntire officiate at our sacrament instead of our Bishop. When I finally reached the altar, I approached the august cleric. I didn't have the name card to give him. I weakly mumbled that I had left it in the pew. With a divine kindliness, the Cardinal bent over and gently whispered, "It's all right. Just quietly tell me the name you have chosen."

In a trembling voice, I quavered, "Theresa."

"All right," he said consolingly. And then, in a booming voice, he declared, "I confirm this young lady in the name of Theresa."

Whew! I was validated, no lightning had struck, and I was now able to proceed on a blessed path. Getting to this point had been a huge Catholic struggle.

BHCS was a stalwart school settled in the midst of comfortable Beverly Hills homes set below Wilshire Boulevard. I attended classes there for only one year, but it was enough to have continued my love of learning and fear of nuns. I can still relate accurate information about Elisha Otis and other great inventors blossoming in the late 1800s and would be a great contestant on *Jeopardy* if they asked questions about those early innovators. Nuns I skirt to this day.

The protected educational and social shields were soon to be broken as I followed my parents' dictum. It was time for reality and for public school. So, for the seventh grade, I began a new view of education and society at Emerson Junior High School in Westwood.

In the fifties, I was still acting quite a bit in episodic TV, film, and radio. When I was absent from school because of work, my mother always told me, "Don't tell your friends where you were." I don't know whether she gave me this advice to prevent jealousy or to keep me from crowing over my acting adventures, but it developed in me a sense of career quietude—never heralding my achievements, creating a low-publicity presence.

Since our home was on the periphery of Beverly Hills, even though we had a Beverly Hills address, my brother Lance went to University High School in West Los Angeles and shared space with child stars such as Tommy Rettig from the original *Lassie* TV show. Our bus would cruise to Frank Sinatra's house and pick up Frank Sinatra Jr. to take him to school. By this time, my sister was married (at nineteen, she graduated from UCLA and was then out on her own adventure) and my brother Bud (nee Hayes) was in the army. I was continuing my entertainment career.

# 15

# Changing Swatches

In 1959, my father received an offer from Robert Bruce, who had the funding and contract to build a tract of homes in San Bernardino, California, to be his architect/contractor. San Bernardino is about an hour and a half from downtown Los Angeles on a good traffic day but miles away from the sophisticated and sometimes tawdry world of showbiz. My father accepted the offer, and it was decided that we sell our Beverly Hills home and move to San Bernardino, orange capital of California. My brother Lance was graduating from University High School, my other brother, Bud, was going to start college, and my sister, Beverly, had two children and was living in Oregon. I would be finishing ninth grade at a new junior high—Golden Valley. At that new school, I met students who remain my closest friends to this day.

My mother thought I could continue my career—after all, the hub of the entertainment industry in Hollywood was "not that far," but it turned out to be difficult and "out of sight, out of mind."

I did go on a few acting interviews, most notably for the lead role in *Gidget*, but most of the time was spent finding my identity as a young woman. I believe by experiencing more or less normal teenage years, I was able to escape the awkward period from child actor to ingénue. I think the opportunity to grow up in a small town with good friends and to be given the opportunity to excel in academics, community, and social activities without the stress of show business saved me from the difficult transition that derails so many child actors. I was free to establish my personality away from glaring lights with a million people watching. The strain of trying to be perfect for a particular part was lessened.

I was able to establish strong friendships. Those whom I met in my teenage years remain my dearest allies. I still see them often—there's nothing like long-time friends who know your history. All my wonderful experiences of growing up coalesced to form a foundation of support that helps me throughout my life.

It is interesting that our small-town high school produced such successful personages. My boyfriend throughout my days at Pacific High School in San Bernardino, Bob Damus, graduated from Dartmouth University and then segued to Harvard Law School. He became General Counsel for the Office of Management and Budget from 1994 until his untimely death of a heart attack at the age of fifty-five. Bob had joined OMB in 1985 as an assistant general counsel and was then named deputy general counsel. He was instrumental in devising budget control legislation, including the balanced budget act of 1997. The country could certainly use him now! He served three presidents well. Bob became a career civil servant and one of a small number of government lawyers to have reached the general counsel level by means other than a political appointment. As President Clinton wrote in his "Statement on the death of Robert G. Damus on November 30, 2000":

> I am deeply saddened by the sudden passing of Bob Damus, General Counsel for the Office of Management and Budget. Bob made invaluable contributions to the common good in his 20 years of Government service, embodying the very finest qualities of our Nation's career civil servants. Bob's fine intellect and the breadth of his knowledge were respected throughout Government and beyond. This administration and the American people benefited greatly from his keen judgment and wise counsel, and he served my two predecessors with the same loyalty, dedication, and commitment to excellence. With a distinguished academic background, Bob chose government service out of a deep desire to contribute to the public good. In recognition of his outstanding service, he twice received the Presidential Rank Award as a Distinguished Executive, the highest honor for career civil servants in the senior executive service. Bob's probity and integrity were unsurpassed. He was a supremely decent man, and his memory will serve as an inspiration to us all.

I second all the kind words of President Clinton.

My rival for Bob in high school, Karen Kuhl, married right out of college and has four beautiful children who are happy and successful adults with children of their own. Karen has thirteen grandchildren. Although her beloved husband of forty-two years, John Stassi, member of the prestigious Duck Club in Northern California and mortgage broker par excellence, died at sixty-seven of cancer, Karen continues with great spirit. She and her friends and family endowed a scholarship at the Christian Brothers School in John's name.

Another friend, Dave Richards, who was my partner in our high school speech and debate class, proffered me the winning line at the end of my summary for our final State Speech Debate Contest when the topic was: Resolved that San Bernardino should become part of the Feather River Water Project. I staunchly proclaimed, "The other side's argument simply does not hold water." We won. After attending Yale University, Dave became a renowned lawyer who filed a Supreme

Court lawsuit regarding ageism. He is also one of the largest collectors of Rudyard Kipling memorabilia and authored a book on Kipling.

My dear friend Heidi Crane taught screenwriting and English at Santa Monica College for thirty years and has produced three movies so far, *13 Conversations about One Thing*, starring Alan Arkin and Amy Irving, among them. Whenever I travel to LA from San Francisco she opens the door of her gracious home in the San Fernando Valley to accommodate me. She calls my beautifully appointed room and surrounds my "vacation house," and it has indeed provided me a respite from my duties and responsibilities to home and family in my Northern California abode.

Taking care of her friends—traveling every day to South Central Los Angeles to the home of one of the school secretaries who worked at Santa Monica College to minister to her in her dying days, for instance—is typical of Heidi's caring and giving personality. She also drove miles to help a pair of her married friends when it was discovered one had cancer after the other had a heart attack; she supported them emotionally and physically until their deaths.

Heidi is also extremely attentive to her dogs, one of whom, Ollie, was a strong rottweiler who weighed more than Heidi and whose legs and hips were genetically deformed. She spent a great deal of time and money to assure a good quality of life for him until those anomalies finally took him to his death. Of her current stable of two black labs and a mutt, one requires special treatment, and Heidi is there for care and support. Speaking of stables, Heidi also has rescued horses and pays for their care, feeding, and housing. She drives an eight-hour round trip to visit, ride them, and make sure they are receiving the attention they deserve. Heidi is giving and altruistic, with a great sense of humor. I am proud to have her as my friend.

Another classmate and friend, Twanette Tharp, sister of famed choreographer Twyla Tharp, became a successful interior designer on Martha's Vineyard and decorated Jackie O's house when she had a home there. Her work has been featured in *Architectural Digest* and other prestigious design magazines.

Marilyn Horwitz lived the reverse order of my life. After attending Golden Valley Junior High School, Marilyn went to a different high school than Pacific High, but we kept in touch through our social clique. Then we went to UCLA together. She got married soon after and had three children right away. She got divorced. At forty she went back to school, received her law degree, and married Don Nelson, Ozzie Nelson's younger brother. She is now partner in a prestigious law firm in Beverly Hills and proud grandmother of six beautiful grandchildren. I pursued my career, did not get married until I was thirty-five, and did not have my child until I was forty-five. Reverse paths, still best of friends.

Steve Dixon, another lawyer, moved to Hawaii and became executive director for the Attorneys and Judges Assistance Program, helping those who became addicted to abusive substances. He found time to write a book about his beloved island home, *The Hawaiian Voyages of the Ono Jimmy*, which has received great reviews. Steve also finds time to sail the beautiful azure waters of the gorgeous island chain on his prized boat. Sometimes he will rendezvous with Linda Brooks, another classmate, who makes her home on the island of Kauai. After teaching in LA, Linda moved to the island and opened a yoga training and massage facility with her husband, Kevin. They became known as those who gave Massages to the Stars with therapeutic treatments to Tipper Gore, Demi Moore, and others who would visit Kauai. After the horrific hurricanes of the 1990s, which decimated their home and business, Linda rebuilt the house and the business and got divorced. She continued working. She now is great friends and companion to Felipe Pomar—past Peruvian surfing champion—and they can be seen riding the waves of the waters in Kauai, blissfully enjoying the exhilaration of the sport in their golden years.

Another friend, Ricky Burrus, became an insurance executive and was happily married to his wife Patty for over forty years. Their children are quite successful. Even after a heart attack, Ricky rode his motorcycle over the rough terrain of the hills of Southern California. As I was completing this book, Rick suffered another heart attack. My dear friend passed on in 2013. Our high school friends gathered with others to pay homage to this energetic booster of life, seldom seen without a beaming smile. He is sorely missed.

My best artistic friends at Pacific were Jimmy Chovick and Vaughn Lewis. Jim participated in plays in high school and at San Diego State. He graduated from UCLA and started a theatrical career. Unfortunately, throat cancer upended him. After radiation treatment for a year and a half, he conquered the disease and is a theatrical fixture in San Diego, having acted successfully in every one of the theater companies there. A wonderfully kind and talented person.

Vaughn, the only person at Pacific who wore sandals and would be termed a "bohemian" in the sixties, changed his name to Alan and followed his artistry into the culinary realm. After managing resorts in the Carmel/Monterey area of Northern California, he and his lovely wife, Kati, purchased a small restaurant in the heart of Carmel and ran the bistro La Boheme for twenty years before they moved to Paris, France, to make that country their retirement haven—ah, so romantic!

Then there is Chris Curtis, son of a judge in San Bernardino, who saves and restores historic buildings in Oakland.

My friend in Orinda, Dr. Bill Olson, after practicing, became Medical Director for United Health Care in Northern California. We dated in high school and recently, as friends, went to a concert headlining Carole King and James Taylor at the Oakland Coliseum, reliving the melodious vibes we shared in the sixties.

Scott Spear entered Pacific in our junior year and was embraced by our group. After college, he created a green environment foundation and was a top farmer in Visalia, California.

Paul Sage, son of the founder of Sage Foods in San Bernardino and other locations in the Inland Empire, lives in Idaho and continues his father's tradition as a retailer and hardworking family man.

Pam Parke was my intellectual friend who was also an accomplished musician. I remember going with her to nearby University of Redlands, where she was taking music lessons. I sat outside the practice room and listened to her beautiful violin music waft through the glass partitions. Pam became a doctor and practices a different kind of discipline in Palo Alto as a respected dermatologist.

Then there is my wonderful friend Ellen. After we were roommates in Rieber Hall at UCLA and she graduated, Ellen married Stan Weisser. I was a bridesmaid at their wedding in San Bernardino and watched in fascination as they stomped on a glass to signify their commitment to each other under a flower-bedecked trellis. She was one of my first friends to get married and has had the longest committed relationship. Stan is a pharmacist. He and Ellen bought a pharmacy/drugstore, then another one, and then another one. Kind, giving, and community minded, they built a successful life together. Ellen, always energetic, was recently honored for her contributions; even in a bad economy, the board on which she sits was able to increase the value of investments on behalf of the pensioners they represent through her expert recommendations. Stan sold the drugstores but remained as a consultant. Then he became a board member of a bank. Recently a building for the Redlands Community Hospital was dedicated in their name. They are generous, kind, and caring contributors; they are generous, kind, and caring friends.

Why such success for these classmates? Was it because of the small-town atmosphere? Where we could go unfettered, without fear of crime, and freely investigate our opportunities? Where we as teenagers could innocently cruise the streets, honking, basking in acknowledgment of our friendship?

The hills and mountains surrounding the small town of San Bernardino protected us from the howling winds. We were also insulated from the harsh realities of urban life. But the valley retained encroaching, unwanted, and growing smog. As we grew older and then left the town, many of us broke through the haze of the tranquil environment and developed a clearer, more complex vision as to how to live our lives.

Our group certainly had our teenage escapades, however. One of them was almost our last as the girls in our clique decided to venture up to Bob Damus's beautiful home in the foothills of San Bernardino. The boys were having an "overnight" and, of course, we girls had to spy on them. As quietly as sixteen-year-old girls could be, we surreptitiously made our way up the slippery slope to Bob's bedroom window, even as we broke twigs and branches. All of a sudden we were startled when the door flew open and there was Bob's father, Shelby, standing with a shotgun in his hands. We veritably flew off the hill and clambered into the car, shakily urging the jalopy to hurry and start. Then we were off!

There was the night that my friend Pam Parke and I decided to go on an adventure. A tract of newly minted houses had just gone on the market. We decided it would be fun to spend the night in one of the fully furnished model homes. I told my mother I would be staying at Pam's, and of course Pam told her mother she would be staying at my house. There were a few people touring the model home when we arrived late in the afternoon. Just as the salesperson started to shoo the people out, I dove under a bed in one of the bedrooms, and Pam dipped under another one. We heard the door lock, and there we were, in our forbidden abode.

The experience was pretty boring and a little scary. I spent a fitfully cold night and was grateful when the sun dawned and it was time to scamper out of the house, proudly able to proclaim we had spent an entire night trespassing.

# 16

## Knots in the Yarn

My high school classmates and I had our innocent adventures and adventurously tried illicit commodities. My first cigarette was attempted sitting on Ellen's curbside. I had three puffs and fainted. But I was determined, so I kept at it and finally could smoke an entire cigarette without getting too lightheaded and passing out. For some strange reason I kept my packs of filtered Kents in a sock in my purse. Unfortunately, one day my mother found them. She was not happy and tried to confiscate them. I fought back, but she won.

There was the heady mixture of Boone's Farm wine and 7 Up, a wine cooler that my friends and I mixed together and gulped out of large plastic glasses. I don't know if I threw up because of the alcohol or the sugary soda, but the few times I drank in high school, I could count on returning home with everything spinning like one of those carnival rides that loses its floor.

It reminds me of the time our "posse" took the bus to Laguna Beach, California, for one of our Easter breaks. The entire two-hour trip I practiced pushing down my fingers into the configuration of an obscene gesture. It took a long time for my innocent fingers to get the hang of it, but by the time I arrived at the beach, anytime someone annoyed me, I was prepared to show off my newly found skill.

It was in Balboa Island that one of my friends introduced me to a friend of hers whose parents owned a beach house. She invited us over, and the entertainment was to practice the art of hypnotism. We sat down, and she attempted to hypnotize me. She told me to do whatever she did, so I followed her motions, dipping my hand into some lotion and then wiping my forehead with my hand, then my cheeks, and then my chin. Nothing seemed to happen. I didn't seem hypnotized at all. And we were hungry. My new friend said, "We'll try it again after dinner." I was certain I couldn't be hypnotized. Too much in control, I thought. Then we all left for dinner.

We climbed the hill to Cliff Drive in Laguna to the famous Victor Hugo Restaurant, now Las Brisas Restaurant. Then one of my friends warned, "Kathy, you can't go into the restaurant."

Feelings hurt, I asked, "Why not?"

She consoled, "All right. Hurry into the powder room and straighten your hair or something, look in the mirror."

I followed her dictate. What was wrong with me? Did I look a mess? I slipped by the maître d' and into the restroom. Staring back at me from the gilt-edged mirror was a face smeared with black grease! Ha ha, really funny joke.

On prom night, my parents were in Needles, California, where they were living while my father built a new tract of homes. I invited friends over for after-prom partying. I drank my first hard liquor, a screwdriver made of orange juice and vodka. I drank another one. Another one went down while I was sitting on the couch in the living room. Then it was time to get up off the sofa. I quickly popped up and promptly fell right back down. Head spinning, I moved more slowly to the bathroom. The rest of the night I was in and out of that small confined and spinning room.

The next morning, I discovered girls in various beds in the house and some boys asleep on the chaise lounges around the pool. My parents had left me under the watchful eye of my older brother Lance, tasked with the unenviable job of overseeing a teenage sister. Lance had returned at 4:00 a.m. from his own adventures that night and stumbled into his bedroom. The next semester my parents moved me to Needles to be with them.

Wild? Maybe. But certainly not by today's standards. There were no drugs. No songs with offensive lyrics. No television where the main characters demean and curse each other. Many of us girls subscribed to the "no sex until we are married" philosophy. Especially us Catholics. But, God knows, there were lots of attempts.

We applauded the spirit of our nation and cheered at our football games. We saw our parents hard at work in their business pursuits. Ellen's parents owned the print shop in town. My father was busy designing homes. Paul's father was running grocery stores. Was it because we had the freedom to make mistakes and to find our own way, study hard, and continue to contribute to our society?

Maybe it's all those things. After forty-five years, my close high school friends and I still have our common foundation on which to rely, and we still care abundantly for one another. We meet at mini-reunions in Napa or for dinners in LA, and we are planning to travel to Hawaii. Our politics are divided now and, being of an age where we really don't care as much what others think, we voice our disparate opinions loudly and passionately. However, if ever any of us is in need, friends are there as soon as they can book a boat, train, or plane.

My high school peers, along with others, helped me immeasurably to survive my theatrical career. Retaining friends is a theme in my family. My sister, Beverly, and her husband, Jim, often have dinner or go on trips with those whom they

My brother Lance zip lining in Costa Rica in 2012.

have known from their earliest days. My brother Bud just went to the seventieth birthday party of his friend Barry, whom he has known for sixty years. Their high school friends from that era surrounded them at the celebration. My brother Lance recently went on a trip to Costa Rica, zip lining. Even though the photo shows his exaggerated terror of the impending journey through the jungle, other pictures show his happiness at being surrounded by his band of friends from junior high school and high school, seasoned citizens now, still enjoying one another's company and history. Friends are so important. Fame, success, money, yes, they are all good, but friends give the ballast we need in life.

My brother Lance with his friends, living life to the fullest.

# 17

# Philosophy of the Threads

I never wanted to be a star. I wanted to be a working actress. I fulfilled that goal with nary a break. Stardom, I had seen, could rob you of your privacy, your soul, and sometimes even your life at an early age.

I worked in film, TV, radio, stage, and voice-over. When film worked slowed down, I started a voice-over career; when voice-over jobs were scarce, I trod the boards in a play; when there were no exciting plays looming, I landed a national commercial—just keep putting it out there. My friend Heidi says that on my tombstone it should be etched, "Kathy's not here. She's out on another interview."

I don't employ fake tears to manipulate myself through life. If tears are shed, they are sincere because of a grief-ridden occasion—someone's death or a situation from which there is no extrication.

My goal in life when I frighteningly realized at age eight that I was a finite being, was to find the answer to *WHY*—why was I on earth? Why were people here? What began our life?

I signed on to the big bang theory, before the popular TV series. The philosophy gave me an intellectual basis on which to survive. I already had my spiritual base. I also had a great fascination with early man—the Neanderthal, the *Australopithecus*. How did they become *Homo sapiens*?

When it came time to find a major in college, I gravitated toward anthropology: that discipline could explain why we were on earth and help me live gracefully and fully in my "place in the sun," I thought. I had already obtained quite an education in acting, theater, and the entertainment business. It was time now to develop my intellect and rely on a different set of skills to give me strength and ballast. My mother, ever practical with her Swiss and Austrian heritage, suggested I get a liberal arts degree for "insurance." She, and then I, thought that to survive in the insecure world of entertainment, it was important to incorporate as many skills as possible: liberal arts, business, and financial skills. So I began college with a "general knowledge" curriculum. Anthropology was one of my first lecture classes at UCLA, with three hundred students at Royce Hall. Wow, I thought, no personal attention here—I really have to apply myself, study in the library, and try not to get distracted by all the interesting new experiences to be found at this small city that was called a university. By the time I was a junior, I had segued to a major in psychology, but finding easier As in speech and debate, speech became my major with a minor in psychology—in the Liberal Arts College. I was still wondering why we were all here but for the time being put my faith in God and evolution, not incompatible concepts as far as I could see.

# 18

## Knitting a Degree

I entered my freshman year at UCLA in September 1963, at age seventeen. In December of that year I reached the golden age of eighteen—I was now considered an adult in the film realm and I could work eight hours a day without a welfare worker making sure I had my three hours of schooling, and I could work overtime.

My entire first semester at UCLA turned out to be overwhelming. Even though I chose to room with my best friend from San Bernardino, Ellen, the cultural difference at the large university from my small-town high school was startling. Ellen and I lived on the women's floor at the new co-ed dorm, Rieber Hall. The change from the atmosphere of the lazy small town of San Bernardino to the hustle and bustle of the immense UCLA campus was quite an adjustment. Bombarded with self-imposed goals, I struggled to get As, lead the freshman squad as Head Pom-Pom girl, participate in the Bruinettes Social Club, continue my extracurricular activities in college, and, of course, date.

Adding to my myriad activities was now additional work in film and television. I was carrying a heavy load of academics, plus trying to adjust, plus working, plus dating. Way too much. I fainted one day and was admitted to the UCLA hospital.

Would I get through this? My mother came to visit me at the hospital bearing a beautiful pink baby-doll nightgown and with concern on her face.

"Too much," she said.

I dropped two of my classes. I was released from the hospital after a three-day stay and admonished to eat more and play less. The experience taught me to alter my extensive activities. I established a more even keel. I could survive this college onslaught, I proclaimed stalwartly to myself.

My parents sold their home in San Bernardino and moved to an apartment in Hollywood. My father went to work again for the federal government, this time with the GSA, General Services Administration. Close by me, my mom and dad provided added support to my active college career, acting jobs and helped me to continue on a strong path. Helped me survive. Family is so important. I am ashamed to say that I took my laundry home each week for my mother to wash and iron for me. Learning laundry methods had not been part of my college curriculum. Also, I figured that since all the children had now flown my parents' nest, wouldn't they enjoy company and something to do? Later on, I saw that this was selfish of me. But my parents seemed happy when I went home for the weekends, I rationalized, and we joyfully ate together, watched television, and caught up on the news of the day.

One of the first shows in which I appeared on my return to Los Angeles from San Bernardino had religious leanings. God welcoming me back into the entertainment fold? Virginia Martindale, who had cast me in three *This Is the Life* episodes as a child, cast me again as a teenager. The episode centered on my character's inability to fit in as a newly transplanted girl to the neighborhood. Typical of the award-winning religious series, it presented everyday problems, sometimes serious world issues (e.g., the Vietnam War), with spiritual solutions. My reel mother was played by the excellent actress Virginia Christine, who later became known as the coffee queen on commercials. The show had attracted other eclectic luminaries such as Julie Adams, Leonard Nimoy, Brock Peters, Adam West, and Dean Jagger, who won a Daytime Emmy Award for his performance in the episode "Independence and 76."

The spiritual threads continued as I was cast in the Emmy Award–winning series *Insight*, produced by the Catholic Paulist Fathers, who maintained a studio in Malibu on the beautiful Pacific Coast Highway. In the episode "The Oleander Years," my brother (John Bennett), mother (played by Tony-nominated actress and wife of Bud Schulberg, Geraldine Brooks), and I had to solve numerous flaws in our relationship. The excellent actor Robert Lansing was along to help out. I had yet to be cast in *Family Affair*, but I appeared two more times in different episodes of *Insight*. Brian Keith also starred in a number of episodes, but we never appeared together. We both shared the Catholic faith and again, the threads of our lives.

The outfit I am wearing in the picture from *Insight* was a source of consternation to my mother. When we were living in San Bernardino, I eyed an appealing wool tweed skirt and top at a boutique. My mother adamantly told me it was too expensive and I could not get it. "But it's perfect," I cried in my most plaintive teenage way. Just as adamantly, my mother said, "No." It was one of the few times I can remember my mother refusing me so strongly.

We returned to the clothing shop a second time. My mother still said, "No." So I saved my money, placed the outfit on layaway, and eventually bought it. It was one of the first times I had gone against my mother's wishes. She had said no. But I really wanted it. So I got it myself. Many times I have had to pursue something with more vigor when it has been denied me—a part, a lawsuit when I have been wronged, cities requiring sprinklers that cost $30,000 when they were not

In an episode of *This Is the Life* with Virginia Christine and a wig.

needed. It made me a fighter to get what I deemed was right. The power of perseverance.

This philosophy would support me when unfortunate events presented themselves in my life. I attacked them all with perseverance and the confidence of my mother and generations before who had said, "Apply yourself, get through this, and believe in your higher spirit, from the most insignificant to the most meaningful plight."

Returning to Los Angeles was a boost to my theatrical pursuits and to my creative spirit. At the end of 1963, I played the part of a high school student in the TV series *Mr. Novak.* This one-hour drama starred James Franciscus and Dean Jagger and lasted two years. Dean Jagger was nominated twice for an Emmy Award for his portrayal of Principal Albert Vane. My episode was entitled "Sparrow on a Wire." It has been written that Novak was reminiscent of John Kennedy in this series with his idealism, earnestness, and look. And in my episode, those particular traits shone through.

I had been attending UCLA for almost three months, and even though I securely knew my path from Rieber Hall past the field and up the steps to Royce Hall, I still ran late on many occasions. It was a Friday morning, and I had taken

In an episode of *Insight*, shown with Geraldine Brooks and John Bennett.

too long washing my hair for the weekend and was rushing to class. On the nearly deserted campus, almost all had securely gotten to his or her seat on time. I saw a student with a radio pressed to his ear and concern on his face. Unable to suppress the news, he beckoned for me to come over to him.

"I'm late," I said.

"Come here!" he insisted.

I did. That's when I heard of the shooting of President John F. Kennedy.

It is said that almost everyone can relate exactly what he or she was doing when the news of Kennedy's assassination was broadcast; the shocking pronouncement can still be recalled instantly in my mind's eye. At UCLA, classes were canceled, and my friends and I gathered around the small television set in Rieber's cafeteria and watched, mesmerized by the horrific occurrence and stunned by all the details of the shattering news.

A special *Mr. Novak* episode titled "Death of a Teacher" aired in 1963. The instructor dies suddenly, and each character in the show deals with the grief in his or her own way, just as we all dealt with Kennedy's death. The show mirrored what was happening in our society at the time. To survive acting or to survive tragedies in our society is a challenge. By having faith in a higher spirit and being human enough to grieve, I believe we can weather whatever whirlwinds and storms we encounter.

I also costarred with Beau Bridges in the "Sparrow on the Wire" episode on *Mr. Novak*, which dealt with social issues and how people related to them—students, parents, and teachers. I believe acting is immensely important in our society—watching actors perform and feel and portray emotions provides an outlet for the culture—a panacea. I appeared in two more episodes of *Mr. Novak* while still attending UCLA.

James Franciscus was often compared with Richard Chamberlain, who starred as Dr. Kildare in the TV series of the same name—indeed, Franciscus was the producers' first choice to play Dr. Kildare, but Franciscus is said to have had scheduling conflicts. Both actors embraced a restrained, thoughtful acting style to which audiences easily related. In the 1960s, I was cast in *Dr. Kildare* as a candy striper, a volunteer nurse's helper, in a four-part episode. The parts were titled "Going Home," "The Tent Dwellers," "A Gift of Love," and "Fathers and Daughters." In all of them I played the character of Tracey Richards. As my mother had been a registered nurse, I fell easily into the role. The award-winning actor/dancer/choreographer Fred Astaire starred as the character Joe Quinlen. Mr. Astaire was warm, gracious, and personable. I brought my books to the set to study while I was acting in the four-episode arc, and we chatted about how important it was to attend college. I remember fondly the experience and the terrific cast and support that surrounded me.

In 1969 I performed in another *Insight* episode, "Mr. Johnson Stays the Course," and worked with the wonderful Robert Lansing again. I am confronted by a gunman (David Macklin) with a threatening dilemma. With the help of June Dayton, who played my mother, and Mr. Lansing, we faced up to the killer with conversation, understanding, and our wiles. We survived. So did many others who were featured in the *Insight* series. It gave actors an opportunity to appear in award-winning quality shows with excellent scripts, direction, and cinematography. Others who lent their talent included Ed Asner, Patty Duke, Carol Burnett, Ron Howard, Cindy Williams, Walter Matthau, Bob Newhart, and Martin Sheen.

In perhaps a shallow cultural vein, but very important to a budding young woman, I admit that I had always wanted to be a debutante. Since my parents were not in high society, I was not involved in a "coming-out" party. Where was I going to find my place to emerge socially in the world? I found it in Hollywood. In 1964, I became a Hollywood debutante and emerged as a belle in the entertainment world. My friend Johnny Grant had advised me on how to apply for the auspicious honor, and after having persevered in my social pursuit, I was accepted with open arms. As a Hollywood princess, I even broke bottles of champagne at topping-off ceremonies such as the debut of the building of the Crocker-Citizen Bank in 1965. It is located across from the Walk of Fame and is now the TV Guide

Appearing with David Macklin in another episode of TV's *Insight.*

Building. We're both still around and a part of Hollywood. Later on, my son would go to Crocker Middle School in Northern California. Strong, steely construction threads.

Johnny Grant became Honorary Mayor of Hollywood, a title he enthusiastically embraced. Having met him at the USO as a child while performing for the military, I also knew Johnny from the legendary Hollywood Christmas parade. I looked forward to this annual event, which proceeds down Hollywood Boulevard in November. I participated in many of the festive procession from the time I was a child, waving and stopping at the KTLA booth to chat with the interviewers. Not long ago, I ran into a fellow former Santa Claus Lane participant. I was attending the Edgerton Book and Film Festival in Wisconsin, where I was promoting my *Family Affair Cookbook*, and I encountered Steve Carlson, my long-ago friend from the parade. He was at the festival to introduce the Disney movie he had appeared in, *Rascal*, about a baby raccoon that had been rescued and chronicled in the eponymous award-winning book written by Edgerton native Sterling North. It had been forty years since Steve and I had met and then dated, but we renewed

As Hollywood Chamber of Commerce princess.

our friendship as if the parade had taken place the previous week. After a few years, the Santa Claus Lane Parade became nationally televised. Then the pageant suffered some financial problems and was up for promoters' and TV grabs, but it has recently returned to its festive route.

Johnny Grant was also very helpful when friends and I were trying to obtain a "star" on Hollywood Boulevard for Brian Keith. Johnny was well known for having hosted more than five hundred celebrities into the Hollywood Walk of Fame circle. He gave me great advice and guided the committee for "A Star for Brian" to the best way to gather support, get financial sponsors, and ultimately secure the star. It was a great day when Brian was given his rightful place on the Walk of Fame, even if posthumously. Daniel Hugh Kelly (his costar on the TV series *Hardcastle and McCormick*), Victoria Keith (Brian's third wife), and I presented speeches in his honor. I was surprised to discover when doing research for this book that Victoria was born the same year as I was! Here is part of my tribute to Brian that I presented at the ceremony:

As a Hollywood princess, I help break ground for the Crocker-Citizen Bank Building in 1965.

As surrogate father to my teenage character "Cissy" on the classic TV series, *Family Affair,* and mentor to me, Brian Keith was a fount of funny anecdotes and great advice. But our relationship started even before *Family Affair.* My first encounter with Brian was when I played a waif to his character, Matt Anders, on his first TV series, *The Crusader.* Brian embodied that crusader spirit in real life—an adventurer, a tough guy on the exterior focused on his goals, yet sensitive with a big heart for children and underdogs. He came to my film rescue in *Family Affair* when I was left an orphan in Terre Haute, Indiana. Uncle Bill and his valet Mr. French took me and my brother and sister under their New York penthouse wing and raised us with understanding, care, and, most of all, love. Brian had that same sense of love and sensitivity in his own life which he shared so generously with me and others. But Brian eschewed publicity. I can see him now up in the heavens, wondering what all the hoopla is about. I'll tell you what all the hoopla is about, Brian. It is about recognizing an excellent actor, family man, and sensitive soul. It is about paying homage to a dedicated and excellent performer.

Now all who come to visit will know what I have known for so many years. Brian Keith is an enduring and luminous figure not only in Hollywood but worldwide. His star will continue to shine and lead.

Congratulations to a most deserving, talented, and stellar performer, Brian Keith, for his rightful honor and sparkling star on the Hollywood Walk of Fame.

At the Walk of Fame star ceremony for Brian Keith with Victoria Keith, Daniel Hugh Kelly, Joe De Santis, Leron Gubler (president of the Hollywood Chamber of Commerce), and Monsignor Sheridan. Clinton H. Wallace/Globe Photos, Inc.

> His unique orb has been shining brightly for quite some time. Brian, you have always been my beacon and light. Your radiance will continue to glow for decades.

It was a wonderful celebratory occasion. The only drawback was that Brian was not there to accept in person this great honor and that Johnny Grant was not present to induct Brian into this stellar Walk of Fame. Johnny died in January 2008; Brian's star was placed on June 26, 2008. But I know Johnny was with us, his dimples playing over his warm smile, looking down with grace from his heavenly arbor. Brian was probably looking down with a smirk, still thinking, and again wondering, "Aah, what's all this hoopla about?"

Shelley Fabares and I at the Hollywood Walk of Fame celebration for Brian Keith's star.
Clinton H. Wallace/Globe Photos, Inc.

# 19

# Adding to the Theatrical Swatch

Bing Crosby. The name conjures a mellow voice, an enduring acting career, a graceful gentleman. In 1964, I was cast in an episode of his family-oriented TV series *The Bing Crosby Show.* This situation comedy, which lasted only a season, costarred Beverly Garland supported by tweeners Carol Faylen and Diane Sherry. My episode was called "The Keefers Come Calling." The roles of the Keefers were filled by singing stars Frankie Avalon and Vikki Carr. I recently viewed some scenes of the show on DVD where I am cavorting, giving my all in a rollicking dance, shades of *This Is Alice.* Too bad there wasn't a *Dancing with the Stars* show then. Having a great time with dreamy Frankie and his reel wife, singer Vikki, plus soaking in Bing's essence made for a memorable time.

As Bing vocalized at the piano, I witnessed in person what made his talent so alluring—the smoothness, melody, and confidence he brought to the musical notes made the song an emotional experience, not just notes being sung. He brought this same talent to his theatrical roles. His demeanor was kind and inclusive.

Anissa "Buffy" Jones later hooked up with Bing for a one-hour ABC color special, "Feelin' Groovy at Marine World," in 1969, when there *was* a Marine World just south of San Francisco. The duo toured the wide variety of marine life and watched water skiers and frolicking dolphins. Music played, and songs were sung by the Rascals group. Bing and his family lived in Northern California for quite a while, so it was a short jaunt for him to go to that shoot. I share neighborhoods with the Crosby estate—my home is not so grand and glorious, but it's still a nice house. It also has had its share of drama, as I will relate later. Bing's wife Kathryn still lives in her Hillsborough manse and has recently resuscitated her singing career, even after she suffered a debilitating car accident. She has quite a bit of perseverance herself. We both recently appeared at the opening of the San Francisco Museum and shared anecdotes. I am proud to say that my photo is hung next to another talent, Steve Jobs. Maybe some of his excellent business expertise will waft my way.

Anissa Jones with Bing Crosby touring Marine World in Northern California circa 1969.

Beverly Garland, who played the reel wife in *The Bing Crosby Show*, is another thread in my life; she appeared on the sound stage next door to the *Family Affair* set. Beverly played Fred MacMurray's spouse in *My Three Sons* at CBS Studio Center in 1972. She was very good in those wifely roles. Beverly and her real husband, Filmore Crank, purchased the Holiday Inn in Studio City and renamed it the Beverly Garland Hotel. It was a successful endeavor and became the venue for the start of a retro phenomenon—autograph shows. Ray Courts and his wife Sharon became the promoters of these shows, which headlined classic stars with vendors hawking movie and TV memorabilia; more about Ray and Sharon later. The shows became quite a success and they continue nationwide. I have attended many autograph shows and am currently working on a Broadway musical about these events. The Hollywood Collectors Show became an outlet for stars to meet their fans and vend photos, DVDs, books, and other articles from their movie cache. But for the time being in 1964, I was in another show happily dancing, with Beverly watching and with Bing crooning.

In 1963, my hair still dark, I played another Indian—this time Pretty Walker to Kurt Russell's Jaimie McPheeters in his TV series *The Travels of Jaimie McPheeters*. I was infatuated with him, but I was a little older, and the connotation of "cougar" had not yet come into common cultural use. Later, I realized the age difference probably would not have mattered to Kurt since he has been with "older woman" Goldie Hawn for years now. I thought it was great fun when my character was directed to cozy up to him in the temporary teepee set up on the TV stage. In the episode "The Day of the Pawnee," Pretty was supposed to have a crush on Jaimie. I really did. But in reel life as in real life, I was rejected. Sigh.

Another western role I essayed in the 1960s was Amy, the waitress in the episode "The Queue," on the TV series *The Rifleman*, which starred Chuck Connors and Johnny Crawford. I observed how easily Chuck and Johnny fell into their roles. There was camaraderie between them that served the show for more than 168 episodes. The warm father-son scenes at the end of each episode mitigated the violence within the body of the shows, which led to a very warm, successful, and long-lasting series. Johnny Crawford was stellar, professional, and conscientious. He was nominated for an Emmy for the series as supporting actor but retained a wonderful down-to-earth quality. Johnny has since gone on to become an exquisite music director, traveling and delighting audiences with big-band music. I recently hosted a show with him on MeTV, the Memorable Entertainment network, which replaced TV Land as the purveyor of excellent classic shows. Johnny and I meshed well and had great fun guiding the audience to the wealth of iconic shows now on MeTV. The network has first-rate talent, such as Neal Sabin and Joe Dale, who keep the interstitials and the rotation of classic series fresh. Soon I anticipate they will add to their production of original shows in the vein of TV Land but continue the family-friendly shows they now air.

Chuck Connors played the character of Lucas McCain in *The Rifleman* with sincerity and aplomb. Born Kevin Joseph Aloysius Connors in Brooklyn, Chuck started his career in sports as a baseball player and then a basketball player. His great height (six-foot-five and one-half) and excellent physique easily made him a top-notch film star candidate. In 1965, I was reacquainted with Chuck when I starred as the character Ginny Pollard in his short-lived western TV series *Branded*. I played the sheriff's daughter in the episode "Rules of the Game." My film father was actor Russ Conway, who had played Fenton Hardy in the series *The Hardy Boys* and had also worked for Fedderson Productions in *The Millionaire* and *My Three Sons*. The irrepressible actress Jeanne Cooper played Chuck's friend, Elsie Baron. Jeanne lived in Beverly Hills with her husband, Harry Bernsen, producer, at the same time as I was living in the town with my family. She always looked beautiful, even walking down Rodeo Drive or one of the residential streets of the city. Their son, Corbin Bernsen, is well known as having played Arnie Becker in the successful TV series *LA Law* and as Henry Spencer in the popular series *Psych*. Thread, here? The producer of *Psych* lives next door to my hospitable friend Heidi.

Johnny Crawford and I host a special for a MeTV broadcast.

In *Branded*, Chuck essayed the part of Jason McCord, an ex-cavalry officer thrown out of the corps because of supposed cowardice. Each week the series showed McCord traveling the countryside to prove his worth. In my episode, Jason McCord is unjustly accused of killing a rival and must again prove he is no coward. He is sworn in as a deputy. In one of the memorable quotes of the season, Jason proclaims, "And as for you worthy citizens of McKinley, you've got a friend to bury, too—a friend all of you helped kill by refusing to uphold the law." Lawrence Dobkin, whom I had first met and befriended on the set of *The Ten Commandments* when he was Larry Dobkin, directed this episode. Larry acted in an episode of Brian Keith's *The Crusader*—such a small theatrical world.

The favorite western TV show I shot was *Big Valley*, which starred Barbara Stanwyck, Richard Long, Linda Evans, Lee Majors, and Peter Breck. Most of the scenes in my episode, "The Royal Road," were with Richard Long, who played my guardian, and Indian teen star Sajid Khan. Sajid had gained fame in the movie *Maya* and then went on to star in the TV series version with Jay North of *Dennis the Menace*. I played a spoiled heiress who rode horses and fell in love quickly. The shoot was convenient as *Big Valley* occupied the stage next to *Family Affair* at CBS Studio Center. However, we traveled to grassy locations, and I had a grand time running over the terrain, riding stallions, and wrestling in the mud. Still an adventuress at heart. My episode was shot in January 1969, and I had been invited to the inauguration of the president of the United States. Not one to miss out on most things, I had accepted the role and the invitation to Washington, D.C. I got strange

Russ Conway and I in the "Rules of the Game" episode of Chuck Connors's TV series *Branded*.

looks when I took off my studio makeup on the plane, redid it for normal evening wear, rushed to the restroom at Dulles, changed into a long gown, and emerged to meet my escort from Philip Morris, *Family Affair*'s sponsor, who had a limo waiting to whisk us to the festivities at the inaugural ball. I didn't care about the looks—I'm used to those—but I see where they got the inspiration for the film *Breathless*.

Like a bridesmaid to a bride as in *This Is Alice*, I became a semi-regular and friend to Patty Duke on her series, *The Patty Duke Show*, filmed in the 1960s. Some of my episodes included "Patty, the Diplomat," "A Visit from Uncle Jed," and "Patty, the Psychic." My pal Dave Stein recently sent me copies of these episodes, and I delighted in seeing how young I looked so many years ago! Patty and I were about the same size and age, and we had lots of fun together. I played Monica Robinson in the series. Patty was extremely professional and . . . fast! She knew her lines and the setup and wanted to complete her work quickly and get on to the next scene. She had and has high energy and is a sterling actress. Patty was a

As Laura Hayden in "The Royal Road" episode of *Big Valley*.

forerunner of playing dual roles as she played cousins on the show: the sweet Cathy from England and the tomboy Patty from the United States; she was quite convincing in both parts. At the time, she was dating Dick Fox, who visited the set often and with whom I became friends later on in life. Recently, I hosted a TV talk show, *Backstage with Barry and Kathy*, and we interviewed Patty, who was appearing in San Francisco in the musical stage play *Wicked* at the Orpheum Theatre. Patty's character, Madame Morrible, wears very heavy costumes and hefty hats. Patty, a seasoned citizen now and five-foot-one, appeared for six nights and two matinees a week, singing, acting, and wearing that burdensome wardrobe. I asked her, "Patty, how do you do this night after night?"

She looked straight at me, smiled, and said, "Determination."

Yes, it's hard to survive being an actress, but if one has determination, staying power accrues. Patty has won a Tony Award and an Oscar for her performances as Helen Keller in *The Miracle Worker* and Emmys when she was older, playing the part of Annie Sullivan in the same story with Melissa Gilbert as Helen.

I was a senior when I tried out for the role of Helen in William Gibson's *The*

With Indian teen star Sajid Khan in *Big Valley.*

*Miracle Worker* to be produced at our high school in the 1960s. I thought I had done a wonderful job on the audition, but Mr. Miller, the drama teacher, had other ideas. He decided to cast a sophomore in the role. Determined, I marched to his office and stated my case: it was my last year to appear in a play in high school, my competition had three more years to act in other plays at the school. I put on my best lawyer act to convince him that I was the best choice for the role. He finally agreed.

After securing the part, I then went around my house blindfolded, attempting to get the essence of someone without sight, running into many walls and doors in the process. It was the night of the premiere of *The Miracle Worker.* During the last scene, I uttered the words when Helen finally makes the connection between the concept of an idea and its expression. Haltingly and with great discovery, I rasped out a word for the first time. "Wah . . . wah . . . water." When I heard my stalwart classmate Danny Rabino cry out and sob in the front row in the theater, I knew I had accomplished my motive and moved the audience. I had made a

Patty Duke, Barry Barsamian, and I during an episode of *Backstage with Barry and Kathy.*

connection. They felt the emotion of what I was communicating and I had the immense satisfaction of knowing I was true to the emotion felt by Helen at that revelatory moment and true to myself.

People often ask me to name my favorite role I have played. I immediately say, "Helen Keller in *The Miracle Worker.*" Even though it was a high school play, the role is so well written and the theme so meaningful, I have to classify it as my best experience. The determination of Helen and of Patty, who originally created the role, and the perseverance of all of us to reach a goal continue to stand as a beacon to me.

While attending UCLA, I skipped some of my classes to work in TV and films. I also tried out for plays at UCLA, even though I was not in the Fine Arts Department at the time. As a freshman I was cast in the play *The Infernal Machine* by Jean Cocteau, which is based on the classic Greek myth of Oedipus. I played the part of Antigone and donned gray Greek robes created by the excellent student seamstresses in the UCLA wardrobe department. I entered the stage screaming that my father had been blinded. The ghost of my dead mother, Jocasta, and I then lead my sightless father, Oedipus, through the theatrical country and offstage. It was quite a psychological experience.

During the rehearsal of this heavy dramatic piece, Harvey Morgenbesser

At UCLA in the role of Antigone in *The Infernal Machine* by Jean Cocteau.

noticed me. He was up in the booth at the back of the theater, running lights. After a night rehearsal, he descended the stairs and came up onto the stage. He introduced himself and became one of my first boyfriends at UCLA. He was older and into the arts. Those qualities were quite exciting to me. But after a few dates of sipping wine in his warm bohemian abode up the canyon in Beverly Glen, it was time to say good-bye to Harvey. The play was over and I was somewhat wary of the hippie culture that Harvey embraced. I went on to other pursuits, adventures, and dates. However, I will always remember Oedipus, Harvey, and that first sip of creative "Jamba Juice."

As a college sophomore, I went through rush to join a sorority. My sister had been a Phi Mu at UCLA, but I decided I wanted to be in a different house, maybe Theta or Kappa. So I went through the process as I would on an interview. Smiling—trying to be charming—I was dropped by both houses. My mother met me for lunch in Westwood after the second day, and I cried at not "making the grade." Always consoling, my mother tried to cheer me with nurturing platitudes like "They don't know what they're missing." I realized later, with some solace, that I had to have "rec letters"—letters of recommendation from past members. I had none. But Pi Beta Phi—a sorority known for cute, peppy girls (as opposed to the statuesque blond, blue eyed Kappas) really wanted me as a member, so they with my friend Jeannie contacted alumni to obtain the required letters for me. I was then accepted, joined Pi Phi and was warmed by the fact that one of my first childhood friends, Jeannie Gifford—classmates from Transfiguration Elementary School—was my pledge mother. She was in the pledge class ahead of me as she had joined the sorority when she was a freshman. Jeannie and I continued our friendship; she became a dental hygienist at University of Southern California. USC is the intense rival of UCLA. I forgave her, as UCLA did not have a dental school at the time. Jeannie works in a dentist's office in the warm and beckoning city of San Diego. Some of my best friends today I also met in the sorority—Mary Halloran and Janet Hamilton, who also sought the warm climes of southern California, Montecito and Long Beach.

As bridesmaid with former roommates Mary Halloran Hampson, third from left, and Janet Hamilton Agajanian (the bride). The dress I wore was used in an episode of *Family Affair.*

# 20

# Gathering Swatches for the Family Quilt

It was in my third year at UCLA when I went on the infamous interview with Ed Hartmann, the writer, creator, and producer of *Family Affair*. Because the series had been presold, the pilot would be the first episode.

The part of Cissy in *Family Affair* had been cast once, but the blond girl the producers had chosen had traveled to Europe on a preplanned excursion and had returned a few pounds heavier; the weight gain gave them pause. Her parents had not yet signed her contract, so the producers were anxious to find someone else quickly to complement the other cast members they had already penned. Brian Keith was to play Uncle Bill, Sebastian Cabot, the valet Mr. French, Anissa Jones, Buffy, and Johnny Whitaker, Jody. Originally the producers, Don Fedderson and Ed Hartmann, had wanted Glenn Ford to play the part of Uncle Bill, but the concept of movie stars appearing on that horrid little screen, television, had not quite taken hold, and Mr. Ford passed on the offer. Brian Keith had gained success as a dramatic actor and by starring in exciting western movies such as *Nevada Smith* and *The Hallelujah Trail*; he had also shown his prowess as an actor by starring in television series such as *The Crusader* and *The Westerners*. Brian had recently demonstrated his comedic and lighter side by starring in the original *The Parent Trap*, a very successful Disney family movie which also starred Hayley Mills and Maureen O'Hara. The role made him an exciting candidate for the part of William Davis.

The producers thought Brian Keith would be an excellent choice for the debonair, manly, yet gentle Uncle Bill. Brian was offered a type of deal that Don Fedderson had originated when he cast Fred MacMurray in another of his successful series, *My Three Sons*. In order to lure movie stars to television, Fedderson promised they would have to commit to only three months of filming and they then would be free to headline movies. As additional bait, the movie star would be given a financial piece of the television show. Almost an offer that could not be refused. And Brian and his agent, Jimmy McHugh, did not refuse!

Brian had just starred in the successful movie *The Russians Are Coming, the Russians Are Coming* and had met a red-haired little boy, Johnny Whitaker, who had a small part in the movie. Brian thought the tousle-haired six-year-old with blue eyes would be an appropriate choice to play in his new series, *Family Affair.* Anissa Jones had already been cast as the character of Buffy. Of Lebanese descent, she had light brown hair and brown eyes, like mine. The stylist dyed her hair blond per the producer's instructions. Although eight, Anissa was tiny for her age and could easily pass as a six-year-old. The parts of the children were originally conceived as a six-year-old girl, a nine-year-old boy, and a fifteen-year-old girl. When Brian introduced Johnny to the producers, they made the creative decision to cast Anissa and Johnny as six-year-old twins.

Terry-Thomas had been offered the role of Mr. French, and they had flown him from England to Hollywood to meet with the creative team. When it got down to the "nitty-gritty" and Thomas learned he was to have to work almost daily with children, he turned down the part. "No kids, no dogs" seemed to be his mantra for choosing roles.

And, then, there I was with my brassy, streaked hair.

After we filmed the pilot/first episode of *Family Affair* in the spring of 1966, I returned and finished my junior year at UCLA. We then began shooting the series in June. To initiate the marketing and publicity for the show, I was sent to CBS on Fairfax Boulevard in Hollywood for the network photographer to shoot cast pictures. I was also sent to the Max Factor studio again and issued another bouffant wig, this time a brown one to match my hair color. I wore the scratchy piece over my short brown hair for the pictures, but by the time June rolled around, my brunette locks had grown out enough so that I could have my own hair styled in Cissy fashion. After the second episode, "Cissy and Jody," the producers decided that a different look was in order. My hair was dyed, and I became a dark strawberry blond for the rest of the season. Was this series really going to be about hair? Well, I guess a stage musical with that title was successful, so maybe so.

The pilot episode of *Family Affair* was titled "Buffy" and concerned a little girl whose parents had died in a car accident. As an orphan, she had been passed to a relative in Terre Haute, Indiana. The relative, Fran Heiger, played by Louise Latham, could not handle the child and deposited her, literally, on Uncle Bill Davis's doorstep. The adorable gremlin ingratiated herself to Uncle Bill, and after Buffy purposefully left her precious Mrs. Beasley doll in her uncle's suitcase, he was persuaded to accept the endearing child into his household. At the end of the episode, Mr. Davis's live-in valet, Mr. Giles French, opens the door to a little red-headed boy, Jody, and a girl with a wig, Cissy. Johnny Whitaker and I spot Anissa Jones and come running into Uncle Bill's luxury apartment with smiles, hugs, and hoots of excitement. We were reunited with our family and our dear sister, Buffy. Preparing for that first scene in the pilot episode, I imagined how a fifteen-year-old girl would feel having lost her parents, been rejected by relatives, and suddenly thrust into a new, uncertain environment. The first moment was of gross

I get my hair styled—lots of attention went into hair on *Family Affair.* Photofest

A hairstyle Kathy would not wear on *Family Affair,* but the session made for a great photo shoot. Photofest

hesitation—which a sensitive fifteen-year-old in those circumstances would surely feel—and an overpowering sense of sadness. It was a basis for the show. *Family Affair* was more a "dramedy" than a sitcom. It did not have pratfalls, or jokey one-liners, or exaggerated comedy. The show was heartfelt, built on situations in which there were tinges of melancholy. The three children were orphans, and the underpinning of love lost was always there. The comedy was realized in the honesty and humor of situation and the innocence of perspective. The writing was subtle and beautifully handled by Austin and Irma Kalish, the story editors with John McGreevey, and the other excellent writers contributing their talents.

# 21

# Piecing the Quilt

My friend John Stephens, the production manager of *Family Affair* and a brilliant maven at organizing shoots, has said that I was the "workhorse" of the cast. With Brian's contract, all of his scenes in all the shows had to be completed first. This dictum meant that the scripts for the season all had to be finished before filming began. With the start of shooting, scenes from maybe three or four different shows would be shot per day to accommodate Brian's schedule. When Brian's scenes had been finished, the production team would then do pickups of the other necessary scenes. It could be a scheduling nightmare, but John, along with the rest of the Fedderson cast and crew, were up to it—with only a few breaches in continuity.

Brian had to complete his filming in thirty-nine days, Sebastian had health issues, and the children could work only eight hours a day, and three of those hours had to be spent in the studio school. There I was—young, healthy, vibrant, and able to work long hours. On occasion, all the masters and two shots would be filmed in the beginning of and throughout the day, including the close-ups of the kids. My close-ups would be saved until the end of the day. Not only did I have to match the emotions of the scenes that had been shot much earlier, but I also had to recapture the fresh glow of morning. Dick Cobos, our excellent makeup artist, was prepared with white makeup to disguise darkening splotches under my eyes. Since the children often had to leave for the day due to their limited amount of time on the set, many times I acted my scenes opposite John Gaudioso, the paunchy, middle-aged Italian assistant director, who stood off camera, usually with a cigar hanging out of his mouth. He gruffly read the lines of my innocent six-year-old sister with an unmistakably heavy Brooklyn accent—what a leap of imagination I had to employ!

On set there are long waits as the camera, lights, and microphones are situated and adjusted. Since there were no computers or iPhones then, I took up needlepoint—it is easy to stop sewing when you are in the middle of a project—

not like knitting, where you have to finish a row. When the AD, assistant director, called, "We're ready for you, Miss Garver," I could easily set down a project and appear quickly. Needlepoint helped pass the time, and I felt a little more productive than just sitting around chatting or staring off. I presented our publicity director, Les Kaufman, with one of my projects depicting the red, white, and blue interwoven word "Peace." The sixties were raging, and even though most of my time was absorbed with acting, publicity appearances, and learning lines, I felt the decade revolving around me like "Pig-Pen" dust motes.

I could not be fully engaged in all the goings-on and sit-ins occurring in the vibrant world outside the studio, but I experienced some of the sixties' revelry in the disco scene. Some of our episodes did reflect the times, with Cissy yearning to join the Peace Corps and trying out the bohemian culture. I was able to experience hippies and also find that free love is not free.

Trying to find a resting area outside the loneliness of my dressing room, I would often go to the canvas schoolhouse, on set where I would work on creative projects with the welfare worker/teacher, Catherine Deeney. Even though I was over eighteen and she had no jurisdiction over me, Mrs. Deeney was always welcoming, and I remember working on a potpourri project with her where I delicately inserted cloves into an orange, creating an organic sachet to scent a room. I could also work on my needlepoint in the relative calm of a quiet place. Being a type A personality, I had to be active. However, the need for quietude from the noisy internal stress of learning lines, acting, and dealing with publicity was essential to my well-being. I wasn't into meditation yet, but I recognized the importance of quieting my active mind and emotions and grounding myself from the whirlwinds and stress of working daily on a successful Hollywood series.

# 22

## Weaving More Stories

The second episode of *Family Affair* explained why Jody and I were deposited on Uncle Bill's doorstop. We siblings had been living separately with different relatives in Indiana, and none of them could or would care for us any longer. The decision was made for us to travel to the big city of New York from our small town of Terre Haute and have the wealthy brother of our mother care for us. The theory was good, but Bill Davis was a traveling bachelor. As an engineer, he had large projects all over the globe to manage. He couldn't take care of three children himself. Oh, of course there was the very competent Mr. French. However, Mr. French had signed on to be Mr. Davis's cook and valet and not to be a "nanny," or "manny," as we might call him today.

Jody finds his way into Uncle Bill's heart, and the bachelor decides to keep the freckle-faced tyke—he couldn't break up a twin set, could he? But what was he going to do with a teenage girl? In a very poignant scene at the end of that second episode, I appear outside of Uncle Bill's office door and overhear that he is contemplating sending me back to Terre Haute. My character, Cissy, feeling lost, sad, and with the poor self-esteem of a newly orphaned and rejected fifteen-year-old, knocks on the door and then enters her uncle's office. She valiantly tells Uncle Bill that she could return to Terre Haute and not be a bother: she isn't like the little kids. Uncle Bill assures her that he loves her; they will manage somehow. After hugs and tears, it is settled that Cissy will stay and all three of the siblings will be together—an instant family affair for Uncle Bill.

Then the series of adventures began.

It was the structure of the show each week to present a problem to solve, work through the problem, and then solve it—classic story structure: problem, a reach toward the climax, and then the dénouement. There was a thinly veiled moral at the end of each show and a dollop of gentle humor, but there was always the thread of love and care, which tied the show together. Not all our shows had

Brian Keith with his instant family of Cissy, Buffy, and Jody.

happy endings. There was one episode, "Christmas Came a Little Early," in which a very ill child is not expected to live until December, so a tree and all the holiday accoutrements are set up in October. The little girl was played by Eve Plumb, who later joined the *Brady Bunch* family. The lessons were how to deal with grief and to learn that sometimes unfortunate events happen in life. We march forward, deal with the situation as best we can, and help others do the same.

Our cast got along very well even though there was little commonality outside of the show. Brian had his real family; he was married to Judith Landon Keith, the former dancer/actress whom he had met in the commissary at Paramount. The first year of the show they cared for their four children, three of whom were adopted, at their Bel Air home. Brian often said he enjoyed doing the show *Family Affair* the first couple of years because the show reminded him so much of his own family.

After a day's shooting in Hollywood, Sebastian returned to his comfortable home in West Los Angeles. His wife, Kay, tended to their youngest child, Yvonne. The couple had two older children, Annette and Christopher, who were out of the house and engaged in their own private lives and careers. Both Annette and Yvonne appeared in episodes of *Family Affair.*

Annette Cabot, daughter of Kay and Sebastian Cabot, appearing with me in an episode of *Family Affair.*

Johnny Whitaker lived with his family in the San Fernando Valley, about thirty minutes from the studio. His father was a high school teacher and Thelma, his mother, usually stayed at home but at times would accompany Johnny to the set. A guardian has to be with an actor under the age of eighteen, so oftentimes a friend of the family would supervise Johnny. His youngest sibling, Dora, was born during the run of *Family Affair,* and baby Dora often was brought to visit.

Anissa—the name is pronounced with a "long e" sound, like "Lisa"—would go home to the family of her divorced mother, Paula, and younger brother, Paul. They lived in the beach community of Playa del Rey. Because Anissa loved to swim and frolic in the nearby waters and because her hair was bleached, sometimes she would appear as—truly, the girl with green hair. Arlene, our *Family Affair* hairdresser, had to do some quick fixes to maintain Anissa's blond locks.

The first year we shot the series, I lived with my parents in a large apartment, now a condominium complex, next to the Hollywood Bowl. The buildings were brand new, close to the studio, with a sparkling pool—but I had little time to dive into the inviting waters. I was too busy learning lines, speeding to the set, and concentrating on the filming. On weekends, for some rest and relaxation, sometimes I would climb the hill above our home, dodge the deer, and sit and listen to the lovely music emanating from the stage of the Hollywood Bowl. My brother Lance had moved to Northern California and was working in sales; my brother Bud was working in Los Angeles, and my sister was married and now had three children. She managed to direct some of the school plays to great acclaim while teaching language arts at Scarsdale High in New York. My father was still working

Johnny Whitaker at home with his large Mormon family gathered at the piano.

Anissa, her brother Paul, and mother Paula at home in Playa del Rey, California.

with the government in the General Services Administration. My mother was my self-appointed assistant and an incredible help as she practiced my lines with me, playing all the different parts as well as making sure I woke up to get to the set on time. It seemed my call was always very early: 6:30 a.m. Well, I was the only one that needed extra time for full makeup and . . . hair.

In my apartment above my parents in the building they owned, with my mother and brother Lance looking on. Photofest

# 23

# Knitting Succeeding Rows

*Family Affair* was a hit after its debut in September 1966. We had an excellent time slot, Monday evenings, 9:30 p.m. PST, right after *The Andy Griffith Show*, albeit a little late for family viewing. But the producers and the executives at CBS had conceived the show to appeal to an older demographic. The episodes would revolve around Bill Davis's escapades as a handsome bachelor and his exploits with the comely women in New York whom he would squire to posh restaurants and plays. The children were to be secondary actors in the plots. But the audience was so taken with the three children and their adventures that the kids became more of the focus of the series. Each character was given his or her episode, and the twins were given an added story, which included them tackling a problem together. Even Mrs. Beasley, the much-loved doll in the series, was given an episode or two.

We were filming in earnest now. The first year we shot at Desilu on Gower Street in Hollywood. Confident that the series would be a success, CBS had ordered a semipermanent set built and a full slate of shows from Don Fedderson—thirty-two episodes. Austin and Irma Kalish were our excellent story editors. They made sure the "bible"—the pages that kept the story line consistent—was followed and that the characters were true to their original concept. Other shows filming at Desilu in 1966 were *My Three Sons*—another Fedderson production—and *The Lucy Show*. I would have liked to meet the fellows on *My Three Sons*, but we were each so busy with our own shows that we didn't encounter one another while working and didn't become friends until later in our lives.

*Star Trek* was also on the Desilu lot. When *Family Affair* first arrived at the same studio as the stellar TV endeavor, I made a point to visit the *Star Trek* set. I was amazed and impressed that so many pages were filmed in one master shot. The camera kept circling, and the actors kept talking. It was truly a memorable and "spacey" sensation.

Lucille Ball sold Desilu to Gulf and Western in February 1967. I wondered whether the sale would mean I would no longer see Lucy traipsing down the streets of the studio. I often would walk by the Desilu offices to see whether I could catch a glimpse of her. I even had a publicity photo taken by the tree in front of her enticing offices.

The new corporate owners merged the Desilu TV Company with the film studio next door, Paramount, and renamed it all as the Desilu Company, Paramount Television. Since CBS was our network and the Fedderson Company had just been renting space at Desilu, Don Fedderson moved *Family Affair* over to CBS Studio Center in Studio City, in the greater Los Angeles area, and onto stage 10. We shot next door to *My Three Sons*, which also moved from Hollywood to Studio City. Republic Studios had originally owned the large area in Studio City on which their stages and offices sat. When CBS took over the lot, this network added new stages and offices but retained some of the old dressing rooms and outbuildings that had been built in the 1930s. My dressing room was in one of the older buildings. It retained the musty smell and the spongy cushions of worn sofas, but I could sense the history and feel the spirited auras of previous actors who had rested, eaten, and studied on my couch, in my room.

Publicity shot in front of the Lucille Ball and Desi Arnaz office at Desilu Studios, in 1966.

We primarily filmed everything on stage 10, which was one of the originals from the Republic days. I always marveled at the peeling paint and creaking doors when I went out to the restrooms and then returned to our set of an ultramodern and sophisticated New York City penthouse. It was a reality check. The juxtaposition of decades kept me alert to the lessons of history.

Don Fedderson added more than modern furniture to our production. He also added a modern concept. Creating a method that movie stars could work on his TV shows, he developed his unique schedule and way of shooting. I guess it worked—the ratings were excellent, one of the top five shows according to the Nielsen rating in our first year. CBS renewed for a second season.

I'm often asked what Brian was like, both on and off camera. The first season he was very communicative; he would entertain with anecdotes and stories while waiting for the scene setups. Brian was enjoying his new series and basking in the confidence that he would be participating financially in its success. His fiscal heart smiled at the knowledge that not only was he guaranteed a full season and a large salary, but he also owned a percentage of the show.

As an actor, Brian followed Stanislavski teachings and was very much a Method actor. He approached his role quite differently from the way Sebastian Cabot did his. "Sabby" embraced a more classic style of acting, one using analysis of scene and character portrayals. He would work diligently over the weekends, assuring that he had learned every line letter perfect, and, then, while on set, would go over the dialogue with the script supervisor to again confirm that he knew all the lines. Brian, on the other hand, would arrive on set, mumble, "What are we doing today?" look at the script a couple of times, and then briskly say, "Okay. Let's do it." He then let the emotion of the moment and the concept of the scene take over. I believe the two different styles added immensely to the dynamic of the show. I had been schooled in a combination of the two methods, and my acting style was a mixture. When I later attended the Royal Academy of Dramatic Art in London, where scene study and analyses are the bases of teaching, I learned more explicitly where Sebastian was coming from theatrically. More about London later.

The children and I would memorize our parts the night before the shooting day. As I have stated—we were given all the scripts for the season before we were to begin filming. Because of the way we shot, with Brian's scenes being photographed first, we might be learning lines from three different stories to be filmed the next day. This process created vigilance, and we were on the ready for the pink pages that might be handed to us when we arrived on set. Pink pages, green pages—these are the colored sheets of script indicating what changes in words or additions and deletions the writers, director, and/or producers thought would improve the story, some even conceived the night before the shooting day. Then we all had to relearn our lines!

The series was generally slow paced. It was Fedderson and Hartmann's styles to engage in long close-ups of the characters. I believe this enabled the audience to get to know the characters and actors in depth. Our faces and behaviors became embedded in the mind of the beholders—the viewers had no choice but to stay with us and become involved in our stories and see the result of the situational conflicts.

Because our series was filmed, rather than taped, there was added warmth to the scenes. Film creates softness around the edges while tape displays a much crisper vision. The sharp and grainy quality of tape reminds one of the harshness of life, whereas the haze of film softly guides one to a different plane of imagined idealism. This haze adds a dreamlike quality where one can easily imagine and find rapport with an ideal family whose members love one another no matter what. I believe shooting on film added to the approachable and likable nature of *Family Affair.*

# 24

# Brian

Brian was an actor with a capital A, not a personality actor. He portrayed his characters with realism, making them exceedingly memorable. His gruffness tempered with his tenderness made him a desired actor and endearing star.

The first year of the show, Brian was very outgoing and embraced his star role and his acting job. The second year of the show, Brian became more introspective. There were troubles with his marriage. His wife at that time, Judith, is a lovely woman, a classic beauty who had studied ballet and is an accomplished dancer. She is gracious and kind; I still have the present of potpourri she gifted me for Christmas the first year of the show. Together, Brian and Judith had five children—Michael and Miriam (Mimi) were their biological children. The family suffered a great loss when Michael died of pneumonia when he was only eight years old. This, of course, was devastating to the family. Judith suggested they adopt. So Barbara, Betty, and Rory came to live with the Keiths (similar to *Family Affair*?). But there were some serious considerations in this particular family structure. Judith liked to go out, participate in charity events, and enjoy the social whirl. Brian preferred staying at home, relaxing, and enjoying simple pleasures. When an article was released with a large photo of the couple in formal garb, with the caption, "Brian Keith and his wife, Judith leave their 21 room house for an evening of dining and dancing without the kids," Brian exploded, according to his niece, Claudia Keith. He thought better of himself than the depiction of him as an avid, fun-loving partygoer. To quote him, "I don't go to the Daisy [a popular nightclub in Hollywood at the time], or . . . give parties under a striped awning out over the lawn with 200 people, four of whom I like." Brian did not want to be known as a socialite. He wanted to be known for the work that he did. Brian was not enjoying the big life. He sold his Bentley, and Judith and Brian divorced.

The third year of shooting, Brian seemed much happier. He had met actress Victoria Young while starring in the film *Krakatoa: East of Java*. The cast included the sterling actors Maximilian Schell, Diane Baker, and Sal Mineo, with Brian playing a dissipated diver and laudanum addict. (Trivia note—Krakatoa is actually west of Java.) I believe Brian wanted to slip out of his family-oriented role of Uncle Bill. His portrayal of the self-destructive Connerly was certainly a changeup. The movie received mixed reviews but was nominated for an Oscar for best visual effects. His future wife Victoria, who was born in Hawaii, played the part of Kiko, one of the enticing Japanese women in the movie. Brian was smitten. Their child, Robert Keith Jr. (Bobby) was born in 1968. Daisy, their second child, was born in 1969. Brian and Victoria married in 1970.

Brian continued to make movies when his acting duties for *Family Affair* were completed for the season. He starred in the movie *Reflections in a Golden Eye*, which also included the terrific talents of Elizabeth Taylor, Marlon Brando, and Julie Harris. John Huston directed this luminous cast from a script based on the novel by Carson McCullers. As an adult thriller, Brian's role as a harsh adulterer again kept him from being stereotyped as the loving family man of *Family Affair.* Indeed, the film dealt with repressed homosexuality, murder, and betrayal—a far cry from Brian's G-rated TV series. Although Brian's performances were based "in the moment," at times he prepared for the technical side of roles. I remember how he carried a lariat over his shoulder to our *Family Affair* set and practiced for weeks perfecting his ability and lassoing skills for *Reflections.*

Throughout his career, Brian embraced roles that showcased his ability and expertise in both drama and comedy. His comedy prowess was especially demonstrated when he played the lead in the warm and enjoyable 1968 movie *With Six You Get Egg Roll*, which also starred Doris Day. The story was a delightful excursion into the life of two widowed parents, each of whom had children to raise. Brian's character, Jake Iverson, had a teenage daughter (shades of "Cissy") played by Barbara Hershey. Doris's character, Abby McClure, had three sons. Handsome John Findlater (sigh) was the teenage boy. The film received good reviews, and the movie reflected the persona Brian had established in *Family Affair.*

Brian continued his comedic ventures with *Gaily, Gaily*, a 1969 movie that was nominated for three Oscars (sound, costume, and art direction). It starred Beau Bridges as a callow nineteen-year-old who leaves his small town for the big city of Chicago. Brian Keith, as Beau's alcoholic newspaper mentor, initiates him into the rousing world of the press. Hume Cronyn and George Kennedy (whose pool table I bought for my home, by the way) provided ample support to this comedy based on the life of Ben Hecht in the 1910s.

Again to keep from being stereotyped and to broaden his range, Brian starred in the war drama *The McKenzie Break* in 1970. From 1942 to 1945, Brian had served in the U.S. Marine Corps; he joined when he was only nineteen years old after finishing school at East Rockaway High School in New York. In World War II, he served as an air gunner and received the distinguished Air Medal for Meritorious Service. Brian had quite an understanding of and bond with the military. He used his experience to great effect in the excellent film *The McKenzie Break.* The

Brian and Elizabeth Taylor in *Reflections in a Golden Eye*, the movie shot on one of Brian's hiatuses from *Family Affair*. Warner Bros./Photofest. © Warner Bros.

story was about German POWs incarcerated in a Scottish prison camp. The movie received good reviews but, as with many of Brian's films, not the recognition it deserved. Lamont Johnson, who incorporated the landscape of Ireland and Turkey to reflect the locale, brilliantly directed the movie. Lamont's thread that winds around my spool of life is that he directed the religious TV show *Insight*, which Brian worked on, as well as the movie my longtime boyfriend David Eyre wrote, *Cattle Annie and Little Britches*, released in 1981. More about David later.

In addition to *The McKenzie Break*, Brian starred in another military-oriented movie, *Suppose They Gave a War and Nobody Came*, also released in 1970. Brian plays retired officer Michael Nace. His role is of a combat vet in charge of community relations in a small town. The film invited the understanding of the trials of returning vets. It received mixed reviews but was lauded for the script and excellent production values. The movie also starred Daniel Hugh Kelly, who later starred with Brian in the successful TV series *Hardcastle and McCormick*. Kelly has stated that he was always a great fan of Mr. Keith, especially after seeing Brian's brilliant portrayal in *Nevada Smith*.

In 1971, Mr. Keith starred in the title role of "John McCanless" in Disney's *Scandalous John*. The movie had piqued Brian's interest; it was a retelling of the

Brian in the movie *Suppose They Gave a War and Nobody Came.* Cinerama Releasing Corporation/Photofest. © Cinerama Releasing Corporation

Cervantes Don Quixote character, who shunned convention and looked to fighting windmills and those who stood in the way of his unique philosophies and desires. The comedy/drama demonstrated how Brian again broke out of a potential stereotype of suave-looking bachelor into the guise of a crotchety, aged rancher. Brian eschewed the sophisticate and anything that reeked of falsehood or pretense. Roles where he could dig down to his true feelings and release them with artistry was one of his favorite theatrical pastimes.

Disney liked Brian. Brian, who spoke his mind, from secretaries to highly placed business executives, would let people know in no uncertain terms whether he thought a script or person was worthy or not. Brian enjoyed playing characters, and Disney provided him with many disparate roles from which to choose. This fed Brian's need and kept him coming back to the studio; Brian had showered Disney with financial and critical success with the delightful *The Parent Trap*, so they were eager to keep him on their financial good side.

# 25

# Brian Gathers His Own Threads

I believe Mr. Keith was a much underrated actor. One of the reasons was his disdain of publicity. He also hated anything which reeked of showmanship. He was one of the hardest-working actors I have encountered, and his focus was on his palette and canvas, not the patina. He would finish one role and start the next as soon as the first was completed. He was restless, and if he didn't have a new project on which to concentrate, he was not a happy man. I believe Brian would have won many more awards for his excellent portrayals if he had participated in more marketing jaunts. Brian was nominated for the Emmy for Best Actor in 1967, 1968, and 1969 for *Family Affair*. Since he hated hoopla, Brian asked whether I would accept the award for him if he won. I happily said I would and picked out a lovely gown and practiced my speech. The award went to another deserving actor, but I still have and covet the speech I would have made for him. Yes, Brian eschewed publicity. On one occasion, he sent his stand-in to take CBS publicity photos in his stead. You will see in a picture that Brian looks a little heavier than normal. The head is Brian's; the body is his stand-in's. Those who knew Brian and have seen him in any of his roles know what an excellent actor and star he was. Brian had the extreme satisfaction of being his own man, of being able to voice his opinion and live life the way he saw fit, good or bad, happy or sad. In all those aspects, he has my supreme respect.

During the series hiatus of the fourth year, Brian jumped into the exciting fare of western films and starred in the comedic movie *Something Big*. The film was directed by Andrew McLaglen and also starred Dean Martin. The masculine movie was just what Brian sought to shake the sentimental morass into which he thought his character in a family series was falling. Brian plays the stiff, gruff cavalry officer of the local outpost in the far West. The movie was an entertaining romp. Dean, a personable outlaw, decides to do something "big" for his last illegal fling. Martin inadvertently steals Keith's wife, Honor Blackman (remember Pussy Galore in the James Bond film *Goldfinger*?), and the chase for Brian to recover his kidnapped

A group picture. If Brian seems a little heavier it's because in the picture, it is Brian's head and his stand-in's body!

spouse is on. Shot in Durango, Mexico, other cast members included Albert Salmi, Ben Johnson, Merle Olsen, and Ed Faulkner. Brian was in his element, outdoors with his macho buddies.

The fourth year we shot *Family Affair*, Brian was amiable, but by the time the fifth year rolled around, the show's slowly revolving wheel had driven him to boredom. I believe the entire cast was experiencing some ennui. Anissa, almost fourteen, tired of playing a little girl dragging around a well-worn doll. Johnny was just mouthing his lines. I was searching for my identity as a young adult. Sebastian was still enjoying his well-defined character, but in looking at scenes from that last year, I see the show had lost some of its snap and luster.

The series death knell rang for *Family Affair* after our fifth year, and I believe Brian was glad to move on. There was restlessness within Brian, and his inner rhythm needed to be met.

The last project Brian dove into before moving to Hawaii for his next television series was *Second Chance*, a TV movie in which he starred as Geoff Smith, a

A photo from the last year of *Family Affair* on the set, where even though we are all smiles, the sense of a downward flow was felt.

rich stockbroker who buys an entire town in Nevada where people can come and receive a second chance in their lives. Elizabeth Ashley played his wife, supported by an excellent cast which included Rosey Grier and William Windom, two of my favorite friends and actors. It was a strong role for Brian, and he embraced it fully.

Brian's next successful TV series was *The Little People*. He and his family moved from California to the Hawaiian Islands to film the show, which also starred Shelley Fabares. Victoria Young, now Mrs. Keith, played the part of nurse Puni, with their children, Bobby and Daisy, also appearing on occasion. Daisy went on to act in additional venues, while Bobby decided to surf the beauteous waves of Hawaii and sculpt original artworks. In 1973, the second year of *The Little People*, the name of the show was changed to *The Brian Keith Show* but it was canceled in 1974. The series had been well received, but alterations in production personnel and in the show itself couldn't build a successful TV foundation on the sandy shores of Hawaii. I thought that the cast was quite good—a family affair with his real wife and children, and they were delightful in it. But TV studio politics plus low ratings squashed the project.

When *The Brian Keith Show* was canceled, Brian returned to his film career.

The first movie in which he starred was *The Yakuza*, written with excellence by Robert Towne and Paul Schrader and released in 1974. The movie starred Robert Mitchum (remember *The Night of the Hunter*?) as the character Harry Kilmer, who commits to doing a favor for his friend, George Tanner (Brian) by traveling to Japan to find Tanner's kidnapped daughter being held by the Yakuza, or the Japanese Mafia. Malibu was the locale of Harry's home; but the movie was primarily shot in Kyoto and Tokyo. *The Yakuza* received great reviews but was not widely seen and is hard to find on DVD. As a side note, the stunts in this movie were done by my brother Bud's friend Bill Saito, who appeared in many movies as an actor and created and executed many excellent physical maneuvers.

After shooting this movie, Brian realized that commuting from Hawaii to the hub of the entertainment world in Hollywood was too difficult, so he moved his family back to California and into Malibu Colony, the beautiful beach enclave in Southern California he had experienced in *Yakuza*. With his new home situated right on the beach, Brian had a splash of the beautiful Pacific waves, a pool on the grounds, and a shorter jaunt to work.

However, just when Brian's family settled in, he was cast in a new series, this time set in England. In 1974, he shot six episodes of the show *The Zoo Gang*, a crime thriller, in London. The series also starred John Mills, Hayley Mills's father, and Barry Morse.

Another TV series followed when *The Zoo Gang* was canceled, and Brian took to the small screen again to star in the TV series *Archer*. Playing the title character, the show was loosely based on the Ross Macdonald books, but only six episodes were shot and shown before this series, too, ended.

Brian then starred in arguably one of his best roles, that of Teddy Roosevelt in the action-adventure film *The Wind and The lion*, released in 1975. This magnificent movie was directed by John Milius and costarred Sean Connery, who broke the mold of the James Bond character. Connery created the robust role of the leader of a Barbary pirate crew, Mulai Ahmed er Raisuli, in the film. But Brian's rendition of Theodore Roosevelt, the dynamic president of the United States, solidified his reputation as a charismatic character actor and further beamed his light as a shining movie star.

Next, in a TV film, Brian created the role of Tank Logan with two leading men with whom I had previous connections—Kurt Russell, from our stint on TV's *The Travels of Jaimie McPheeters*, and Cameron Mitchell, whom I knew from the film *The Barney Ross Story*, in which I played his stepdaughter, Noreen. The macho trio made movie magic in the film *The Quest*.

The film *The Mountain Men*, released in 1980, starred two of my favorite actors—Brian and Charlton Heston. Even though the film was more of a "man's" movie—not to be sexist, heaven forbid—I loved the adventurous story, and I loved the acting and the character of these two highly talented men. Brian performed in more films and in the TV miniseries *Centennial* before he hit TV series gold again with the three-year run of *Hardcastle and McCormick*, which costarred Daniel Hugh Kelly. Brian, in his sixties, played the crusty retired judge Milton C. Hardcastle, and the handsome Kelly played his last defendant, Mark Paul "Skid" McCormick. The story followed the duo as they teamed to follow cases that had been dismissed from the court because of technicalities. The series was quite well received, and Brian was always happy when he had steady work.

I believe that Brian's compulsion to work and to get paid well were the primary reasons he accepted roles in the short-lived series *Pursuit of Happiness* and then *Walter and Emily* in 1991. The inimitable Cloris Leachman played Emily Collins, with Matthew Lawrence and Christopher McDonald rounding out the cast in that one-season series. Brian also accepted the starring role in the TV series *Heartland* and was able to work with his daughter Daisy, although this series lasted only ten episodes.

Brian was then off to do guest-star roles in TV shows before taking on voice-over spots. The threads of our lives again intertwined when we both worked on the animated TV series *Spiderman*, in 1995–1997. Brian played Uncle Ben. I played Miss America (you can look like anyone when you're animated), Madeleine Joyce, and . . . a Gila monster.

Brian had been diagnosed with lung cancer in 1996; he then learned that the

Charlton Heston and Brian Keith in *The Mountain Men*, 1980. Columbia Pictures/Photofest. © Columbia Pictures.

disease had spread to his adrenal glands. Depressed because his precious daughter, Daisy, had taken her own life in March 1997, he was suffering. In a haze of medication, having been given just two weeks to live, Brian committed suicide. He shot himself at his home in Malibu on June 24, 1997.

Brian was refreshingly blunt and very much his own man. In death, as in life, Brian deigned to control his own destiny as much as he could. A wonderful actor, a dedicated father, and a staunch personage, Brian shall long be remembered.

In more of the speech I gave when he received his well-deserved star posthumously on the Walk of Fame in Hollywood on June 26, 2008, I stated:

> Love was what Brian was all about—love—for his family, his friends, his coworkers and whomever needed him. I remember on the set when we learned that Bobby Kennedy had been shot. I was so distraught and tearful. Brian comforted me with a hug and supportive words—it was so typical of Brian to sympathize and understand.
>
> My family and I salute Brian on this well-deserved honor of a star on the Hollywood Walk of Fame. I can envision Mr. Keith looking down from heaven, casually standing to the side of the pearly gates wondering what all the hoopla is about.
>
> We all know, Brian. Your light has been shining brightly for some time. Now all who come to visit or learn of this special accolade will recognize what I have known for a long time. You are a brilliant star.

Handsome, versatile Brian Keith.

# 26

## Sebastian, the Manny

Sebastian was somewhat as he appeared—formal and ever striving to be a gentleman. He was born in London, England, and arrived at his acting career later in life. After his father lost his business, Sebastian dropped out of school at age fourteen to help the family, pursued small jobs, never returning to an educational path. While driving Frank Pettingell, the famous Englishman who starred in *Gaslight* and *Becket*, Sebastian became interested in acting and started absorbing the theatrical jargon around him. He finally bluffed his way into some small parts in England.

Sabby immigrated to the United States and began acting on the stage. Then, finding film and TV more suited to his tastes, he established himself as a character actor known for his elegant and upper-class portrayals, ironically since he was born in a Cockney household. But he was a consummate actor, taught by experience and honed by directors with whom he worked. Portraying many roles in TV and film, he eventually landed a part in the two-season run (1960–1962) of *Checkmate*. This intriguing series was one I enjoyed immensely as a child. The show was about a firm of detectives, tasked with protecting their clients. It also starred the handsome leading men Doug McClure and Anthony George, and was set in San Francisco. Sebastian played the part of a British criminologist, Dr. Carl Hyatt.

In 1964, Sabby appeared for Fedderson in one of the episodes of *My Three Sons*. The Fedderson Company was prone to use people who had worked in its other shows, such as *The Millionaire*, because it already knew the actor's work. After the episode of "The In-Law-Whammy," in which Sebastian guest-starred as Tom Morrison in *My Three Sons*, he appeared in other TV episodics and began recording voice-over roles. Disney was enchanted with his polished English accent and cast him as Bagheera the panther in the animated *The Jungle Book* in 1967 and as narrator for the *Winnie the Pooh* franchise.

Sebastian was approached to take the role of Mr. French in *Family Affair* after English actor Terry-Thomas had turned it down. Sabby, too, had misgivings. He did not want to be typecast, and the role of a gentleman's gentleman or butler had stereotypical connotations. But the salary was high, and Sebastian was also offered a percentage of the earnings of the show. Since he had a wife and three children and a fondness for steady income, he took the role. He was glad he did, although there were rumblings along the way of jealousies; for example, his trailer had to be the exact same length as Brian's, and he had to be sure he received his adequate share of promotional appearances.

When *Family Affair* ended, Sebastian tried to shed his recognizable character of Mr. French, but the persona was so embedded in the culture by then that he found it difficult to dismiss the image. Sebastian had created such a memorable character that he couldn't escape. He had worn the same type of formal attire all five years—oh, there were a robe or two and a very loud flowered shirt he donned when we filmed a couple of episodes in faux Tahiti—but the gentleman's gentleman suits he wore were unforgettable.

Throughout the five seasons of the series, I tried to alter my image as much as I could. I changed my hair and clothing styles as the years passed. I didn't want to become typecast. And I was allowed to grow up a little. "Cissy" began the series as a fifteen-year-old. Five years later, she was just eighteen. I'd like to use that math in real life. Catherine Patterson Davis grew from the problems of adjustment from country life to enjoyment of city life, from emotional teenage crushes to more mature feelings—even to deciding whether she should wed an Austrian prince. Then there was the young adult decision of whether or not to join the Peace Corps. Because "Cissy" changed in so many ways, she did not have a consistent persona. Therefore, some people remember her as a more amorphous character. However, if you were a young man at the time you saw *Family Affair* or its

Sebastian taking an arrow for the *Family Affair* cause.

reruns, you definitely remember the girl with the differing hairdos and the colorful, short dresses.

Anissa wore the same twin ponytails for five years—the producers opting only a couple of times for change. Johnny had longish red curly hair which was primarily the same length throughout the run of the show. Brian went from varying shades of blond and gray to differing toupees but was basically consistent in his look. Sebastian had the identical beard and uniform throughout the five years. The continuity of character and wardrobe is a hallmark of a long-running TV series—in movies there are usually more character and development changes in their shortened time constraints.

When the series ended in 1971, Sebastian fought to alter his image. He accepted a role as the host of the occult thriller anthology series *Ghost Story*. As his character, Winston Essex, Sebastian welcomed the audience into his sinister mansion and introduced them to stories ranging from voodoo to vampires. Cabot had definitely tried to shrug his Mr. French image.

In 1973, he was cast in a made-for-TV movie remake of the classic film *The Miracle on 34th Street*, which originally starred Edmund Gwenn as Kris Kringle with the young Natalie Wood as Susan. Guess what part Sebastian played? Of course, the hearty hirsute character of Santa Claus. Sabby had to shave his now famous whiskers for the role. "But St. Nicholas had whiskers," you say. Yes, but the makeup artists could not dye Sebastian's beard white enough nor fill it out enough to look like Santa's. They had to paste on a false, bushy, snowy white beard. With his warm laugh and hefty carriage, Sebastian made an extremely believable and likable Santa Claus. He had had some training when his character of Mr. French donned an anomalous red velvety Christmas costume for an episode of *Family Affair.*

After his role as Kris Kringle in *The Miracle on 34th Street*, Sebastian worked for Disney again. This time on *Man, Monsters, and Mysteries*, a live-action documentary, which also starred Sterling Holloway as the voice of the animated character, the Loch Ness Monster. Sebastian then participated in some shorts in the seventies and recorded the role of the narrator in the animated holiday film *The City That Forgot about Christmas.*

Sabby was a delight and very professional. I liked being with him. Even though at times he could present a crusty exterior, he had a warm and tender spirit, as did all the members of the cast of *Family Affair.* Sebastian had an inviting little house up near Victoria, British Columbia; he and his family would often go there for rest and relaxation. In 1977, Sebastian was visiting his beloved home at Deep Cove when he suffered a severe stroke. He was rushed to the hospital in Victoria, but they could not save him. Sebastian passed away on August 22 at the age of fifty-nine.

I attended his funeral at the Westwood Village Memorial Park Cemetery in California, where Brian was later interred; Mr. Keith was placed just a few feet from Sebastian in 1997. Perhaps they still share their common connection. Sebastian was an excellent actor, a warmhearted family man, and an inspirational friend to me. I doff my theatrical hat to him and will always keep a fond place for him in my heart.

Sebastian in a rare costume change, playing a likable Santa to the twins.

Photo of a *Family Affair* Christmas with the entire cast.

# 27

# Anissa, "Buffy"

Anissa Jones, the sweet "Buffy," was an enchanting child. She was eight years old when she captured the heart of the producers and then the TV audience of *Family Affair*. Anissa was tiny for her age and easily passed for the six-year-old the producers were searching for to portray Brian Keith's younger niece. Coincidentally, "Mary" Anissa Jones was born in Indiana, the state in which her character of Buffy was also conceived.

Anissa, her parents, and her brother moved from Indiana to California and settled in the casual beach town of Playa del Rey in 1960. Her mother, Paula, escorted her precocious daughter to an open audition for a cereal commercial and the adorable munchkin secured her first job. Anissa was bright and personable, and for the first few years sincerely enjoyed acting in *Family Affair*. When the show became a stunning success, Anissa was whisked away for frequent publicity appearances. I believe the tiring traveling and promotional stints took quite an exhausting toll on the little girl. Besides aptly learning her lines nightly, studying three hours a day for schooling on the set, and filming her scenes, she also was called upon to deliver a weekly interview or two on set. On the weekends, the Fedderson Company's publicist would book her at Toys "R" Us stores, parades, and other venues. A host of products was coming into wider use as a source of income for successful shows, so the owners of *Family Affair* jumped on the marketing bandwagon and released licenses for lunch boxes, paper dolls, coloring books, View-Masters, and other products. Anissa, Johnny, and I plugged them all. But in my opinion, it was quite a lot to ask of a small child to hawk merchandise in addition to her strenuous shooting schedule.

In the first episodes of *Family Affair*, Mrs. Beasley, the doll, provided Anissa's character with much comfort. Buffy's parents had been killed; she had been sent to relatives who weren't particularly happy with their new boarder, and she had been separated from her twin brother, Jody, and her older sister, Cissy. Buffy had

Adorable Anissa Jones, on the pilot episode of the first year of *Family Affair,* 1966.

been deposited at the front door of a large Manhattan apartment to live with an uncle whom she had seen on only a few occasions. Everything was confusing to her, and she sought solace with the doll. Mrs. Beasley, dressed in a country frock of blue and white polka dots, sporting an apron and "granny" glasses, would listen in rapt attention to the little girl and stay for hugs as long as the small child needed comfort. When Uncle Bill decided he couldn't keep Buffy and it was necessary for him to leave on a business trip, he discovered that somehow Mrs. Beasley had stowed away in his luggage. In a very tender moment, Bill Davis, now Uncle Bill, changes his mind and decides the orphaned girl and the doll can remain in the Davis household. At the end of that heartwarming and touching premiere episode, the doorbell rings, and two more Patterson children, Jody and Cissy, stand at the doorstep. Espying their missing sister, Cissy and Jody run in for a tight reunion embrace with Buffy. Mr. French, eyes skyward, plaintively cries, "My heavens, I *am* a nanny!" One can almost imagine Mrs. Beasley with a widening smile on her plastic face.

*Family Affair* dealt with personal and family situations with understanding and love. Brian's scripts usually concerned girlfriend problems, settling work disputes,

Anissa modeling her clothing line on one of her many photo shoots.

or trying to deal with the children's predicaments. Sebastian's scenes dealt with the adjustments of being a nanny since he had been highly trained as an exclusive gentleman's gentleman. In later episodes, more of Mr. French's personal past was investigated to the great delight of all concerned. The children's situations dealt with helping others, learning lessons, and growing up. My scripts dealt with boyfriends, teen problems, and maturing from an innocent girl to a young woman.

The faux twins were not allowed the luxury of growing up as I was, albeit at a slowed pace, and stayed as young children for five years. Nowadays, when Disney does a series with teenyboppers, the producers shoot three-years-in-one while the "tweeners" remain the same age for which they were cast.

Toward the end of *Family Affair*, Anissa was getting tired of lugging Mrs. Beasley around. She was a teenager and was trying to establish her identity. Her identity wasn't as a little girl in pigtails with a doll: it was of a big girl with curly brown hair who knew her mind and had her own sensibilities. Indeed, even in some of

Sebastian realizing that, yes indeed, he is a nanny.

the episodes in the fifth year, the doll was left behind in New York as the family traveled to different locales.

When the series ended, Anissa had amassed $70,000, a good deal of money; her parents, after a contentious divorce in 1965, were battling for custody of her, and Mary Anissa Jones was through with show business. She turned down the starring part of Regan offered to her by author William Peter Blatty for *The Exorcist* movie. She just wanted to be a "normal" teenager. She began attending regular public school at Westchester High, near her home at the beach, but unfortunately, the teens she found as friends there were taking drugs. Childhood custody of Anissa was awarded to her father, John P. Jones, in 1973, but he died of heart disease shortly after he had won the long guardianship battle. Anissa returned home to live with her mother and her brother Paul but shortly afterwards moved out to stay with a friend. She began skipping school and worked at a doughnut shop at the beach. In 1976, she became a legal adult. I went to her eighteenth birthday party, which was held at her mother's home in Playa del Rey. Anissa looked happy and relaxed. She was surrounded by her teenage friends and blew out all the candles on her pink and white birthday cake in one huge breath. Paula took me aside at the party and asked whether I would call Anissa and spend some time with her, as she feared Anissa had gotten in with the wrong crowd, who were taking drugs. I promised I would but also explained that I was leaving the next day to go to Virginia to appear as Eliza Doolittle in the musical stage show *My Fair Lady* for a six-week run, but I would get together with Anissa as soon as I returned.

The day after her eighteenth birthday, Anissa received her *Family Affair* money, the portion that had been saved in trust and bonds. Tapping into some of the lucre, she bought a blue Ford Pinto for herself and a red Chevy Camaro for her brother. Now a young adult, she also rented an apartment for both of them. In August 1976, Anissa went to a weekend party at a friend's house in the beach town of Oceanside, about ninety miles south of Playa del Rey. In the late morning, she was found in one of the bedrooms, unconscious. Her friends, who had checked on her earlier and thought that she was sleeping, didn't know what to do when they rechecked their small friend. Anissa wasn't breathing. The teenagers panicked. When the medics finally arrived, they found Anissa inert. She had passed away from a lethal cocktail of cocaine, Quaaludes, PCP, and Seconal.

I learned of her untimely death while I was still working in Virginia. The announcement was heartbreaking. That dear Anissa, a young woman of such talent and promise, lay dead, alone, in a guest bedroom was shocking. Attempting to understand the loss of this precious life, I could not fathom the details. The actual report on her demise heightened my confusion: the coroner from San Diego stated

Anissa as a teenager.

it was the most massive overdose he had ever encountered. Was she depressed? Was she lonely? Did she take her own life? Did she just not calculate how many drugs a small body could absorb? These questions will forever rack the depths of my heart and mind. Anissa, and her alter ego, Buffy, will eternally be remembered as the sweet young girl with bouncy pigtails who was alert with a quip or a comforting glance, with her Mrs. Beasley held tightly in her tiny fingers.

Anissa was cremated and her ashes spread over the Pacific Ocean near her home. Such a sad ending to the life of a bright, beautiful, and talented girl. It is dangerous being in the entertainment business as a child and even more difficult to survive.

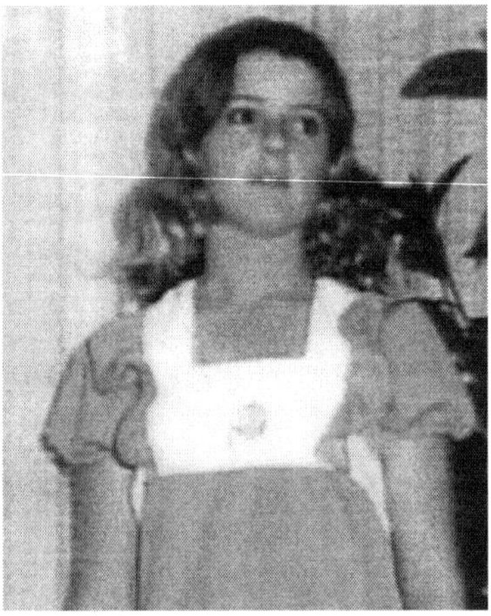

Photo of Anissa growing up.

# 28

# Johnny, "Jody"

Johnny Whitaker's story is similar to Anissa's as he attempted to make the difficult transition from child star to successful adult. Johnny was the fifth child in a Mormon family of eight children. His parents lived in a comfortable house in the valley of Southern California. Johnny's first taste of show business came as a toddler when he appeared in an OK Used Car commercial. After his mother, Thelma, secured an agent for him, the six-year-old was cast in the film *The Russians Are Coming, the Russians Are Coming*, where he met Brian Keith. Brian had just signed papers to star in a new television series, *Family Affair*, and he thought the young boy might be good for the role of Jody. Even though the original idea was to have a six-year-old girl and an older sibling, the producers thought Johnny strongly resembled Anissa. They decided the two curly-haired moppets would make a strong and appealing pair. Anissa and Johnny got along well on the set, but coming from different backgrounds and Anissa being older than Johnny, they spent little time together outside of working or doing publicity appearances. As the years progressed, Johnny physically outgrew Anissa, even though he was younger, but they were still believable as twins and were still able to relate to each other on some level.

The children and I supplied our own wardrobe the first season, and Thelma, Johnny's mother, was usually on the set darning socks for her family or mending clothes. Anissa's mother, Paula, was on the set also, overseeing her daughter and being the proverbial stage mother.

An excellent acting coach was supplied for the children; she helped Johnny cure his lisp. It was quite cute when six-year-old Jody would say "Uncle Be-oo," being unable to pronounce his *Ls*, but as Johnny grew older, the producers thought it more professional and in the interest of clarity to have him pronounce his words correctly.

Johnny enjoyed working, but like Anissa, most of his time was spent with

Johnny and Anissa on set.

studio school tutoring, family obligations, and/or publicity jaunts. The five years passed quickly for him and then it was over.

After the series, Johnny did three projects for Disney, *The Biscuit Eater*, a 1973 movie that was a remake of the 1940s movie of the same name, *Napoleon and Samantha*, about a boy, a girl, and a lion, starring Michael Douglas and Jodie Foster in her first film role, and *The Snowball Express*, about a father (Dean Jones) who moves his New York–based family to Colorado to renovate an inherited hotel into a ski resort.

Johnny then did the memorable musical movie rendition of *Tom Sawyer*, appearing in the title role. The Sherman Brothers (Richard and Robert) had adapted Mark Twain's book and scored the film. The movie costarred Jeff East as Huckleberry Finn and Celeste Holm as Aunt Polly. Johnny reunited with Jodie Foster (from their Disney outing of *Napoleon and Samantha*), who created the memorable role of Becky Thatcher in *Tom Sawyer*. This is the last on-camera movie in which Johnny would appear until 2013. In 2015, threads were pulled as I rewove the part of Aunt Polly into the stage adaptation of the Disney film version of *Tom Sawyer*—more about that later.

The Sherman Brothers also wrote the music for *Sigmund and the Sea Monster*, a 1973 TV series produced by the prolific and successful team of Sid and Marty Krofft (*HR Pufnstuf*, *Land of the Lost*). Johnny played Sigmund, a teenager, who along with his younger brother, Scott, played by Scott C. Kolden, discover a sad sea monster, essayed by costumed little person Billy Barty. The watery creature, complete with hanging seaweed, had escaped from the ocean because he didn't want to scare people, which was a condition if he wanted to remain with his fearsome family. The innocent little monster finds refuge and adventure when he meets Johnny and Scott. The Stuart brothers' goal in the series is to hide the sea monster from their parents and from the sea monster's parents.

*Sigmund* lasted only thirteen episodes, and then Johnny was off on a Mormon mission for two years to Portugal. He returned to the United States, attended Brigham Young University, met and married Symbria Wright, and then got divorced after four years of marriage. He was not happy when Symbria tied the knot with his supposed best friend.

Floundering, Johnny moved back to California from Utah and found a job repairing computers at CBS and then joined his sister Dora's theatrical agency.

Unfortunately, like Anissa, Johnny got hooked on drugs and alcohol. He spent and lost the money he had left from his youthful acting pursuits. Penniless and almost homeless in Los Angeles, his close-knit family decided to do a drug and alcohol intervention. They told him, "Either get off drugs or we are divorcing you as a family." He got off drugs. Taking classes and attending rehab, Johnny was then able to get a drug counseling certification so that he could advise others on how to live without narcotics and alcohol. Yes, acting is hard—especially for children trying to make the transition. But Johnny survived and is helping others to live a clean and sober life.

A recent photo of Johnny.

# 29

# Mrs. Beasley, Played by an Unknown

Mrs. Beasley was a charming character. Buffy's "very favorite friend" was the first "old lady" doll to achieve film prominence. The soft, huggable toy became a symbol of comfort and love to many millions in the audience. I remember a conversation I had when I played a part in the TV movie *The Siege at Ruby Ridge*, which starred Dennis Quaid and Laura Dern. Laura told me that she was a big fan of *Family Affair*, and when her parents, Bruce Dern and Diane Ladd, were getting a divorce, Mrs. Beasley was her constant companion, providing her with continuing comfort and warmth during that difficult time. At autograph shows, I have heard many versions of that tale. The huggable doll had taken on a comforting persona and made a long-lasting impact on many fans.

Buffy and her surrogate toy grandma had many adventures throughout the series. One time, Mrs. Beasley was rushed to the doll hospital when Jody inadvertently pulled off her arm. The guilty moppet waited anxiously with the family until the treasured friend's limb was sewn on and then proclaimed, "Good as new!" by the doll doctor.

Then there was the time Mrs. Beasley went missing and the doll, by now having taken on humanoid characteristics, became the intense focus of a frenzied search. The comforting little old lady was finally found on top of a dirty metal garbage bin as Mr. French had accidentally knocked her from the heights of the apartment's balcony. Mrs. Beasley had dropped many stories, rapidly descending to crash unceremoniously in the refuse area. She was retrieved, cleaned, and later lived to tell about it in a Mattel version of a talking toy doll. Thank goodness she survived!

# 30

# Other *Family Affair* Family

## John Williams

*Family Affair* had outstanding talent performing in recurring roles. An excellent actor, John Williams, filled one notable spot, that of a different Mr. French in Sebastian's absence during the first year of the show. I was recently at the Hollywood/Chicago Autograph and Collectible Convention in Rosemont, Illinois. Many fans came up, asking, "What happened to Sebastian Cabot? Why was he replaced in the first season?"

Sebastian had a problem with his hand, and it became necessary for him to undergo wrist surgery. The producers had to find someone to carry on in his stead. I believe they made a great choice in casting the superb actor John Williams, who had starred in *Dial M for Murder* and as Audrey Hepburn's father in the award-winning film *Sabrina*. I loved *Sabrina* and I loved John. He was a tall, thin Englishman with warm and proper decorum, just right for the temporary replacement of a gentleman's gentleman. Sebastian's operation and recovery did not take as long as John's stint on our show, but because of the way we shot—to accommodate Brian—John starred in nine episodes in 1967 as Mr. Nigel French, Mr. Giles French's cousin from England. John was very professional and an extremely good actor. I believe it is always difficult coming into an established series and taking over for another actor, but John's innate graciousness and talent saw him through in a winning way.

In one of the episodes, Cissy encounters yet another opportunity for young love in Mr. Nigel French's nephew, David, played by Martin Horsey. Mr. Williams had many lovely scenes with his nephew and me. David had stopped in New York on his way to the West Coast to study to be a dentist. Neither Cissy's nor Mr. Nigel French's interventions could persuade him to stay nor to follow in a gentleman's gentleman's polished footsteps. David continued his journey westward. And Cissy continued her quest to find true love in the next episode.

Again, the threads are always fascinating to me. Mr. Williams was a guest star in Sebastian's TV series *Checkmate* in 1960 and also guest-starred in Fedderson's series *My Three Sons* for three episodes. The threads tied together to create a satisfying starring bow on a highly successful series package for the gracious Mr. Williams.

## Gregg Fedderson

Gregg Fedderson was a recurring character as my boyfriend Gregg from 1969 to 1971. Gregg was a very handsome partner, yet being three years younger than me, I didn't think of him as a real boyfriend. Gregg did, however, and began courting me offscreen.

Gregg had not graduated from high school, and I was almost finished with my studies at UCLA, but he had a sophistication and ardor that I had yet to master. Being born into a successful and wealthy family had given him confidence and savoir faire. He treated me to exquisite dinners at the Coconut Grove, several beautiful Beverly Hills restaurants, and other posh eateries. Gregg presented me with an elegant necklace with a gold-and-diamond heart pendant engraved with, "All my Love, Gregg," that I cherish. When Gregg and I did scenes together, sometimes I would get tickled and start to giggle, I think from repressed sexuality. And, because Gregg did not have much experience as an actor, he would sometimes flub his lines. I was used to being very slick and quick, completing a scene in one take. Gregg many times would get distracted. John Stephens told me he remembered one specific time when he was called down to the set from his production office because of one of the scenes Gregg and I were trying to complete. I remember it well. We were up to seventeen takes. I think it might have been a record on *Family Affair*. By the time Gregg got all his lines right, I would start to anticipate that he would flub them, and when he didn't, I started laughing and flubbed mine! We were finally able to wrap the scene . . . and the day . . . in twenty takes. I did learn a valuable lesson from that experience: concentrate, focus, and keep your mouth shut when you have to giggle.

Mr. Fedderson was not pleased that his handsome young son was dating "the help" and tried to put a stop to our romance. At least, Cissy got fewer lines when we were dating off camera. I didn't want anyone to think of me as a fortune hunter or someone robbing the proverbial cradle. I was very fond of Gregg; there was an ingenuousness and naturalness about him that was *so* endearing! But I had the intuitive feeling that our relationship was not going to last. Plus, I was quite secure that I could make my own way in life. I also knew that I was smarter and better educated than Gregg, sometimes difficult in a long-term liaison. We ended our innocent fling, but I continued to be friends with Gregg; I adored his gentle humor, sensitivity, and basic good grace.

After *Family Affair*, Gregg married a beautiful blond girl and they started their life together full of hope and promise. But they were soon divorced. Gregg lived a while in Hawaii, but he seemed lost. He worked at a yacht brokerage firm and was somewhat successful. When his father died, Gregg found that he had been severely reduced in his inheritance. I think this snub and ostracism added to his stress and depression. He died too young, at the age of fifty-three, of cancer, but he will live on in my heart and as a light in my soul.

## Nancy Walker

Nancy Walker was cast in the semiregular role of Emily Turner in the fifth and last year of our show. The producers thought the tame *Family Affair* needed a lively injection, and Nancy seemed to be the droll nurse to give it. Her part was as a maid to Mr. French's staff of one. Playing her well-hewn character of brash "commoner" from such series as *Rhoda* and *Macmillan and Wife*, Emily was to be a prod to Mr. French's staid ways and a foil to Sebastian's humor. But Nancy brought an element that was foreign to the gentle ways of *Family Affair*. Indeed, Nancy used to complain that she had to alter her tried-and-true quick comedic timing. Don Fedderson's film style was to show long close-ups and slow reactions. Nancy came from vaudeville, and she went for fast-paced humor and large takes; her style just didn't quite mesh with *Family Affair*'s comedic technique.

Gregg Fedderson and I at the Ice Capades. Our relationship was anything but frosty.

Nancy Walker, who played Emily during the fifth season, with Sebastian and Brian, trying to solve a problem in an episode of *Family Affair*.

Nancy's character did bring to the show a very handsome companion for Cissy. Peter Duryea, son of actor Dan Duryea, whom I had enjoyed watching on his fifties TV series *China Smith*, played Emily's son, Jim Turner. In the *Family Affair* narrative, Emily had taken the job with the Davis household to help put Jim through medical school. Jim, the young intern, was a fresh breath of air to me: the first couple of seasons, my "boyfriends," such as the singer Eddie "High Hopes" Hodges, were younger and maybe right for Cissy but did not ring Kathy's romantic bell. Then along came Peter—older, handsome, and very appealing. We had great screen time together and brought my character to new heights!

## Heather Angel

Heather Angel essayed the part of Miss Faversham, a polished female English nanny as opposed to Mr. French's disdainful rendition of a manny. Heather had had quite an illustrious career in film, having starred in *The Three Musketeers*, *Lifeboat*, and *Bulldog Drummond* before she joined the cast of TV's *Family Affair*. She added a lovely touch of class to our show and displayed her excellent acting in eighteen episodes.

## Sherry Alberoni

Sherry Alberoni (remember my competition for *This Is Alice*?) played the recurring part of my perky teenage friend Sharon. We had great times together and got along exceedingly well. I respected Sherry's talent, and she has had a long career in show business, so we had a lot in common. After *The Mickey Mouse Club*, Mousketeer Sherry continued to act, doing guest spots on another Fedderson show, *My Three Sons*, and starring in the short-lived series *The Tom Ewell Show*. She then began a voice-over career. Sherry recorded the voices of characters on such animated series as *Super Friends* and *Josie and the Pussy Cats*. My friend is now a grandmother, enjoying a lovely life in Southern California with her husband of over thirty years and continuing to make appearances for Disney. We still see each other on occasion and exchange proud Christmas cards.

## Other Members of the *Family Affair* Quilt

During the five-year run of *Family Affair*, the show hosted a handful of wonderful guest stars. One of the most memorable ones was Robert Reed of future *Brady Bunch* fame. In the episode "Think Deep," the children are awestruck by this handsome teacher. Brian didn't particularly care for Mr. Reed or his style of acting, and if Brian didn't like someone, everyone knew it. Mr. Keith was not one to mince words or emotions. Brian never met a child he didn't like, but adults were different. If a woman was cast to play one of his many girlfriends and he didn't like her, Brian just wouldn't look at her during the scenes—or he'd look as little as possible. Those relationships were not destined to last as a recurring part

Sherry Alberoni (former Mouseketeer), who played my pal Sharon on *Family Affair*, and I.

for the actress in the series on or off camera. I think Mr. Reed merited about two quick glances and one long look from Brian.

Veronica Cartwright (from Hitchcock's *The Birds*, and the sister of Angela from *The Sound of Music* and *Lost in Space*) guest-starred along with Jamie Farr (*MASH*) as hippies when Cissy decided that she needed to venture forth to discover what the flower-power culture was all about. She came, she saw, but she did not conquer the new wave and was quickly back in the non-pot-smoking and secure arms of the Davis family.

In the "Somebody Upstairs" episode, Anissa and I were able to demonstrate some of our heretofore unheralded talents. Guest star Joan Blondell played a famous Broadway actress who moves into our New York apartment building. Buffy and I are star-struck and want to be triple-threat actors, just like the exciting diva. We rehearse and then perform for her in an effort to garner some attention for our idea. I play the piano while Anissa and I sing "Let Me Entertain You" with gusto in Joan's lavish apartment. We were eventually encouraged in the show not to give up our day jobs and reminded about the sacrifices one must make in order to be a star . . .

Anissa watching as I play the piano in the episode "Somebody Upstairs."

Ann Sothern was another guest-star delight. Most of her scenes were spent with Sebastian because the story centered on their mutual admiration. As the character Florence Cahill in the episode "A Man's Place," Ms. Cahill entices Mr. French to join her in opening a restaurant named Our Mr. French. The issue of being a servant was also discussed. Although the restaurant was a success, *our* Mr. French missed the family, so his budding relationship with Ms. Cahill and the restaurant were both short-lived. However, I will long remember the graciousness of Ms. Sothern. After all, she was one the first movie stars I met when I joined the entertainment business and when I appeared on her star vehicle, the TV series *Private Secretary*.

In one of my favorite episodes, my friend and future *Vanities* costar, Linda Kaye Henning, was a guest in "And Baby Makes Eight." Married to one of the Fedderson sons, Mike Minor, for five years, Linda is most well known for her delightful portrayal of Betty Jo Bradley in the long-running TV classic series *Petticoat Junction*. Linda is a warm and delightful person whose father, Paul Henning, was the successful producer of *Beverly Hillbillies*, *Petticoat Junction*, and *Green Acres*. The folksy shows he wrote and produced probably stemmed from his Missouri roots. He and his wife, Ruth, donated a conservation area and state forest near Branson. Linda is now docent for the Griffith Park Zoo, and we continue our friendship over the phone and at occasional autograph shows. "And Baby Makes Eight" was written for the fifth season of the series and emphasized how I was maturing. It also embraced some of the world's roiling events, including the Vietnam War.

Another one of my favorite episodes combined acting and drawing. Painting is an enjoyable pastime of mine, and the writers incorporated the talent into the *Family Affair* episode "A Member of the Family." Cissy is taking an art class, and Mr. French's feelings are hurt because he doesn't think he is included in the exhibition. It's just that Cissy wants to surprise him with caricatures. Seeing my faux family members every day while shooting *Family Affair*, it was easy for me to capture their individual essences in the caricatures I drew and colored for the episode.

Myrna Loy was another famous actress who graced our show. I had loved her in the *Thin Man* movies with William Powell and was excited to meet the star. In *Family Affair*, she played Adele, a maid, in the episode "A Helping Hand." Although somewhat tentative, she was an absolute joy to work with. Charming, talkative, and professional, she provided a glimpse back into the heady days of studio movie stardom. Mr. Williams and she got along "famously."

The Oscar-nominated (for best actress in a supporting role for *Some Came Running*) Martha Hyer added a touch of glitter to our show as well as a silken thread, as she also appeared with John Williams in the movie *Sabrina*. In the episode "Star Dust," Ms. Hyer guest-starred as famous actress Carol Haven. Cissy, of course, was quite impressed with the beautiful star, as was I. She mesmerized the entire family, especially when we went on a shopping spree for a non-birthday party and she played charades with us. It looked like we were going to get a mother

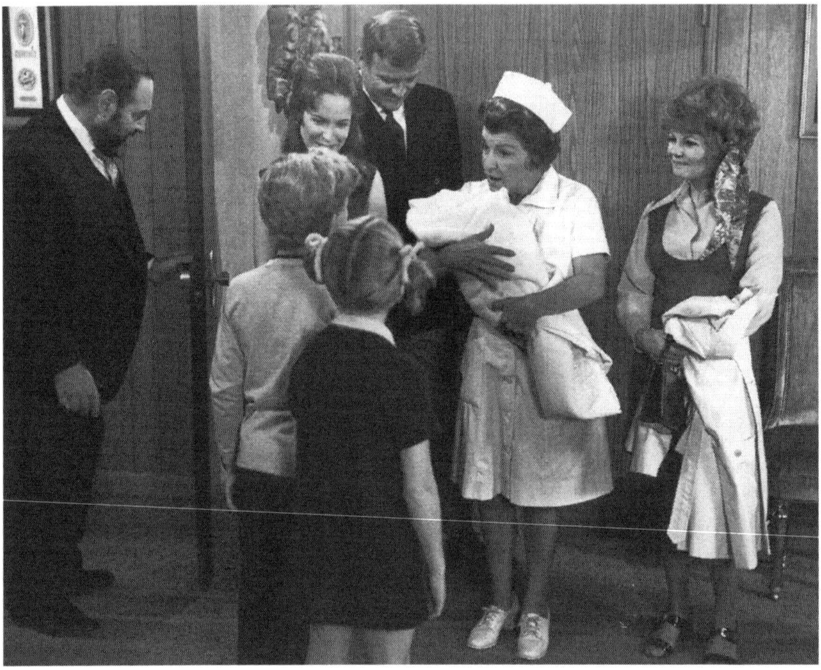

A family portrait with Nancy Walker as Emily along with guest-star Linda Kaye Henning and a faux new baby.

for our family until Uncle Bill's heart was not beating with the same fondness we all held for her. When the glamorous star was about to turn down a part that would take her to Spain for a year, Uncle Bill encouraged her to go. I think she got the hint. Although we did hear from the diva via a package of goodies sent from España, we didn't hear from her again as a guest star. But I certainly enjoyed working with her.

Then there was Ida Lupino. She was beautiful and intelligent. I learned that Mrs. Howard Duff was born in London. She was perfect to play the part of Lady Marchwood, the wealthy widow whom Mr. French had known in England when she was but a humble barmaid. There was great chemistry between the two. Indeed, Sebastian and Ms. Lupino and been childhood friends in England. She was glad to be returning to acting as she had spent over ten years directing. She stated to Bob Thomas from AP, "I like it. I like being able to come on a set and worry about my own lines instead of concerning myself with five thousand other details." I had a slim tie to Ms. Lupino. Besides meeting and working with her on *Family Affair*, I re-created the role she had originated on TV's *Twilight Zone*'s "16 Millimeter

During *Family Affairs*, I enjoyed my leisure time painting. Photofest

Shrine." When this television episode was adapted for radio, I starred in the same role Ms. Lupino had originated. Ida Lupino's *Family Affair* episode, "Maudie," was so popular that a second episode featuring Ms. Lupino was ordered, "The Return of Maudie." She returned with great warmth and graciousness.

Jackie Coogan knew all about child actors. In the 1920s, he was the highest-paid young thespian in Hollywood. When he came of age, he found he was penniless. I have mentioned the "Coogan Law" that was passed, which reserves a percentage of a youngster's pay in an untouchable bank account until the child has reached the age of eighteen. Jackie appeared in the "Fat, Fat, the Water Rat" episode as a blue-collar worker down on his luck. In one unusual episode, the twins were allowed to get dirty, wear everyday clothes, and play with "the other kids." It was a poignant episode, and Mr. Coogan was great in his role; this appearance occurred soon after he had starred in *The Addams Family* as Uncle Fester. Thankfully, Mr. Coogan was finally able to earn money in the entertainment world and keep it.

As the character Julie Madden, actress/songstress Kaye Stevens was hired for the episode "The Unsound of Music" to help teach Buffy to sing for glee club. It turned out to be a losing cause as the whole family agreed that Buffy had many talents, but vocal ones were not part of her skills repertoire. Kaye was very vibrant and even gave me her contact information. It was my introduction into "networking."

Caricatures I drew for the *Family Affair* episode "A Member of the Family."

## THE FAMILY *FAMILY AFFAIR* QUILT

Besides our illustrious guest stars, we had other notable actors appearing in our *Family Affair* series. Nepotism is rampant in Hollywood. And why not? A child models his or her behavior and actions after parents and family, and if parents are in show business, it seems the children are likely to put at least a small footstep through the door of entertainment. During the first season of *Family Affair*, Don Fedderson's wife Tido, who was the mother of Moyna Minor, Mike Minor, Gregg, Darr, and Dana, held sway over the Fedderson household. A former actress, she appeared in many of her husband's shows. She also was a lovely hostess and seemingly brought luck and success to *Family Affair*. After her divorce from Don, she moved into her Palm Springs home and treated Gregg, me, and our friends many times to dinner at the exotic Trader Vic's there.

Brian's wife, Judith Landon, an actress and ballet dancer who later owned a dance studio, appeared appropriately in the *Family Affair* episode "Ballerina Buffy"

Guest star Myrna Loy (*The Thin Man*) in the *Family Affair* episode "A Helping Hand" with John Williams, who replaced Mr. Giles French as his cousin Mr. Nigel French in the first season.

On a *Family Affair* shopping spree with guest star Martha Hyer with Buffy, Jody, and Mr. French.

Guest star Ida Lupino enjoying a joke with Sebastian Cabot on *Family Affair.*

In the "Fat, Fat, the Water Rat" *Family Affair* episode, Buffy and Jody repeat the eponymous ditty as Mr. French and guest star Jackie Coogan watch.

Brian Keith and guest star Kaye Stevens react as Buffy tries to warble some musical notes. CBS

as Margot Dunbar, Buffy's ballet teacher. She also provided a love interest for Brian—perhaps typecasting, but they divorced soon after. It seemed to be catching as Tido and Don Fedderson filed for divorce in 1969.

Joan Vohs, wife of our astute production manager, John Stephens, appeared as Buffy's teacher in the episode "The Unsound of Music" along with Judith Landon (Keith), a double hit for nepotism in *Family Affair.* However, John and Joan remained married, and Joan appeared again as Miss Cummings in five episodes. Joan was always very gracious when I would visit her and John at their home in Tarzana. She sent great Christmas cards until her death in 2001.

Annette Cabot, Sebastian's daughter, appeared as Brian's secretary and in four other roles in *Family Affair,* and Sabby's daughter Yvonne appeared in some episodes also, but as an extra.

My brother Lance appeared as a news reporter in one of the episodes, but his footage was left on the cutting room floor, shades of *The Bad Seed.* Too much competition for Brian maybe, or perhaps the episode was running long, which happened frequently. Many scenes had to be cut or rearranged to fit that precious twenty-two minutes.

Anissa's brother appeared as an extra, and Johnny's assorted brothers and sisters also appeared as extras in the series.

A row of nannies with Mr. French in the first episode. Tido Fedderson, Don Fedderson's wife, can be seen at the end of the park bench.

# 31

# A Quality Garment

One of the reasons I believe *Family Affair* was so successful—many other similar family-oriented sitcoms had been created—was because the show was cast so well. The actors and characters liked one another, and the love shone through: it was excellent chemistry. In subsequent attempts at shows in this genre, people disdained or insulted others in the family. Why watch people belittling one another? Is that a goal to be reached, an ideal to be sought? If that is a reflection of the times and reality, should we not strive for a better way to communicate?

Why not entertain with positivism—offer the audience a reachable goal instead of disdaining those we love? For crass humor? Or would gentle chuckles and laughter be a better path for entertainment? Our show did have an element of fantasy because, in some ways, it was an idealized family with the care and concern that each character exhibited. But the feelings toward one another on *Family Affair* were genuine, and I believe that true camaraderie was a primary element that made it a hit. Additionally, the show engaged experienced directors, writers, and producers, all of whom built the foundation of the show's success. Because of the nature of our shooting schedule, the same director had to be employed for the entire season. After the single-show pilot was filmed, which was directed by James Sheldon, the premiere season was helmed by William D. Russell. Mr. Russell had gained fame as the director of several successful TV series, such as *Father Knows Best*, *Dennis the Menace*, and *Hazel*. He seemed an apt choice to launch our new family show. However, Mr. Russell had suffered a stroke and was recovering while managing the first year of *Family Affair*. After he received a nomination for an Emmy for Best Director for our show in 1967, he retired and unfortunately died the next year, 1968.

Our subsequent director stayed with us the rest of the run, Charles Barton. I loved Charlie. Mr. Russell was somewhat demanding and a little distant, but Charlie was a friendly leprechaun who was always ready with a smile and a hearty laugh.

He had gained fame as director for the Abbott and Costello films and had great comic sensibility. Charlie directed episodes, as did Mr. Russell, of *Dennis the Menace* and *Hazel* but also family movies such as *The Shaggy Dog* and *Toby Tyler* for Disney and the TV shows *Amos and Andy*, *The Gale Storm Show*, *McHale's Navy*, and *Petticoat Junction*. A thread tying *Petticoat Junction* to *Family Affair* is that Mike Minor, Don and Tido Fedderson's son who played Steve Elliot on *Petticoat*, was the brother of Gregg Fedderson, who played my boyfriend both on and off the set of *Family Affair*.

The writers were also terrific. The first year, Austin and Irma Kalish and Ed Hartmann had the immense task of assuring all the scripts by various writers demonstrated the theme, concept, and feeling of the show. Austin and Irma were the story editors that first year. They were well known in Fedderson's world and had first written for his series *The Millionaire*. They also wrote for Fedderson's *My Three Sons*. After the initial season, they continued to write scripts for *Family Affair* but went on to other writing and producing chores. They were executive producers for such shows as *Good Times*, *227*, *Facts of Life*, and *Valerie's Family*.

Edmund L. Hartmann was a screenwriter and producer of the first order. He had written seven comedies for Bob Hope, including *The Lemon Drop Kid* and *Sorrowful Jones*, which was a remake of *Little Miss Marker*. Mr. Hartmann adapted the original story by Damon Runyon and wrote the screenplay for Bob Hope in the starring part. My friend Mary Jayne Saunders played in the remake in 1949 as the little girl who is left as collateral on a bet. Sometimes it seems there are no new ideas. A friend of mine told me recently that he thought there are really only seven story lines and they just keep getting told and retold. Mary Jayne appeared with me in the 1964 movie *Kiss Me, Stupid*, directed by the legendary Billy Wilder, starring Dean Martin and Kim Novak. We were enthusiastic autograph seekers but didn't get our proper credits in that movie (where *were* our agents?!). Mary Jayne met and married Jay Johnstone, a major league baseball player for both the New York Yankees and Los Angeles Dodgers, and retired from show business.

Ed Hartmann and Edmund Beloin both wrote Bob Hope's movie *My Favorite Spy*. Beloin was joined by Henry Garson (who had adapted Gore Vidal's hit play *Visit to a Small Planet* into a screenplay for comedy king Jerry Lewis) to become the writers/producers with Ed the first year of *Family Affair*. They also wrote Bob Hope's *Paleface* with costar Jane Russell. Another thread.

In 2010, the third year into my San Francisco talk show, *Backstage with Barry and Kathy*, Barry Barsamian and I traveled to Jane's home in Santa Maria to interview this icon. More about Ms. Russell later.

Ed did not write the sequel to *Son of Paleface*, which again starred Bob Hope and Jane Russell, but since he had established the root story, he received credit for his contributions. Ed also wrote and produced shows for Abbott and Costello, including the film *Naughty Nineties* in 1945, which was tagged "A Showboat Full of Laughter." I believe that is where Ed met Charles Barton. In the fifties Ed served as president of the Writers Guild. He was not only smart, intellectual, and politically savvy but also a raconteur of the first order. I liked him immensely. He took an interest in his actors even though he was in his office most of the time, and I did not see him on the set regularly. Ed suggested that I join the Book-of-the-Month Club and recommended I read the nonfiction best seller at the time, *The Double Helix*, which told the story of the discovery of the molecular structure of the nucleic acids—DNA and RNA, the particles of life. As I related earlier, one of my philosophical bases is to find the essence of our life on this planet. *The Double Helix* guided me to the scientific understanding of microbiological elements that comprise our universe. DNA came into popular knowledge when the book was published in 1968. James Watson was one of the discoverers of the specific structure of the molecule. Along with Francis Crick and Maurice Wilkins, they won the Nobel Prize in Physiology in 1962. One can hardly turn on a crime show today without DNA being mentioned as a lead to discovering who committed what or what contaminated whom. It was fascinating to me in 1968 as an entry to understanding our universal beginnings.

Besides recommending books to me, Mr. Hartmann gave me tips on acting. He said that acting is through the eyes—the window to the soul—where most emotions and feelings are expressed. Look at Al Pacino's performance in *The Godfather Part II* as a good example. If you have watched *Family Affair*, you will see the long close-ups and heartfelt emotions in the eyes of the characters, following Mr. Hartmann's and also Mr. Fedderson's styles.

Ed was also a great host and invited Henry Kissinger, the former US secretary of state, to our set in 1969 to observe filming, along with his son, David, and daughter, Elizabeth, and to have lunch at the studio. We must have made a theatrical impression on David as he later became involved in the entertainment world. He was copresident at NBC Disney and then became president of Conaco, Conan O'Brien's production company.

Mr. Kissinger was given the Nobel Peace Prize in 1973. I thought he was charming, diplomatic, and charismatic. Very warm and friendly. Mr. Hartmann had arranged a special catered lunch for the cast and select production team members from the studio. I will never forget how Ed guided the conversation. There were many egos present, and they seemed to find it necessary to regale the visiting political dignitary with tales about themselves. Mr. Hartmann interceded with the gracious and diplomatic words that "perhaps we could hear what Mr. Kissinger has to say." Bravo, Mr. Hartmann!

Besides being a film writer, Mr. Hartmann produced the Fedderson TV series *My Three Sons*. From this success, he gleaned the voice of his audience and created, wrote, and produced the successful *Family Affair*. During our run, he also wrote the pilots for two other Fedderson shows, *To Rome with Love*, which starred John Forsythe, and *The Smith Family*, which starred Henry Fonda. These series followed Fedderson's formula of casting movie stars in his TV shows, but these series were short-lived. The culture and TV viewership were changing to more "realistic"-oriented shows in the late 1960s. The brash humor of *All in the Family* was replacing the gentle humor of *Family Affair*. After CBS canceled *Family Affair*, Fedderson offered the show to ABC. The network was just about to sign the papers for additional episodes of *Family Affair* when it was presented with a new family series. This show had more children, one of whom looked a lot like Buffy with her bright blond pigtails but was much younger, and two comely looking adult stars. Instead of taking the older established but waning *Family Affair*, ABC opted for the new, fresh *The Brady Bunch*.

I stayed in contact with my dear friend Ed when *Family Affair* ended and visited his Asian-decorated home many times. His love of Japanese culture surfaced several times in Eastern-themed shows on *Family Affair*. One of the special episodes was about a bonsai tree titled "Mr. Osaki's Tree." An elderly Japanese gentleman gifts the family with a miniature tree, which he says has paralleled his life. Then, as he is about to depart to his home country, he takes ill, and the bonsai begins to wither. The children are very upset, as it seems Mr. Osaki is also dying. There is a wonderful moment when the small tree begins to lift its withered arms. Mr. Osaki is called, and he too has recovered. The touch of Japanese mysticism served the international feeling of the show well, and there was another heartfelt ending to our sentimental show.

Once, after the series, Ed and I had a memorable lunch together at the Beverly Hills Crest Hotel, and in that relaxed atmosphere I got to know even better the gracious man who had first asked me why my hair was turning green in his audition office so many years previous.

Besides the extreme talents of Ed Hartmann and other producers on our show, an additional reason *Family Affair* did well was because it was one of the first shows to be broadcast in color. How exciting to see a luxurious penthouse colorfully projected in a family comedy! Just to make sure the audience realized the show was presenting something new, *Family Affair* opened with a brilliant kaleidoscopic image, turning and displaying the beautiful hues about to be experienced. The vibrant opening was accompanied by the engaging strains of Frank De Vol's inviting, upbeat tune. Frank was a well-known composer by the time he created music for *Family Affair*. As I have said, the Fedderson Company liked to use people that it had tested. Actors, crew, and creative personnel on *Family Affair* had all passed the theatrical exam. Music was no exception. Frank had previously composed the theme music for the TV series *Richard Diamond, Private Detective*, *Grindl* (starring the legendary Imogene Coca and with Charlie Barton directing several episodes), and Fedderson's *My Three Sons*.

Even though the company began with a large slate of thirty-two episodes a year for *Family Affair*, we finished our season quickly. The alacrity with which we shot was due in a large part to our excellent production team, led by John Stephens, the production manager who was able to schedule the odd way we shot, brilliantly taking advantage of the same locales to shoot all the scenes that used a particular space. Because of his efficiency in scheduling, all of the cast members, then, were able to take on other projects when the season was completed.

# 32

# Weaving an International Quilt

*Family Affair* was an international hit and was received with accolades in many countries. It was the first American television show that was allowed in China; it appeared on that Eastern front in 1970. Many foreign translated shows were created, some of which were entitled *Cher Oncle Bill* in France, *Lieber Onkel Bill* in Germany, and *Mis Adorables Sabrinos* for the Latin market.

Not only was the show itself globally successful, but ancillary products created for the show were also big hits. There were paper dolls, color forms, trace and color books, View–Master sets, and a myriad of different coloring books with Mrs. Beasley, Buffy, Jody, and the whole family. There were watches and alarm clocks, dolls and ornaments. The plethora of products extended to the literary market, where *Buffy's Cookbook* found an audience, as did German, French, and Israeli books that based their stories on *Family Affair* and its main characters. The show became a collector's haven, and one can still find treasures on eBay and through private collections.

It was a time when the merchandising of shows was taking hold, and the *Family Affair* products grabbed on with great strength; I believe it is one of the reasons the show is still so widely and fondly remembered. As a child, if you were lucky enough to own a Buffy or Cissy ensemble—you have memories of where you wore it and what happened then. If you colored in one of the many *Family Affair* coloring books, the kinetic and creative energy you used is tucked away in your memory bank and can be withdrawn, relived, and enjoyed once again. The feelings remain if you still have your Mrs. Beasley doll or some of the other quality offerings from the beloved show. Les Kaufman, publicist for *Family Affair*, and the CBS marketing team seemed to know about "branding" before it gained such wide acceptance in our verdant social media age. There was even a series of *Family Affair* comic books created—a mini four set by Gold Key, which I fondly take to comic conventions and sign for fans.

A German book of *Family Affair—Lieber Onkel Bill.*

A Buffy collection was specially created. The popular little girl was just what the country needed in a time of rapid change, counterculture movements, and the Vietnam War. The quest to escape from the tensions of the times built a firm foundation of fans for the blond-headed tyke. And so there were Buffy costumes, Buffy saddle shoes, Buffy wigs, and Buffy carrying cases. Children, parents, and collectors shared in their pursuit to be a part of a sweet fantasy personified by the beloved character. The products showed the image and likeness of all the actors on *Family Affair.* Paula Jones has said that the share of Anissa's take on the merchandising was very slim but also that she didn't really care about it. Anissa Jones, as Buffy, went along with the photo shoots and the publicity appearances, but not happily, and it took a troublesome toll on her. The time it took to be a certain character at a certain place took away from her natural development and, as I have stated before, when the show was finished, Anissa was finished with show business. She just wanted to be normal and be with her friends.

An Israeli book of *Family Affair.*

One book of a four-part comic miniseries for *Family Affair.*

Classic paper dolls from the *Family Affair* series—some still available on eBay, but for an increased price as the value has vaulted.

A doll made from Anissa's likeness, complete with a mini Mrs. Beasley.

# 33

## Puzzling Together the Pieces

My mother was an avid crossword puzzle solver, and her love of games was passed on to me. I enjoyed playing Scrabble, Concentration, bridge, and other games with my friends and family. When game shows emerged on TV, I was right there to participate in them. From *The Match Game* to *Street Smarts*, my competitive spirit jumped in, and I was out to win.

The shows not only tested my intellectual mettle, they were fun, and I also got to meet people and celebrities I would not normally have met. *Hollywood Squares* is a good example. From the handsome John Davidson to the elegant Zsa Zsa Gabor, I always had a great time appearing on the show. Well, Jim Backus could get a little lecherous, but by then I was learning to handle myself in Hollywood.

Peter Marshall was the Emmy Award–winning host of *The Hollywood Squares*, and his great bonhomie and spirit is alive and well today. In 2007, I had the honor of "roasting" him at the Game Show Congress V in LA, produced by Steve Beverly, and Peter was "game" through it all.

I see him on occasion in LA or Palm Springs, and he always has a warm greeting with that special smile. In his friendly but revealing book, *Backstage with the Original Hollywood Squares*, Peter explains "The Lox Box":

> No jokes were ever written for the bottom center box. We called it the lox box, or the Carol Lynley box, because that was where we usually put the pretty girl off some new television series or someone we feared might be boring. This spot was one that didn't get much action so most of the time the star just sat there for half an hour like a lox, and that's how that particular square got its name.

In the photo you will see that I am sitting in the bottom center box. That was my first appearance. After that I sat in a different box. The producers had been surprised when this lox added her own garnishment—not capers and onions but

The *Hollywood Squares* show with me in the Lox Box.

humor and energy. I was recalled many times to appear on the show but didn't sit in the lox box again. The creators even started writing jokes for me.

Peter's favorite one-liner from the show was uttered by George Gobel. To quote:

Peter: What is the definition of the word "gobbledygook?"
*George: That's the stuff you'll find in the corner of a turkey's eye.*

In the photo you will see I am seated close to Burt Reynolds—talk about personable and handsome. We got along very well, and then he asked me to join him for a weekend in Big Bear, in the mountains of California. Silly me. I didn't go. Sometimes I wonder about my decisions.

The show *The Dating Game* supplied some other excitement. I was to select which bachelor would be my escort to an exciting locale. On the first show in which I appeared, I selected whom I thought would be an interesting date from three contenders seated behind a screen. Our destination was to fabulous Rio de Janeiro via a long plane ride to Brazil. We were to have a chaperone. The nanny turned out to be a twenty-one-year-old girl named Sam. I actually was older and more experienced than our caretaker. But that was okay since once we got to Brazil my cute guy was more interested in other cute guys. I still had a good time and loved going to Corcovado but was dismayed at the sight of the dismal hovels stealthily erected as quickly as possible during the still of the night on the beautiful hills.

The second appearance on the show led to a trip to Madrid and San Sebastian, Spain, plus Lisbon, Portugal. My date seemed more interested in sightseeing, and we weren't really all that attracted to each other, but it was a wonderful travel experience. Well, maybe not for my brother Lance. He happened to be in Europe at the time I was in Spain, traveling around in a yellow Volkswagen nicknamed Lemon Drop that he had rented with his bud, Tim. Tim had to go back to the States, the car had to be turned in, but Lance and I agreed to meet in Lisbon. In his travels, Lance had heard that Cascais and Estoril were beautiful places to visit and close to Lisbon. We could take the train to see these culture-filled seaside villages. So we met at the Lisbon train station from our different travels at 3:00 in the morning. I was exhausted, plus I had lots of luggage in tow. But my brother insisted we did not need a hotel and could put the luggage in a rented locker. So we spent the rest of the evening on a cold hard wooden bench in the train station, quite a contrast to having spent my time in luxurious accommodations in the Basque region of San Sebastian.

The seaside towns we visited were lovely, and then we returned to Lisbon, stumbled onto a centuries-old building that housed a highly rated basement restaurant, and indulged in slices of a succulent roasted whole pig. The next morning we visited the exquisite carriage museum and then the Monument to the Discoveries, where at the time I was able to climb and stand with the great Portuguese explorer stone statues. The next day it was time for Lance to get me to the airport.

I gathered my belongings from my hotel room and then . . . I couldn't find my airplane ticket. It was a first-class ticket—nothing but the best for these game show winners. After an extensive search, pulling things willy-nilly from my bags and right before I decided I had to call the network, the ticket fluttered into my hands from atop the hangers in my carry-on bag—to Lance, it was like manna from heaven. He now would be able to fulfill his role as big brother and get me to my plane on time. He helped me get all my luggage together, and then we rushed to the airport. When we got there we found the flight was delayed and so decided to get breakfast and a farewell coffee. Refreshed, we slowly started to the gate and then heard a blaring announcement: "Kathy Garver to Gate 5, your plane is leaving, Kathy Garver." We each looked at each other in horrified amazement and then sped down the aisle of remaining gates. My gate was closed. It was before the days of intense security, but Lance was willing to do almost anything to see me off; he adamantly insisted to the flight agent that I had to get on that plane. After a few quick calls, I was allowed to go through the gate, where a waiting car speedily delivered me over the tarmac to the foot-tapping flight attendant standing at the top of the stairway to the giant bird. I could almost hear the sigh of relief from my brother. He was glad to be rid of his little sister, but as the plane took off I looked out the window and could see a faint outline of him bravely waving and mouthing, "Safe travels."

# 34

# Charitable Threads

In the seventies, my main project was to graduate from UCLA. Along with that goal I wanted to be involved with charity work. I became youth chairman of the March of Dimes and traveled the country extensively with the warm and intelligent Louise Roy Sellars, the MOD youth coordinator and stepmother of the famed theater director Peter Sellars. As the charity's spokesperson, I delivered TV and radio interviews and met with the press to garner attention for the needs of babies with birth defects and the organization that served them. The experiences of putting myself forward to help those in need helped to ground me and also gave me the wonderful emotional feedback of having done something special for my community. The responsible position helped me survive the egotistical energy that stardom sometimes develops in young actors. I gave speeches to thousands of people in various venues, including Rotary Clubs and youth conventions. I explained the strides that had been made in helping to prevent birth defects, which had become the focus of the March of Dimes in the 1970s. I tenderly held babies with serious anomalies and met their courageous families. I felt the pain they were going through yet saw the hope and strength they exhibited when dealing with their collective challenges.

Sometimes one does not know the effect one has or will have through time. My appearances stayed with many of those whom I had met. In a speech I delivered to a March of Dimes/Rotary Club rally in the 1970s in Knoxville, Tennessee, Jay Allen, my publicist at the time, suggested I include some writing by Rod McKuen, also one of his clients. I quoted the poem *An Outstretched Hand* from Rod's book *Lonesome Cities*:

> Each of us was made by God
> And some of us grew tall
> Others stood out in the wind
> Their branches bent and fell.

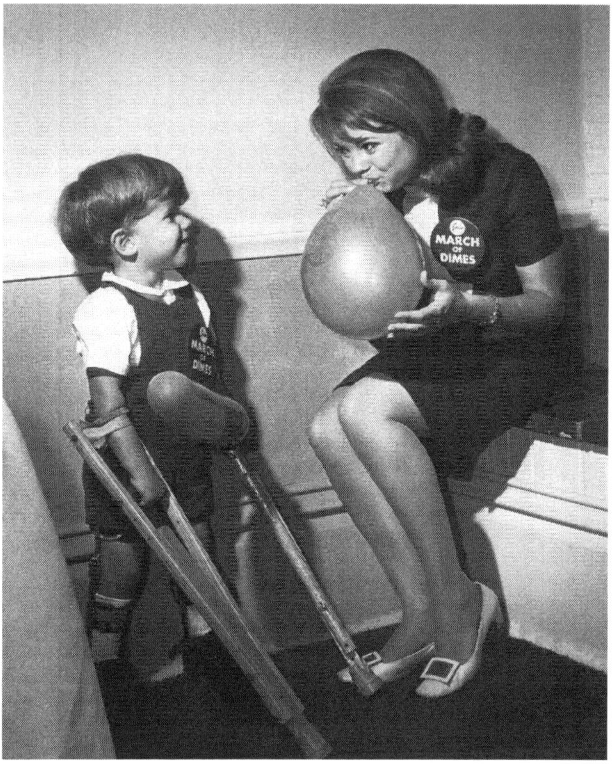


With the March of Dimes Poster Child of the Year. Photofest

Those of us who walk in light
Must help the ones in darkness up.
For that's what life is all about
And love is all there is to life.
Each of us was made by God
Beautiful in His mind's eye.
Those of us that turned out sound
Should look across our shoulders once
And help the weak ones to their feet.

It only takes an outstretched hand

I felt the poem was apropos of my feelings for the March of Dimes and would further my attempt to inspire others to put forth their charitable hands.

Evidently, a young man in the audience was quite moved by the speech because he later told me that he had quoted the same poem in a graduation speech

Holding up a March of Dimes sweatshirt at a youth rally in Tennessee.

he delivered. He also presented me with a picture he had taken the day of the MOD rally that depicted me smiling and holding up a March of Dimes sweatshirt. He had kept that photo safely tucked away for forty years. When Gerald Maloy cast me to play "Amanda" in the wonderful Tennessee Williams drama *The Glass Menagerie,* he presented me a blown-up version of his prized snapshot as a gift. What a treasure. Our mutual admiration of Rod McKuen and his sentiments tightened invisible threads between us, as did our love of theater. The youth, now a grown man, became my esteemed director/producer in 2008 where, as associate professor and head of the Theater Department at Walters State College in Tennessee, he formulated the classic play to be presented to the students and community. It was a thrill to be acting in the award-winning *The Glass Menagerie* as Amanda, guided by the superbly talented Mr. Maloy. There were lots of lines to learn, but what a fantastic experience to walk the boards saying the beautiful words of Tennessee Williams . . . in Tennessee! I could feel the emanations from the actual place where Williams wrote his wonderful words. And as I worked on the play, I felt and created Amanda's despair for a time gone by and the southern ways to which she clung as she and her time as a sweet magnolia wilted.

In 2012, Gerald Maloy again appeared theatrically in my life. I was booked to star in a new stage production in Owensboro, Kentucky, *Absolutely Dead*, written by Michael Walker, which had won the Best Play Award in the International Mystery Writers Festival. It has been my experience that events happen in cycles and for prescient reasons. The week after I was booked for the mystery play, Gerald called and asked whether I could star in his new musical stage adaptation of the Disney classic movie *Summer Magic* in Morristown, Tennessee—three hours from Kentucky, and opening a week after *Absolutely Dead*. I knew it would be difficult to learn the lines, blocking, and songs so quickly after I had just completed another assignment, but I really wanted to do the musical. So Jerry sent me the script and blocking ahead of time, and I was able to rehearse a week in town so that I could be ready to tread the boards as the strong mother figure Margaret Carey. I happily told Gerald I'd love to complete his cast.

The 1963 *Summer Magic* film starred Hayley Mills, Burl Ives, Eddie Hodges, and Dorothy McGuire as Margaret Carey. The movie was based on the novel *Mother Carey's Chickens*. Disney had adapted the book as a musical with the Sherman brothers writing the score and the songs. My talented friend Jerry thought it would make a wonderful stage musical, so, he set about adapting the music and the movie script for a theatrical presentation. After dealing for months with Disney and polishing his adaptation, the *Summer Magic* stage musical was finished, cast, and

As Amanda in the stage play *The Glass Menagerie*.

on the boards. What an accomplishment. And those threads! Eddie Hodges had appeared in one of the *Family Affair* episodes and now, living in the South, came to the *Summer Magic* opening along with the talented songwriter Richard Sherman and the delightful Mary Costa, the original voice of Disney's *Sleeping Beauty*.

Threads around another spool tightened when the talented Jerry created a new theatrical presentation about Tom Sawyer. More about *River Song* later.

# 35

# Musical Sheeting

I loved singing the title song in *Summer Magic*, but warbling is usually not my forte. In the 1970s, I started and ended my pop recording career. I was on hiatus from *Family Affair* when I appeared on an episode of *American Bandstand* with Dick Clark and met Chuck Ashman, manager of singers/songwriters Tommy Boyce and Bobby Hart. Tommy and Bobby had composed the musical theme for *The Monkees* TV series as well as the hit song "Last Train to Clarksville," among other successes. Chuck, a lawyer, was promoting their career. He also became Zsa Zsa Gabor's manager and my manager as well. It was an eclectic client group. Chuck booked Tommy, Bobby, and Zsa Zsa into Vegas into one of its major hotel venues and it was quite a show.

It was also the time of startling space exploration and the Lunar Excursion Module (LEM) had just been created to rendezvous directly with the moon. Chuck, ever the one with stellar creative ideas, thought it would be an excellent idea for Tommy and Bobby to write a song about another lunar explorer, Lem, the orphan reindeer, and for me to sing it.

Chuck had created Aquarian Records, to which Tommy and Bobby were signed, and so my recording production was completed under that banner. After Jimmy Haskell arranged the song, we recorded at the Hollywood Sound Factory with Dave Hassinger as the engineer; he also owned the studio. The opus was a delightful Christmas ditty with a choir of children assembled to do backups.

The day we were to record, I jauntily entered the studio on Selma Avenue, which hosted such stars as Linda Ronstadt and Ringo Starr. In the studio, I confidently started singing the lovely lyrics, which I had memorized, in a soft, mysterious tone when I suddenly heard a loud voice yell, "Stop!"

Startled, I stuttered and asked, "Wha . . . what?"

"You're off-key," Chuck shouted into the microphone behind the muting glass where the engineers and producers watched and listened.

"Off-key?" I replied, flabbergasted.

I had always thought I had a great voice. I played the piano, sang in the Shrine Auditorium as a child and in front of thousands, but I was off-key singing this simple song? Maybe I was a quarter-note flat, but as Dick Van Dyke has said about his singing, "It makes for a unique sound." I buy into that. But Chuck wasn't buying into it, and neither was Ed Justin, another song writer/promoter, or Dave, the excellent engineer. According to the sensitive sound equipment, I guess I was a little tiny bit off. No big deal, right?

Chuck had another bright idea.

"Why don't you just recite the lyrics in rhythm?" he asked, encouragingly.

"Say them?" I replied indignantly.

"Yes," he emphatically replied.

"Okay," I gave in.

And thus was born one of the first rap songs!

Here are a few of the infamous lyrics for "Lem (Lunar Excursion Module), the Orphan Reindeer":

> In the very midst of nowhere, Santa signaled, "Whoa!"
> He'd spied a tiny reindeer struggling in the snow
> As Santa raced to save him,
> He shouted and he waved
> And the tiny little reindeer cried with joy
> Knowing he was saved.

The reindeer was rescued, and you'll have to listen to the recording to know what happens next and what space has to do with it. The audience of *American Bandstand* found out as Chuck set up another appearance for me and I performed "Lem" on Dick Clark's program. Dick loved the performance, and I gave him one of the plush toys Chuck had had created to go along with the song so that he wouldn't forget the rapper and the reindeer.

"Lem, the Orphan Reindeer" was reissued in 2003 as a CD and is online at luxuriamusic.com. The recording has the dubious honor of being included in *Dr. Demento's Radio Christmas Show* for 1987 and in his *Novelty Christmas* CD. It certainly was a novelty.

I wouldn't sing again until I took on the starring role of Eliza Doolittle in the musical stage presentation of *My Fair Lady* in Virginia in 1986. By then, I had done my musical math and fixed the flat quarter-tone.

With Lem, the Orphan Reindeer, and Dick Clark on his *American Bandstand* TV show.

As Eliza Doolittle in *My Fair Lady*.

# 36

# Camo

In 1970, Sarah Selby, an actress who had played three different characters on *Family Affair* during our five seasons, invited me to go on a USO tour to the Far East with her. The USO was quite familiar to me as I had been performing at the Hollywood Canteen on Selma Avenue in Hollywood, dancing and singing for the soldiers since I was a young girl. This excursion was to be a hospital tour; we were to go to Korea, Japan, Guam, Okinawa, and the Philippines and meet with the wounded warriors. I briefly thought about it and then gave Sarah an emphatic "Yes," and she began to arrange our trip. The time we were to leave was during the hiatus of the series and toward the end of the Vietnam War. Many of the young men we would visit would have been medevacked to the medical centers. I tried to gird my heart to meet these brave young men, just taken from the jungles, wounded and in pain. On the first visit, I experienced my initial heartbreak at seeing these valiant soldiers who had given an arm or a leg to assure that freedom would prevail. I so respected and admired their dedication and bravery.

It was the month before Christmas when Sarah and I left on our journey. Most of the young men I met expressed their desire to return to their families so that they could enjoy the holiday season together; it seemed to be foremost in all their minds. They wanted to leave the horrors of war and be embraced by the comfort, warmth, and care of those who loved them. Where they would be safe.

In Okinawa, I approached one young man in a small hospital room. I entered quietly and then smiled at him, trying to cheer him up; he smiled back and then released a small, shy laugh. I can still see him in my mind's eye. He seemed to establish a spiritual connection with me, thanking me with his eyes and then extending courtesies, overriding his obvious physical discomfort with the painful loss of his leg. We talked softly about Christmas and about his family back home. I will never forget the incident or the impression he made on me.

The day I was writing about the experience for this book, a remarkable occurrence happened. For a week I had been trying to put the previous encounter into heartfelt words—the reality of the communion of souls, the unforgettable mark this episode made on my life. The last day of my writing week and finalizing this happenstance, I checked my e-mail and saw an address from someone I did not recognize, but curious, opened it anyway. I have reprinted it here for you with permission:

> *Hello Ms. Garver,*
>
> *I have often thought about your visit to the hospital in Okinawa in 1970 and how much it meant to the troops and especially to me. I just wanted to say thank you for caring at a time when it seemed like no one did. I was shot in Vietnam on November 13, 1970, and I was in a hospital room with a triple amputee. We were both 18 at the time and were both in a lot of pain but when you came into our room we forgot everything and we felt like, wow. We've watched you on TV and now you're here sitting next to our bed talking to us like a regular person and you were so beautiful. I will never forget your visit and I hope your life has been a happy one. You made a lot of us guys happy. Thank you again for taking the time out of your life to make a lot of memories.*
>
> *Truly yours,*
> *Bill Yarbrough,*
> *Marion, Ohio*

How amazing, I thought, that this person, who was present in my mind and on paper, would find me over forty years after we met and e-mail me at the very same time I was writing about our meaningful encounter. This mystical occurrence strengthened my belief in synergy, the ether, and most of all the power of significant shared memories of God and the soul.

Another memory I hold about my USO tour was not as serious but demonstrates the graciousness the military extends to its out-of-town guests. Had it not been for radar and the conscientiousness of the army, I might not have been here to tell my tale.

One part of Sarah's and my trip took us to Clark Air Force Base in the Philippines. I had finished the rounds of a hospital there, and one of the young soldier escorts and I got along very well. He described the surrounding landscape to me and, noting my affinity for the outdoors, mentioned that there was a beautiful waterfall near the base. He volunteered to take me there on a hike. Sounded good to me. He brought me camo and a green hard hat and we took off across the base and into the jungle. The terrain was gorgeous, and we were having a good time enjoying the scenery and our small snack. We hiked and hiked. And then we hiked some more. I thought that the cascades were a lot closer than my erstwhile guide had indicated. Hungry and very thirsty, I asked him how much farther it was to the falls. He finally turned to me and shamefacedly confessed, "I'm sorry. We're lost."

"We're . . . what?"

On a USO hospital tour in Okinawa.

"Sorry."

I was thinking, "I'm exhausted, I've trekked miles all the way through the mosquito-infested jungle, not even seeing the falls, and he just mumbles a little 'Sorry?' "

Hosting a visiting star from the States and then losing her was not good news for anybody. As we were panicking and wondering what to do—no cell phones and no walkie-talkies—we decided to keep trekking through the brush. I could barely take another step: large blisters had commandeered my tender feet. Then we heard the faint thrum of a helicopter above us. We looked up and then realized that the base had literally sent out the troops! Thank goodness! And this before TV's *Survivor.*

My guide was more than embarrassed. It was very expensive to dispatch those military whirlybirds. It also put a quick end to the glimmer of a soldier/star relationship. I just hope my escort was not demoted for losing his way and almost his charge in the dense jungles. I never did tell him I couldn't walk for three days after our futile excursion to the falls of Shangri-La!

# 37

# Sparkling Ties to Publicity

Much publicity occupied our time during the course of *Family Affair*. As the success of the show grew, so did the amount of time required to feed the media with the stories and the happenings of the cast.

Photos from *Family Affair* and its stars graced many magazine covers in the sixties and the seventies. Articles appeared in domestic and international print media. A photo and subsequent cover was honored as one of "Our 50 Greatest Covers of All Time" by *TV Guide*. I had an "Ask Kathy" column in *Photoplay* and *Seventeen* magazines. I was called on to help promote cosmetics, clothing, and of course our show. The experiences were fun, but we were rarely paid extra for our appearances—it supposedly was just to help promote our images and that of the show. The policy was changed the last year, when we each made separate deals to hawk our clothing lines and other merchandise.

Although there were many arranged dates for publicity events, my brother Lance was oftentimes my escort. Indeed, my friend John Stephens used to say that he wasn't my real brother—he was just a cover. But actually, it was my real brother, and Lance was gallant enough to forbear the glare and glamour to watch out for his little sister. I think he actually had a good time at most of the events.

Sebastian and I cohosted the J. L. Hudson Parade in Detroit, broadcast by CBS. I got a disparaging look from Sabby when I promoted my recording, "Lem, the Orphan Reindeer." My manager had told me to talk about the newly released Christmas ditty, and adhering to the dictum to follow directions given by authoritative adults, I did what I was told. But there is a picture depicting Sabby and me commenting jovially on the parade for prepublicity. We got along well despite my shameless self-promotion. I recently watched the Macy's Thanksgiving Day Parade and found that nowadays every announcement about a float bespoke of how wonderful songs, characters, and/or shows were that the floats depicted and of the host's projects as well. Promotion has advanced since the sixties! The fleece I am

*Family Affair* pictured on one of *TV Guide*'s "50 Greatest Covers of All Time."

At a publicity promotion for makeup.

With Clint Ritchie and my brother Lance at a publicity event.

wearing tops a woolen maxicoat that was a gift from my manager. He had bought the beautiful garment for me as well as a long, black, pleather maxicoat from the exclusive Bergdorf Goodman in New York. I thought the coats so extravagant; I later found out it was my money that had paid for them. But I survived.

Sabby and I hosting the J. L. Hudson America's Thanksgiving Parade in Detroit.

When I went to visit my high school sweetheart, Bob Damus, who was going to law school at Harvard in 1968, he invited me to dinner at the luxurious Ritz-Carlton Hotel dining room in Boston. I was wearing a very short pink minidress that was also rather low cut. The maître d' out-Frenched Mr. French in his expression of horror at my revealing but, I thought, very chic wardrobe. Thank goodness I had the gray Bergdorf maxicoat. Donning the stifling wool over my delicate rose dress, I was accepted and allowed to be led to the antique polished table set with crisp white linens to enjoy my elegant dinner.

# 38

# Lacy Love Life

While I was shooting *Family Affair*, I went on some interesting dates with intriguing young men.

In many ways the role of "Cissy" was an amalgam of the writers' vision of my teenage character and me. The personae became very much intertwined. I was somewhat of an innocent in the sixties. I did not try drugs, although, I must say, I did enjoy trying different types of liquor, rejecting martinis and embracing scotch and water. I am now a dedicated wine drinker—love that resveratrol plus living close to Napa, California, acclaimed viticulture center.

My parents and a brother or two carefully vetted my dates and the young men I went out with to make sure they were respectful of my family values and me. I never had trouble with supposed "casting couches." Maybe it was because I was an established actress by the time I was a young woman and did not have to grovel for attention or jobs. I was experienced, polished, and blessed. I went to auditions with the confidence of an intellect and the talent of a trained professional. I don't know what I would have done if a casting director or producer had made any untoward advances. I had values ingrained from my parents, my church, and my peers. It was working. Why change it? Either that, or I just wasn't sexy!

Ah, I do remember one time when there was a cute six-foot, dark-haired handsome extra on the set of *Family Affair*. He flirted with me while explaining he was attending Southern California University. He was working as an extra as an alleged hoot. I thought he would be fun to go out with. We went to dinner and then we stopped at the beach at Malibu. We sauntered down the sand to the surf, and then he laid out a towel for us to rest on. I guess one would call it—attempted date rape. I freaked and ran down the beach, found a pay phone and a taxi, and that was the end of him and the start of a wiser Cissy/Kathy.

*Photoplay* and other precursors to *People* and *US* magazines were on the stands, and my PR person, Jay Allen, set up photo shoots and appearances. Jay was well respected and went on to great fame in the book industry as a publicist with clients such as Robert Ludlum, Maya Angelou, James Clavell, and as mentioned, Rod McKuen, among others. He was quite devoted to his clients, and Rod dedicated the poem *An Outstretched Hand* to him—the ode used in the speeches I gave for the March of Dimes. A literary thread.

I enjoyed the photo sessions set up by Jay with the likes of Dack Rambo (*Guns of Will Sonnet, Dallas*), Michael Christian (*Peyton Place*), Dennis Cole (*Felony Squad, Bracken's World*), Schell Rasten, and Yale Summers (*Return to Peyton Place*), handsome young leading men at the time. None of these handsome fellows, however, evolved into much serious dating. However, I found some of my own romances despite my busy schedule.

There was Clint Ritchie. I met him on Highland Boulevard near the 101 freeway in 1968 when I was returning home to my parents' house from an interview. We were living in the large Hollywood apartment complex the Highlands, built in 1966. I was driving my maroon Oldsmobile Cutlass I had bought the year before. Clint pulled up in his little gray Mercedes. Harking back to days of cruising in San Bernardino, I felt an iota of comfort—my friends and I had always glanced

With handsome bachelors of the day Michael Christian (*Peyton Place*) and Dack Rambo (*Guns of Will Sonnet*). Frank Edwards, Fotos International

With intriguing Dack Rambo at the race car track.

at other cars and curiously peered to see who was cruising the streets and whether we knew them. When Clint smiled at me through his car window and then started driving beside me, innocently and comfortably, as in the early sixties, I smiled back and then pulled over at his request; we chatted and then exchanged phone numbers. We found we had a lot in common. He was an actor and under contract to Twentieth Century Fox along with Lyle Waggoner. Lyle, starring in some sci-fi movies, was spotted by Carol Burnett and became her suave announcer on *The Carol Burnett Show*. Lyle later won fame in the part of Major Steve Trevor in the comic-strip-turned-TV-series *Wonder Woman*. Clint and I started double-dating with Lyle and his wife, Sharon. Once, I went to Carol Burnett's house for Sharon's baby shower. Carol entertained us in the kitchen when she related a story about her own pregnancy. She told us she was sitting on a tall stool when she leaned over to get a glass of water. Carol said and illustrated that she was so front-heavy that, as she reached to grab the glass, she leaned and leaned until her whole body went with

With handsome Schell Rasten, who later married Charo. Photofest

her—a very funny visual image. Two children later, Sharon, Lyle, and I still exchange cards whether they are in their home in Westlake, their hacienda in Mazatlán, or their chalet in Jackson Hole, Wyoming. They all look great!

Clint was a "manly man" who smoked pipes and exuded male charm. He was very handsome to boot. Developing quirks special to our relationship, he used to gently take my cheeks in his hand, purse my lips, and then goad me to say "bubby chub." I'm not sure why, but it became "our thing." We went to lots of parties and had great dinners together. At the time, he was starring in such movies as *The St. Valentine's Day Massacre* and *Bandolero*. Clint was an excellent horseman and especially enjoyed filming *Bandolero*, which also starred James Stewart, Dean Martin, and Raquel Welch. Later, he starred in the TV series *Thunder*, another western, as Bill Prescott. In his long-lasting TV series *One Life to Live*, he played the character of Clint Buchanan.

Ever the outdoors man, Clint bought some land in Grass Valley, close to Auburn, California, and named it Happy Horse Ranch. And he was a happy man. Clint loved to participate in the hundred-miles Tevis Endurance Horse Cup, which starts at Squaw Valley and ends near Auburn. His ranch was once used as a locale for his soap opera, *One Life to Live*.

With erudite Yale Summers on a publicity date in New York City.

Clint had an unfortunate accident in 1993. While riding in his tractor on his property, he hit a tree, pierced his lung, and broke several bones. He recovered, but in 2009 after having a pacemaker implant, a blood clot traveled to his brain, and he died in late January of that year. A charming, funny, and engaging man, I very much enjoyed our times together and miss his unique ways. When we drove to Palm Springs one weekend, we stayed at my close friends Ellen and Stan's house in Redlands, and I discovered my macho man's endearing nature—what a love. But at that time, it was too late; I had met David Eyre.

On a plane back from the Mardi Gras festival in New Orleans in 1970, I was saying good-bye to my gracious hosts and noticed some uniformed men standing nearby. Pilots, opting to deadhead on my plane, I thought. I was attending UCLA during our hiatus from *Family Affair* and as a multitasker had taken all my books and papers with me to the Mardi Gras city to try and find time to cram in some studying. In the jazzy town of New Orleans, I had found no time and was desperate to get some work done. After the plane took off, I realized I had packed all my

Boyfriend Clint Ritchie and I out to dinner. Photofest

necessary books in my suitcase, which now resided in the hull of the plane. I talked to the off-duty pilot sitting next to me, haranguing him with my problem. "Not to worry," he said confidently. He disappeared when we made a stop in Dallas and later triumphantly appeared with my suitcase and the books. I was flabbergasted and impressed that this handsome young man could be so resourceful. Our relationship didn't stop when the plane landed in Los Angeles, and we began a romance. I found out that he was not a pilot but in the military, home on leave. He told me he had been quietly cursing the young strawberry blond who could not seem to say good-bye to her friends. He had been anxiously waiting to discover whether he had secured a seat on our plane. When he finally got settled, he just wanted to get some sleep. Endlessly prattling about my mislaid texts, he figured if he retrieved my books for me, maybe I would be quiet and he could get some rest.

David was my first grown-up love. While we were dating, he went back to Vietnam as part of the Navy SEAL support team. One time when he again was on leave, he booked a motel on Wilshire Boulevard around the corner from where I

Clint and I exploring the beach in California. Photofest

lived in an apartment with my roommates, Mary Halloran and Janet Hamilton. As former Pi Phi sorority sisters, we decided to room together after our graduation from UCLA. They were both teaching elementary school, and I was commuting to the set of *Family Affair in* the early seventies.

After he called to tell me of his arrival, I brought David over some cookies and beer. He opened the door, and I let out a big gasp. I had never seen such a dehydrated, exhausted person. His lips were chapped so severely that he could barely open his mouth; his fair freckled face was dotted with peels of skin, and bright red patches sprouted all about his arms and face. He had just returned from two weeks of grueling training with the SEALs, the Sea, Air, and Land team who are the US Navy's principal special ops force and part of the naval special warfare command. My heart went out to him, and I immediately went to the store to get water and more beer.

When David finished his military commitment, we continued to date. Released from the navy, he rented a place in Venice, California, with his University of Washington buddy, Rick Marshall. Rick was quite jealous that I was making more money than him, as he thought an emergency room doctor in Marina del Rey should be making far more than a mere "actor." I survived his jibes, but it did hurt my feelings. I felt I, too, had earned my way. David primarily ignored Rick's barbed insults.

Now on native soil, David had a gigantic period of adjustment from the military and Vietnam. He was sensitive, and the war had taken a tremendous toll on his psyche and soul. PTSD, posttraumatic stress disorder, had not really been known then, and David, independent warrior that he was, would not have sought help even if offered.

He was floundering. He wanted to be a writer but did not have a trust fund or independent financing to pursue his dream. He was one of the most innovative and creative people I had encountered up to that time. We dated for three years, enjoying picnics, premieres, and dinners, but time was moving on and David had still not found his niche. I suggested he get a "real job," but that was not in his mind-set. It begat a huge conflict in our relationship. Finally, the day he put on a suit to apply for a nine-to-fiver, without my knowledge of his quest, I broke up with him. Aware of the insecurity of being an actress, I wanted someone with whom to share my life, someone who would have more secure employment than I as well as someone with whom I had a strong emotional tie: I wanted a normal person. I was to find that there is no such thing as a "normal person."

David did become a successful screenwriter and novelist known especially for his movie *Cattle Annie and Little Britches*, which starred Amanda Plummer as Annie and Diane Lane as Britches. Headlining were Burt Lancaster and Scott Glenn, with Rod Steiger as Marshal Tilghman. Nice cast. The movie was heralded as "an excellent family western with outstanding dialogue in a great script." David went on to write other screenplays, such as *Wolfen*, and TV specials such as *Roots: The Gift* and *The Rescue of Jessica McClure*, which I thought was one of his best outings. However, at the time when we were dating, I was getting anxious. I wanted to get married and begin my own family affair.

# 39

## One Spool Empties

*Family Affair* ended in 1971, and when the series was finished, I considered my next move.

I guest-starred in an episode of the TV series *Adam 12* (Kent McCord, Martin Milner) where Barbara Hale (*Perry Mason* and mother of William Katt, who was *The Greatest American Hero*) played my mother. Her real husband, Bill Williams, also guest-starred in this episode, "Pick-Up." I was cast as the recalcitrant teen Paula Jessup who gets into all kinds of trouble, not the least of which is buying and selling drugs—very un-Cissy-like. I hoped this might change my image, but one episode of a different TV show, even one as popular as *Adam 12*, did not do the trick.

To take the next step toward adulthood and to change my image of sweet Cissy, my manager decided I needed a new "brand." Taking out an ad in the *Hollywood Reporter* and *Variety*—the two largest entertainment print media of the day—I was presented as the next sex bomb to tease the bright lights. However, the producers weren't particularly buying this transition.

What to do? I had graduated from UCLA with a major in speech and a minor in psychology by continuing to go to the university during the hiatuses from the series. I contemplated being a lawyer and so took the LSAT (Law School Admission Test). I was then accepted to both Loyola and UCLA law schools in California. At that time, I was offered a starring role in a play in Texas, a comedy entitled *The Ninety Day Mistress* by J. J. Coyle, and a proposal to be the assistant to James Caan on a new movie, *T. R. Baskin*.

I had learned that being a lawyer was not about truth and justice, two concepts I had held to be the highest in my value structure. One of the main reasons I originally wanted to be a lawyer was that I believed so mightily in the truth and thought that an attorney could help in peeling back the layers to the crux of a case or situation and present it genuinely and winningly. Then I discovered that my

Kathy, Martin Milner, Barbara Hale, and Kent McCord in the "Pick-Up" episode of *Adam 12*.

The attempt to change the image of sweet Cissy.

ideological and romantic notion of truth was sullied by being a lawyer. Not only was truth not at the basis of being a good lawyer, but to be an excellent attorney, one had to circumvent it and present the most compelling argument. One was triumphant through excellent presentations and formulating scenarios that best helped one's client. One had to be manipulative; one had to be convincing, whether or not who or what was being represented was honest and true. That was not for me. I abhor manipulation—whether it is through falsehoods, tears, or over-the-top dramatics to achieve one's wants and wishes. After dropping the law school idea and learning that I would basically be babysitting Mr. Caan and act as his gofer on the movie, I decided to star in the play. I trundled off to Texas and had a grand time creating laughs and continuing my acting pursuits.

# 40

# Winding Another Spool

On the return from Texas, I decided it was time to buy a house. My parents had dutifully set aside my money in an interest-bearing savings account—even though I was over eighteen when I started the series and they were under no obligation to do so. I remember vividly going to my bank in Baldwin Hills to withdraw the entire amount of my savings. It was a goodly sum, and the teller said, "I think you should talk with the bank president."

"Why?" I indignantly remarked. "I can't withdraw my own money?"

She answered, "It's what I am supposed to say when an amount like this is to be withdrawn—it's protocol."

"Okay," I said, thinking it might be interesting to meet the president of anything.

The bank teller led me to the executive's office. He asked why I wanted to withdraw the entire amount from my Bank of America savings account. I told him I wanted to buy a house. He thought that was a good reason to take out the money but still tried to dissuade me from removing all my funds from his care. After we chatted a while, he offered me a job at the bank. I countered that I was going to remain in my acting career but thanked him for his faith in my monetary ability. He issued me a cashier's check, and I was on my way to home ownership.

After looking at several different properties—in Beverly Hills and up Benedict Canyon—I found one that I thought might have a good resale value—not my first choice of homes, but one I thought to be a good investment. The three-bedroom, two-bath ranch-style house in Sherman Oaks, right off Mulholland Drive, had a great view of the San Fernando Valley. Above me on Mulholland lived my friend Gloria Loring, who was at the time married to Alan Thicke—the transplanted Canadian enjoying popularity with his talk show, *Thicke of the Night.* Their son, Robin Thicke, is currently riding at the top of the pop music charts with such hits as "Blurred Lines." Wilt Chamberlain also lived up the block from me—in a much more expensive and custom-built home with *very* tall ceilings.

I bought the charming rancher with the large family room and separate dining room and started to furnish it. My mother went with me to buy my Danish modern dining room set for the formal dining room, and when she helped negotiate a deal and we agreed on a price, I started to pull out my checkbook.

She said, "No, don't do that."

"Why?" I asked. "I have enough money."

She said, "Yes. But you have to establish credit and this will be a good way to start."

"Oh, credit."

Ah, my monetarily savvy mother—I learned a lot about finance from my mom.

It seems I have trouble with homes on hills with good views. I had been living in my Sherman Oaks house for one year when I left to go to Utah to star in the play *Under the Yum Yum Tree.* My six-week theatrical contract was almost up; the show was closing that Sunday. Saturday night before the play, the phone jangled in my hotel room. Picking it up quickly, I listened to the startled voice of my neighbor breathlessly informing me that the soggy hillside of my house was steadily tumbling down and about to inundate the home below. "What?" I exclaimed. I could do nothing until the next day, when my contract was up and I could get a flight back to California.

Los Angeles had suffered from torrential rains in 1974. Waters gushed down canyons, and the lots on my street, created by some overly ambitious contractor who had leveled the hill, allowed the resulting dirt to cascade clumsily on either side of his mechanical blade. The dirt had not been compacted. When I bought my house in 1973, I thought the hillside looked fine and didn't even think to have a soil test.

When I returned home to the morass, I saw that a large portion of my hill had dangerously slid down and had done severe damage to the house below, breaking my neighbor's rear sliding glass doors and inundating their home. Thank goodness the family was not there at the time of the disaster, as the water had crashed into the interior of their infant's nursery.

The canyon flood area was declared a national disaster, and indeed it was. But even in my twenties and single, I took the proverbial "bull by the horns" and investigated what could be done to restore the property. Since it was "an act of God," I was not responsible for my neighbor's damage, but to repair my own home, I took out the 3 percent loan that was offered by the government, managed by the Small Business Administration. I replaced my retaining wall and fence and redid the patio. I staunchly repaid the loan.

Despite earthquakes and rains, it was a good time to buy in Los Angeles in the seventies. I bought two rental properties. My mother and father had purchased a home on Sierra Bonita Avenue off Sunset Boulevard in Hollywood after they had moved from the Hollywood Highlands. Ever exploring, my creative mother found a house for sale on the next street over from her in the course of one of her walks.

The California bungalow sat on comfortable Curson Avenue, tucked between Franklin and Sunset Boulevards with La Cienega and La Brea Boulevards serving as its west and east perimeters. I later found out that Charles Laughton, the actor/director with whom I had worked on my first movie, *The Night of the Hunter*, had lived a block above this house on Curson with his wife, Elsa Lanchester. Ah, threads.

My mother thought it would be a good idea if my older brother and I joined together to buy the house; Lance had graduated from college with a degree in business and was about to become a relator. He later became a real estate maven, owning the successful company Motel Brokers, USA and buying and selling commercial properties. He could help with the sale and management of this residential venture on Curson. So Lance and I entered into a lifelong real estate partnership with that initial house.

My personable mother had made friends with Poppy, the woman who lived next door to the first house that Lance and I bought on Curson. When Poppy decided to sell her home, my mother was the first one Poppy called, and my brother and I again went in as partners to buy our second well-located home. We found eager renters and were able to retain the houses, then refinance them, and eventually exchange them for other rental properties in California.

The next house I bought was with my husband, and it was reminiscent of the primary residence I bought high on the hill in Sherman Oaks. I love views, but

*Money Magazine* photo of my brother Lance and me in front of one of the two rental houses we bought together in Hollywood. Tony Costa, Time Inc.

the idea of purchasing another home as if I were an eagle sitting in an aerie needed further investigation. I found that steel pylons had been securely drilled into the bedrock for the foundation; our new purchase was not going anywhere, even with the Northern California earthquakes that occasionally rattled nearby. Other adventures occurred with the house, however, that I will relate later on.

David, my husband-to-be, in my house in Sherman Oaks with my cocker spaniel, Daisy. Tony Costa, Time Inc.

# 41

# The Fiber of the Business

One spool of my life that continues to be unwound is that which spins around my different entertainment pieces. One piece is an interview. You go on an audition hoping you will get the job, and then you're told: "You're too tall," "You're too short," "You're too fat," "You're too thin," "You're too dark," "You're too blond." Then—"You're not a big enough celebrity," "You're too big a celebrity for this part," and on and on. There are some parts I *almost* got that I really would have liked to book. There was the part of April, news reporter, on the animated *Teenage Mutant Ninja Turtles* series. The audition came when I was enjoying a great amount of success in my voice-over career, especially in animation. Jeff Danis represented me in the voice-over department at ICM (International Creative Management), a very prestigious talent agency in Beverly Hills. I thought I did a great job on the *Turtles* interview. I had used one of the news anchors in LA as my prototype for the April role. The next day, I anxiously waited to see whether I had secured the part, which would mean steady work and lots of residuals—always good for an actor. Actors are very high on the angst list: one of the largest stress factors is the loss of a job—actors are always losing jobs, even when they get one—they do it, and then they are out of a job again. Will they get their next job in time to pay their mortgage? As my jealous neighbor dismissively said with disdain about the twenty-six-year-old single lady who bought the house next door to her in Sherman Oaks: "Ah, you know actresses—chicken one day, feathers the next!"

Yes, it's hard being an actress.

So I vigilantly waited by the phone to see whether I had survived the critical review of my audition and succeeded to be a regular cast member and star in the new cartoon series. Then I waited some more. Finally Jeff called and declared, "You had the role and then the producers decided at the last minute to cast a younger voice. You *almost* got the job," he added consolingly.

"Almost?" I thought. Hmm. Why didn't the producers just ask me to give a younger reading? I can do that easily. Why didn't Jeff say, "You didn't get it," or "They went in a different direction?" I could have swallowed that information a lot better than having my hungry hopes high and then being told that I was going to have to go back on unemployment: I was within an inch of getting this steady work and then the producers at the end of the process decided they wanted someone else with a younger voice.

Ugh! That experience did teach me a new lesson, however. From then on, whenever I went on an interview, I would ask the casting director/director/producer, "Would you like it any other way?" This is a very important question and helps involve them and also helps me get the job. I can massage my performance around to expectations.

I have a strong faith in God's way. I am always solaced even if I have a disappointment about losing something. Maybe I will get a better part that would have shot at the same time. Maybe someone else needed or deserved the job more than me. Perhaps there is something to be learned that I can utilize in another part of my life. Perhaps it is God's plan. I survive to rationalize.

I just read a statement by Robert De Niro, or maybe it was Al Pacino—I always get them mixed up—I actually think it was Pacino. Anyway, he said that he was never disappointed if he went on an audition and didn't get the job: "You've got to think of things as an opportunity. An audition's an opportunity to have an audience." I buy into that.

After *Family Affair* was over, a friend of mine, Danny Ben Av, whom I had met through Tommy Boyce and Bobby Hart, approached me to do a special appearance. Danny asked whether I wanted to go to Israel. With a Sagittarius sun sign (willing and eager to take on new adventures), restless, and free at the time, I eagerly said, "Yes!" Danny had written a musical stage version of *Family Affair* and wanted me to star in it. The play was titled *Ha mishpacha she ka zot*, that a kind friend of mine, Yael, instructed me on the spelling—loosely translated it means "Family Again." This Catholic girl agreed to go to the dangerous, strife-ridden country of Israel during the 1973 war and to learn Hebrew phonetically to sing and act in a touring company of *Family Affair*, Israeli-style. My series was the number one show in Israel at the time. Danny was sure it would be a sellout. Shows were planned for Tel Aviv and Haifa. Danny was right: the stage show was an incredible success, and the theaters were filled to standing room only. The cast was comprised of Israeli actors who looked like the American *Family Affair* TV counterparts. There was a rotund Mr. French, replete with great black beard, a handsome Uncle Bill, and two adorable children who played the parts of Buffy and Jody. I, of course, essayed my own role as Cissy—too much fun! There were also personal appearances—one was in a garden setting, and there were so many people it took on the excited but controllable complexion of an energized mob.

Then there was the magazine layout that Haim Saban set up. I was to go on an arranged publicity date with a young Israeli star, and the resulting photos would be used in a popular Israeli photo magazine, similar to the US *Photoplay* magazine of the seventies. Haim had contracted to pay me a large sum. I went on the date, the photographer snapped the pictures, but did I ever get paid? I waited for Haim at the end of the shoot to appear with my money; I waited for him at my hotel lobby; I waited for him at the airport. I finally had to board the plane for London. This incident was one of the most disappointing experiences I had yet to encounter. I was so naïve. I actually believed that people followed through with what they had promised. Silly me. I glanced out of the airplane window after another no-show at the airport by Haim and cried most of the way to London.

# 42

# Throwing Threads to the Wind

When I arrived at Heathrow Airport, I had second thoughts about returning to the United States. I had felt so blessed that I had experienced such a successful series and career. My friend Alison Arngrim, who enjoyed fame as Nellie Olsen from *Little House on the Prairie,* said in an interview that only one-half of 1 percent of people are so graced to have starred in a successful TV series. But I was not feeling graced now. I felt depressed about the nature of people and the nature of the business. I decided to stay in London and decide what my next step was going to be. Again, being the adventurer that I am, I decided to enroll in the Royal Academy of Dramatic Art. I had already graduated from UCLA with a bachelor's degree in speech and gone back to get my master's in theater arts, but I felt that I had not yet "suffered for my art." I needed to suffer more. Life had been too good to me. I hadn't survived enough hardships.

I looked for a place to rent in London and found one in Chelsea, a tony part of the city, which I leased. It was a dark, Dostoyevsky-type basement space, even though the house above was light and beautiful. There was only a modest radiator to warm my modest rooms. Ever chilly, one night I was standing close to the small heater. I smelled something acrid and looked to the back of my long flannel nightgown. There was a fiery eruption scorching my flowery hem! Who knew that English sleepwear did not have fire retardant? I rushed to the bath chamber and splashed icy water onto the hearth. No more heater that night, my rapidly beating heart kept me warm. I gratefully survived that conflagration.

I wired home and asked my parents to forward me some money and clothes. As usual, they complied with support and alacrity. But I was by myself and feeling lonely. I usually like to be by myself—paint, write, and be devoted to a role. But a foreign country and the incident with Saban had left me rattled, and it was taking an emotional toll. I decided I had to find something to do quickly. Since I was a member of the Screen Actors Guild in the United States and a known former star of a

TV series, I was able to sign up for classes at the Royal Academy of Dramatic Art and learn from the fabulous teachers there. English theater and styles of acting are different from many of America's acting techniques. While I had studied sense memory with Uta Hagen and the Stanislavski Method in New York, in London we did scene study and analysis and diction and clarity. It was a much more intellectual approach to frame a performance. After this experience, I combined the two methods to formulate what I believed to be the strongest style for my acting.

I love the snow, and while I was in London, I decided to go to France for some alpine skiing. It was toward the end of the season, and the snow was icy with some grassy patches at the bottom of the hills. I slipped on one of the patches at the end of a very exhilarating but long day of schussing. In a daze, I lay in an icy scrub where I had fallen. I thought I had gone to heaven because as I looked up, there was this snow princess, complete with a panting, furry St. Bernard by her side who had a covered thermos roped around his neck. Having been knocked out, I thought I was floating on a lofty cloud. When my senses began to recover, I realized there really was a St. Bernard and a woman dressed in snowy white fur. That must have been some grog she had given me. I survived my lonely, bruised, snowy excursion with frosty fanciful memories.

Rome was on my list of beautiful cities to visit while I was staying in England. I never got to Florence or Venice; travel to those beautiful cities is still number one on my bucket list. I bought a cheap plane ticket while I was in London and flew to the Eternal City. On one tour, I descended into the catacombs of Rome and felt age-old emanations from countless martyrs. The Vatican was spectacular, and I was privileged to see Michelangelo's masterpieces and even glimpsed Pope Paul VI when he appeared on Sunday to bless the crowds that had gathered in St. Peter's Square. Forward young Italian men pinched me, and it is true that there really are many handsome lotharios in Rome. Then, I felt, it was time to return to the United States.

# 43

# Red Velvet Curtains

Because I had been performing in theater and scene work at RADA in England, I felt imminently drawn to do stage when I returned to the United States. I immediately began starring in stage plays. The magnet was strong as dinner theaters were booming, and I was an apt star because of my fame in *Family Affair.* The plays were not of Shakespearean quality but did help me to develop my comedic acting talents. I starred in such fluff as *The Ninety Day Mistress*, *Under the Yum Yum Tree*, *Star-Spangled Girl*, and *Sunday in New York*, among many others. It was fun, and it paid well, but I was lonely. Sometimes my mother would accompany me; we had a great time. Many times, I took my loving cocker spaniel, Daisy, with me. At Pheasant Run Playhouse in Aurora, Illinois, where I starred as Robin in *Under the Yum Yum Tree*, my mother and I swam in the indoor heated pool at the hotel complex and had the best bacon and tomato sandwiches I had ever tasted. The reviews of the play were good, too: "Kathy Garver as the naïve Robin Austin is perfect in 'Under the Yum Yum Tree.'"

I am proud to say I never received a bad review while doing these comedies. For instance, from the *Bossier Press* in a review of *The Ninety Day Mistress*, it was printed that "Kathy Garver gives an excellent characterization to the part of Leona Hastings. As petite as she is, she commands the stage throughout the production." When I portrayed Sophie in Neil Simon's *The Star-Spangled Girl* at the Cherry County Playhouse in Traverse City, Michigan, the reviewer from the *Record Eagle* enthused, "Kathy Garver bubbles. The scene in which the analyst tests her threshold is great!" And when I starred at the Robinson Theater in Illinois, the reviewer wrote: "No one can outshine Miss Garver. Her rendition of 'Sophie' in 'The Star-Spangled Girl' is marvelous."

When I reprised my role as Robin at the Hayloft Theater in Lubbock, the *Lubbock Avalanche Journal* published, "Kathy Garver has a wealth of talent. She is a comedienne Par Excellence."

From the *Shreveport Journal*, when I played Leona at the Beverly Theater (the show then went on to New Orleans): "Kathy Garver wowed them Friday night in 'The Ninety Day Mistress'. There was a packed house." Allen Case, who was to become my dear friend, costarred with me in *The Ninety Day Mistress* in St. Petersburg, Florida, at the Country Dinner Theater. The review stated: "Miss Garver is just the right combination—she balances rationality with emotion—the 'new' woman with the Eternal Female and looks both cute and sexy as she does it. She and the role are made for each other." And Allen and I seemed to be made for each other as well.

Case had gained famed as the deputy, Clay McCord, in the western TV series *The Deputy*, which ran for two seasons from 1959 to 1961 on NBC. The series costarred Henry Fonda, in one of Hank's few TV appearances. But as Marshal Simon Fry, Fonda was not in all the episodes. The show revolved around Allen, but Henry's name and reputation, as well as his excellent ability as an actor, had been used to draw viewers to the show. Even so, *The Deputy* lasted only two seasons and Allen was out, like the rest of us actors, looking for a new gig.

Some more of those wily threads wove through our relationship. Allen began his career as a singer. He had a beautiful voice and first appeared on *The Arthur Godfrey Show* in New York. He segued into Broadway and off-Broadway musicals,

Allen Case and I having fun onstage in the romantic comedy *The Ninety Day Mistress.*

adding acting to his resume. In 1959, because of Allen's fame in *The Deputy*, Columbia released a long-play recording titled *Allen Case—The Deputy—Sings*. It is a compilation of beautiful romantic songs, such as "Bewitched, Bothered and Bewildered." The threads? Besides being "bewitched, bothered and bewildered" by Allen, Frank De Vol, who had composed the theme music for *Family Affair* as well as musical scores for fifty films and multiple TV series, conducted the orchestra for Allen's recording.

More threads unrolled as the makeup person, Jack Barron, and the hair stylist from *The Deputy* were engaged for Fedderson's *Family Affair*. Henry Fonda went on to star in a Fedderson-produced TV series, *The Smith Family*, that ran for one season, 1971–1972, and costarred Janet Blair with Ron Howard. The show occupied the stage across from stage 10, where we were shooting *Family Affair* at CBS Studio Center. The set had just been vacated by the Fedderson series *To Rome with Love*, which had starred John Forsythe, running from 1969 to 1971.

Allen also starred in the one-season series *The Legend of Jesse James* from 1965 to 1966, which also starred Christopher Jones as Jesse James. Allen taught me a lot about acting and life. We had great times together driving in his big white Lincoln he dubbed "The Marshmallow." But Allen was no marshmallow; he was a kind, giving, and talented man. He died too early at the age of fifty-one of a heart attack while vacationing in Truckee, California.

I continued working and continued being lonely. Traveling to New Mexico, I appeared at the Albuquerque Little Theatre in a diverting comedy, *The Voice of the Turtle*, in 1979, which costarred Allan Hunt. Allan is most well known for his role as Riley in *Voyage to the Bottom of the Sea*. Allan was a delight, and he and his wife and I became good friends. I returned to Albuquerque to star in another play—this time as the character of Joanne in *Vanities*—but more about that later. For my first appearance in New Mexico, I starred as Sally in the excellent play by John William Van Druten. It was written: "Kathy Garver is perfect as the somewhat naive actress Sally Middleton in '*Voice of the Turtle.*' She comes across as a 5'2" bombshell as the young sweet star-struck girl from Joplin." I am actually only five foot one, but I will accept any height exaggeration!

I believe I was able to garner such excellent stage reviews because of my extensive training and my stint at UCLA. I had a bachelor's degree in speech, but I returned to obtain my master's degree in theater arts. Since speech was in the College of Letters and Science and theater was in the College of Fine Arts, it was necessary for me to take some undergraduate courses to fulfill the requirements before attaining my master's. One of the most fearful times in my life was when I stood on an extremely tall ladder trying to adjust a carbon-arc klieg for my class in lighting design. "Just don't look down," I said to myself. "Don't look down!" I didn't, but I felt queasy the entire time I was on the high, shaky ladder. The palms of my hands showed fingernail print tattoos whenever I had to adjust a light.

But I survived the class and went on to appear in plays at UCLA and to learn

Allan Hunt and I enjoying acting in the play *Voice of the Turtle.*

from excellent instructors about scene study and improvisation. I remember creating bodacious skits about the politics of the time.

Also, during this time, I was attending parties and going to publicity events. I met the lovely actress Brenda Scott, who worked steadily in the 1960s and 1970s, primarily in TV westerns but interspersed with film and drama shows. She married the actor Andrew Prine three times—at some point they were determined to get it right. Brenda became one of my best Hollywood friends and taught me about antiques and design. She later opened her own store on Ventura Boulevard in Studio City, highlighting her own unique vintage treasures. At one point during one of her separations from Andrew, we went to a small dinner party in Malibu. O. J. Simpson was there and was quite taken with Brenda. Luckily, she said no when he asked her out on a date. She eventually successfully married the erudite and talented Dean Hargrove, who wrote and produced many successful mystery TV shows, including *Columbo*, *The Father Dowling Mysteries*, *Jake and the Fat Man*, and *Matlock*, among others.

I would stay with them in their beautiful home on my excursions to LA in the eighties and nineties. It was always a treat to partake of Brenda's fabulous cooking and their sensational holiday parties!

One party I attended was hosted by the mother of my friend Darby Hinton (*Daniel Boone*), Marilynn Hinton, at her lovely home in Bel Air. There, I met a person who was to become very important in my life, James Doolittle, not General James Doolittle, but the impresario Jimmy Doolittle. Although quite a bit older, he escorted me to many of the shows he produced at the Huntington Hartford Theater, where he served as general manager and producer. The theater was eventually renamed the James A. Doolittle Theater in his honor. We also went to many pretheater dinners, especially to the Brown Derby, which was across the street from the Huntington on Vine Street in Hollywood, and to such 1970s green and pink decorated posh restaurants as L'Orangerie. Through Jimmy, I hobnobbed with many interesting people, such as Zsa Zsa Gabor, Charlton Heston, Harry Belafonte, and Anthony Hopkins. I thought our best times were dining out alone at heralded Hollywood eateries where he shared his extensive knowledge of theater production and we discussed world affairs and gossiped about the stars of the day. We also dined at friends' homes, such as at Esther Williams and Fernando Lamas's in Beverly Hills and at Sheila and Joe Barbera's of Hanna-Barbera animation fame. Joe sat on the board of the Huntington Hartford in Los Angeles, and Jimmy and Joe had a great relationship. Jimmy was a wonderful companion. I learned a tremendous amount about theater from him, and we coproduced two touring companies of the play *Vanities* that were quite successful.

Jimmy Doolittle and I painting the town with Joe and Sheila Barbera, Zsa Zsa Gabor, and Ron Postal.

The first tour was to Albuquerque, to the engaging Albuquerque Little Theatre, where I had previously appeared. Our cast included my friend Linda Kaye Henning of *Petticoat Junction* fame. We received excellent reviews, and I enjoyed putting all the pieces of the theatrical puzzle together with Jimmy. Ever penurious, I opted not to get insurance when we trucked the set to New Mexico from California, where Jimmy and I had produced *Vanities* at the Spreckels Theatre in San Diego, and—wouldn't you know it—the truck driver had an accident. It was a very expensive lesson to learn. I miss Jimmy's kind and gentle ways, but his name lives on in a scholarship given to USC—yes, we had many discussions about which was the better school—USC or UCLA!

Jimmy filled many lonely nights, but I was still looking for the person with whom I could make a life and have a family. So many people found it so easy to find someone, fall in love, and get married. Where was my love-mate? I just wanted someone normal, someone who could provide me a base. I was not looking for someone to take care of me or to pander to me. Just someone I liked, with whom I could live passionately, and with whom I had common interests.

The successful James Doolittle/Kathy Garver production of *Vanities* with Eda Zahl and Linda Kaye Henning in Albuquerque, New Mexico.

# 44

## Creating My Own Threads

As a child and teenager, I had been a happy-go-lucky, friendly girl. After the first year of *Family Affair*, people began stopping me in the street, recognizing me, asking for autographs. I was rather taken aback by this attention; I had been quite protected as a child actor. When they asked for a signature, I thought, "Why do they want an autograph from me?" I gave it to them but still wondered. Then my publicist said, "It makes people happy." So giving an autograph became like giving a present, and I made friends with the concept.

However, more people started stealing little pieces of me, and a business manager stole $10,000. Celebrity wasn't all it was cracked up to be. Would it crack me up?

With the disillusionment of my Israel experience, the death of my beloved costar Anissa, and the theft of some of my wealth, I became focused on my work, studies, and maintaining business clarity. Yet there was something serious bubbling under all my activity. When I was in London, I felt very lonely. I was away from friends and family and not accomplishing anything significant, still in a learning mode. When I returned to the United States and was traveling and starring in plays, it was difficult being on the road. Something was definitely missing. When I would return to my home in Sherman Oaks, I again was all alone. I would sleep late, get up and go to the gym, wait for the phone to ring, and watch TV—no computer then.

I dated, but nothing clicked. One night a man whom I was dating, a psychologist, came to pick me up from my home for an event and, while I went to get my purse, amused himself by looking at all the art I had hung on my wall. He said to me when I returned, "Do you realize everything on your walls depicts a single figure?" I had not realized it, but all the pictures, whether I had painted them or had bought them, showed a lone image.

One of the worst moments came when I burst out crying uncontrollably. I was by myself watching the dramatic movie *The Old Man and the Sea* on TV in the darkness of my living room. I commiserated with the old man and felt like him, utterly alone in a vast, waving sea: I was that old fisherman, adrift in an unending ocean, waiting, waiting.

I decided that I had to do something about this loneliness thing. The weekend of my decision, I went to Palm Springs. I had just purchased a condo with my brother and decided I should do some more decorating for it.

My friend Arlene Golonka (*Andy Griffith Show*) was in Palm Springs as well, and she asked me to give her a call when I arrived. She was attending a music industry event, and she thought we could get together. I had been playing in a lot of celebrity tournaments that the enterprising publicist David Mirisch had organized. I was in great tennis shape, feeling healthy and athletic. But I arrived in Palm Springs in a sorry mood of desolation. Arlene called and said to come over to the Riviera Hotel and join her and her boyfriend, Tom, to play some tennis. They would supply the fourth for a game of doubles. I packed my car, as I had to leave that night to return to my home in Sherman Oaks and figured I would leave from the Riviera. In my little two-seat maroon Mercedes 280SL, I drove to the hotel with the thought pressing in my head: the next man I meet I am going to marry.

I rendezvoused with Arlene and Tom courtside and waited for our fourth. "Where is he?" I anxiously thought. Finally, onto the court galumphed a six-foot-three very handsome man in his early thirties. I thought, "This is the next man I am meeting; we are going to get married."

The intense tennis game began. Even though I am only five-foot-one, I pack a wallop of a serve and could scamper quickly all over the court. My partner, whose name I discovered was David, and I were beating our opponents, and after I aced a serve, he said, "Ah, finally, a woman who can play tennis, I'm going to get married!" "What?" I thought—and then chuckled delightedly. We finished the game as victors.

After the tennis match, David asked whether I would join him for the music industry banquet that evening. I had already packed my car and was ready to be on the road, but I thought about twenty seconds and then quickly said, "Sure!" Arlene let me get ready and change in her hotel room, and I met David for the evening's event.

After the entertaining buffet, we had coffee at a nearby Sambo's café and started chatting. He told me he had to catch a plane back to his home near San Francisco the next day from LA. I quickly told him that I had to go back to LA and would be happy to take him to the airport. He said that he had his golf clubs with him and other luggage. I said, "No problem!" He rented me a room at the hotel and then kissed me good night and said he would see me the next day.

That morning I hurriedly smashed all my suitcases together, shoved things into every corner of my car, and created enough space for the incoming clubs and luggage. We began our journey but stopped to have lunch and play miniature golf on our way to LA. I saw him off at the airport, and that was the beginning of our long-distance romance.

While we were dating, I continued my career. I was primarily acting in plays at the time, and David flew to meet me at a couple of the venues.

I starred in *Vanities* with Priscilla Barnes (*Three's Company*) and Canadian actress Brenda Bazinet in Calgary, Canada, at Stage West Theatre. David flew to the province of Alberta, and we had a great time skiing in Banff on my days off. He enjoyed the play and got along famously with Priscilla, who he thought was adorable, funny, and personable. She is a delight to this day.

David then joined me in Albuquerque, New Mexico, where I was starring in *The Voice of the Turtle*. On my two days off, David and I took the short jaunt to Bishop Ranch. Renting horses one day, I was having a lovely time galloping through the dusty terrain. The horses started climbing up the rocky hills. Then it was time to descend a craggy, narrow trail. My horse started down the mountain.

"Come on, David," I shouted to my hunk.

"I'm coming," he said. "Giddyup," he told his horse. The stubborn stallion stood stalk still. "Giddyup," he repeated, gently kicking El Diablo in the sides. The horse still would not move. "Okay," said my David. "Stop." And the horse did exactly as he was ordered.

More good times followed, and David and I were growing fonder and fonder of one another. He was hesitant about tying the proverbial knot. He had been married once at twenty-one and has a son, Scott, from that short-lived, one-year marriage that ended so quickly in divorce. That's one of the reasons he was single at thirty-three—marriage shy. But when we both turned thirty-five (I am three months older than David), I said, "Look, I am not getting any younger. What's happening with this relationship?" I was still lonely in Sherman Oaks while he was living in the quaint town of Saratoga, in Northern California—six hours away by car.

David was working with a music company called GRT, General Recorded Tape, and his company requested that he go on a European trip to expand its home recording market. Now, David is one of the best salespeople you will ever meet. He's personable, engaging, and excellent at sealing the deal. He could sell insurance, cars, or dogs. But he didn't and still doesn't know much about technology. To aid him on his European trip to expand the international market, his company assigned a high-tech person to accompany him. And David assigned me to accompany them both. So David, Lloyd, and I set out on a fabulous European adventure. David told his secretary to book all the best hotels; he felt comfortable in doing this as his company owed him unpaid bonuses and the company could make it up to him by booking a luxurious trip to the Continent.

One of our first stops was Munich, Germany. I had a grand time shopping while Lloyd and David went to their business meetings. Then we were off to the Alps. We drove many hours and finally arrived in the dark of night. We were hosted by one of the company's business clients at their home at the foot of a large mountain near Munich. When I awakened from my deep sleep, there was a light snowfall as I looked out the paned-glass window. I was amazed and delighted to discover an immense fairy-tale stone castle on top of the mountain beckoning with its romance. After a hearty Swiss breakfast, David, Lloyd, and I rented a horse-driven sleigh to ascend the sloped long drive up to Neuschwanstein, one of the magical homes of mad King Ludwig, Louis II. The castle was magnificent, and I can still envision the beautiful glazed windows, polished wooden floors, and plush furnishings. It was quite a romantic tour.

The romance continued as we flew to Austria. My favorite episode of *Family Affair* is "Waltz from Vienna." In the story, I meet an Austrian prince who proposes marriage, but silly person that Cissy is (sometimes I wonder about that girl), she turns him down and returns home to be with Uncle Bill and the kids. I admit that I am an unabashed romantic. And my grandmother was born in Austria, but I had not visited this picturesque city. David and I checked into the most beautiful and expensive hotel in Vienna. We were escorted like royalty to the mezzanine floor and shown our exquisite suite. The rooms glowed with the sheen of extensive silk bed coverings and shimmering drapes. The bathroom was lined in gray and white marble with heated towel racks standing at the by. "Wow," I said in a not-quite-appropriate exclamation for my over-the-top luxurious surrounds.

The next day David and Lloyd went on their business rounds, and I took a bus tour. The guide pointed to the hotel where we were staying and said, "And *this* is the most beautiful hotel in the city, the Imperial Palace. The mezzanine floor suite is reserved only for royalty."

Gulp. "They must have made a mistake," I thought. I returned to the hotel,

In one of my favorite episodes of *Family Affair*—"Waltz from Vienna"—no *Dancing with the Stars* back then.

and they *had* made a mistake, but they said we could stay in the suite one more night before actual royalty arrived.

That evening was the grand opening of the Viennese opera. Through the concierge, David was able to garner some special tickets. We dressed quickly and bustled down the street to the opera house. We were late to our box seats. We had become separated and David, salesman that he is, had talked the usher into seating him, even though he was late, confident that I could find my way, independent lady that I am. But after rushing to the restroom, I was really too late and stood watching the beautiful opening musical strains on the TV monitor in the lobby. When I finally met up with David, he said he was bored, didn't like it, and couldn't understand a thing they were saying. "It's being sung in Italian—*Fra Diavolo*. It *is* opera," I stolidly told him. David has a hard time even with operas sung in English. *Fra* was a comedic opera, but David didn't see the humor in it and wanted to leave at intermission. Since I was hungry and also somewhat tired, I acceded, and we decided to go to the famous Sacher House restaurant down the street from the opera. We entered and were somewhat surprised that it was so empty. The six waiters I saw stood as arctic penguins in the cold, elegant room. It had been touted as one of the best restaurants in Vienna, albeit expensive, but I thought, "Where is everyone?" David and I stayed and were graciously seated at a romantic table for two. We must have been stunned because neither of us said a word for a while. When we did, the sounds echoed in the cavernous room. I thought it best not to disturb the stillness. We ordered quickly and then ate even more rapidly. We paid the bill and surreptitiously left. We later found out that the dinner rush was *after* the opera. I have never felt so uncomfortable in a restaurant in my life. I heard that pin drop.

Our next stop was in Holland. I so wanted to see Anne Frank's birthplace. I had performed a scene from the *The Diary of Anne Frank* in college for which I had won an award, and I felt very close to Anne. David and I were able to take a tour, and I felt the invisible waves of survival history flowing from that small house in Amsterdam. We also went to the Van Gogh Museum and I bought a reproduction of his famed *Sunflowers*, which I shipped home and still gaze upon in all its artistic, emotional, and crazy energy.

# 45

# Chasing Windmill Fibers

More than anything on our trip I wanted to see a windmill. As a child I had been given a pair of wooden shoes, and I cherished them. And when my sister got married and we had the reception at our home in Baldwin Hills, I wore my communion dress as flower girl and it had a Dutch-styled hat to accessorize it. I was irrationally disappointed that I had grown out of my clogs and I no longer had them; I still felt like a little Dutch girl. I have always had a fascination with Holland. In Amsterdam, we booked a tour to see the beloved windmills; I was so excited to go on the tour that David and I arrived at the meeting place an hour early. We decided to order and sip a cappuccino in the corner café while we waited for the van. Finished with the warming beverage, we strolled down to the corner and were told that the car had already left! I was so upset; I started crying. It was the primary site I wanted to visit in our entire European excursion. David comforted me and said, "Let's go to the Zuider Zee." Most frigid experience of my life. I know why the little boy's finger was stuck in the dike: it was so cold there it froze in place.

Our next stop was warmer; we went to Aruba. David and I decided to go snorkeling, so we hired a boat and set out to enjoy the beautiful seas. However, it was so windy and the waters so turbulent that I was buffeted about and the fish flipped topsy-turvy around me. However, the good thing about Aruba is that I was finally able to see a windmill. Yes, on an island near Venezuela, there were my windmills. I learned Aruba is a Dutch island.

I was to experience more windmills in my life—visiting the beautiful windmill in San Francisco from WWII and then when I went to Holland again: Holland, Michigan. I had begun a successful career in audio-book recording, and one city where I did much of my recording was Grand Haven, Michigan, for Brilliance Audio. I was fascinated by the Michigan waterways and the abundant greenery of the small, quaint village of Grand Haven. One time, when I was in town for a week of recording, I rented a bike and rode down to the levee every day after work. At night, I was able to experience the "singing fountain"—maybe a bit hokey by some standards, but I marveled at how the music was set to the cascading waters and pulsating lights. I felt entranced and relaxed, mollified by the experience.

Close to Grand Haven is a village settled by the Dutch, appropriately named Holland. I was blessed to be there one time during tulip season. A kind friend of mine from Brilliance volunteered to drive me to the special town. Not only were there beautiful flowers blooming in the most colorful arrays but also an actual working windmill, which had been brought over piece by piece from the "real" Holland. And it was open for tours. I was in Dutch heaven. The weather was nice, so it wasn't a Dutch oven. I know. Low groan.

Upon our return from Europe, David and I felt very good about our romantic trip and decided we should return, especially to France. I planned an exchange of my home in Sherman Oaks with a doctor's beautifully furnished apartment in Paris as well as his chalet in the French Alps, contacting a vacation trade club. We were off on another dreamy trip.

Paris was gorgeous but very expensive at the time. And we were so jet-lagged that we slept through one entire day before we were able to venture forth with any energy or enthusiasm for the Louvre and other museums that I dragged David to. His delight was in the restaurants. My culinary-minded sister, who makes a gourmet pilgrimage to Paris each year, made a list of the best restaurants for us to enjoy. We went to Maxim's, Pré Catelan, and La Tour d'Argent. La Tour d'Argent is heralded as one of the best duck restaurants in Paris or anywhere for that matter. I had always loved ducks as pets, so it was hard to eat one, especially when the waiter gave us a written history of where our duck was born and raised and who its friends were. I would have preferred not to know the duck's name and siblings. But it certainly was an elegant restaurant. Expensive, too.

Driving the car, which was included in our exchange package, I hoped that the Parisians in California were treating my little Mercedes as well as we tried to treat their small French car. We traveled on the scenic roads from Paris to Cannes. Now, everyone knows that Paris shuts down in August, as that's when all the workers take vacation and go to Cannes or other gorgeous and popular beach resorts. Everyone except us. So there we were, with no reservations, virtually hat in hand, going to every hotel, motel, and *auberge* in the beautiful seaside town trying to find a room for the night. No room at the inn. Finally, in our last effort, we paid an exorbitant price for half of a suite, the living room half with a pull-out bed. But we were in Cannes, and we went to the beach, and it was fabulous.

Then I insisted we go to Provence, and David was glad we did. What a charming cobblestone village we found. I still have some of the unique pottery that I bought in St. Paul de Vence. One glazed piece was a small statue of a duck. I felt better that I could fairly honor one that I ate. As we dined at La Colombe d'Or in this medieval town, the waiter told us tales of Chagall and Picasso and showed

David and me where priceless art by these renowned painters was hung randomly on treasured walls. The crowning glory of the trip was when we traveled to Monaco. David had made a reservation at one of the most beautiful hotels there, the Vistaero. We had an exquisite view of the bay. I remember the well-dressed waiter bringing a tray covered with crisp white linen to our beautifully decorated room. On the silver salver sat crunchy croissants atop Limoges plates. Little jars of jam and a bright red rose in a small crystal vase centered our brunch. We had a great start to an eagerly anticipated tour of the romantically rumored city of Monte Carlo. We were blessed to be in the sparkling city on the final night of the international fireworks competition. We watched in inspired awe as rockets flared and exciting bursts of light brightly dappled the skies. And then David proposed. I don't know whether it was the beauty of Monaco or the excitement of the luminous fireworks, but he mumbled out the famous words, and, as art sometimes imitates life, our marriage has been like that fiery evening ever since. Sort of like Cary Grant and Grace Kelly in *To Catch a Thief.*

# 46

# Tying the Knot

David and I returned to the United States and started to plan a wedding. My fiancé was still living in Northern California and I was in Southern California, so some compromises had to be made. He suggested that we move northward and that I rent my house. I was ready for a change, so I agreed. I don't know why.

I was starring in a play in Texas and had a little time between performances and so was able to shop. I bought my wedding dress in Lubbock.

My friends Dr. Tim Dalton and his wife, Sherry, offered the use of the beautiful Bel Air Country Club to hold our wedding reception. I thought that was a grand idea.

I am Catholic and David is—well, he's Christian, but he really never went to church. To please me, he agreed to go to catechism classes so that we could be married at Good Shepherd Church in Beverly Hills. But it was going to take a year to get married in the church, and after three years of dating, I was anxious for commitment. We decided to be married by a cleric and a judge at the club: it seemed we had both marriage corners covered. We started planning for the invitations, food, and music—all the wonderful things I had anticipated since a child.

We would greet the guests in the foyer of the Bel Air Club on an early Sunday morning and then invite them to walk down the flower-strewn carpet and be seated in front of the rose-bedecked arbor. After the wedding ceremony, the invitees would return to the foyer and be handed chilled mimosas in crystal glasses at eleven o'clock in the morning to give them a heady start to the festivities. Actually, we needed the large room we were using for our ceremony to be vacated so that it could be transformed into the reception room, complete with our buffet table and dance floor. We wanted the guests to enjoy themselves during the wait. No wonder I heard so many lovely comments about our wedding being one of the most beautiful our guests had attended: most of them were already lightheaded from the champagne before they even entered the brunch area.

Taking a picture with the wedding dress I bought in Lubbock, Texas, where I was starring in the play *Under the Yum Yum Tree.*

Both David and I are very romantic. We agreed on having a beautiful ice sculpture of a swan to grace the laden buffet table plus a harpist to provide lilting music for our guests. My accomplished singing friend Jan Armstrong would regale us with melodious tunes, and then doves would be released at the end of the ceremony. That all actually went pretty smoothly, but the doves were itching and cooing to take flight. And David put his morning jacket on too soon, and rings of sweat defined the underarms of his nervousness. My sister, the maid of honor, had forgotten to get her long green taffeta skirt hemmed. And the best man had not paid the limo driver in advance and had to round up cash at the last minute while David and I anxiously sat on the bumper of the limo's open trunk, bravely smiling as though we had planned this ignominious end to the fabulous wedding we planned to start our new life.

The morning after our blissful honeymoon night at the Bel Air Hotel, I returned to my home in Sherman Oaks to meet my friend Sally and let her in so that she could remove the refrigerator I was giving her. She was late, and I meandered around my home saying goodbye like Emily in the play *Our Town.* David brunched on savory eggs benedict in the elegant dining room of the Bel Air Hotel.

David and I celebrate at our wedding in 1981 at the Bel Air Country Club.

That was typical of what would eventually describe our marriage—me doing the work while he sat enjoying what he wanted to do—but as long as I was able to do whatever I wanted and go whenever and wherever I wanted and maintain our love and trust, that type of relationship was good for me and him. And we have been married for thirty-four years as of 2015.

We started our honeymoon, which was to drive up Highway 1, the beautiful coastal route from LA to San Francisco. David proffered that we had already had our real honeymoon in France, and I was too happy to argue and instead enjoyed the wonderful sea sprays wafting through the window as we made the trip up the gorgeous Northern California coast to our new home.

# 47

# Invisible Threads through the Air

Living in Northern California while continuing a career with the hub of the entertainment world in LA proved challenging, but I secured an agent in San Francisco and ramped up my voice-over career. Flying down to Hollywood for an interview to create the role of Firestar in the new animated series *Spiderman and His Amazing Friends*, I initially met with the producers. I flew down again to interview with cast potentials, such as Dan Gilvezan, auditioning for the part of Spiderman, and the wonderful man of a thousand voices, Frank Welker, as Ice Man. We were all hired. We proved to be an engaging and successful triumvirate; the series has had a long life. Cartoon shows are wonderful vehicles for actors as they are attractive to successive generations of fans. And those fans that originally saw the series as children are loyal. I have been to many comic book conventions signing autographs, and the Spiderman fans can eagerly tell me all about each episode.

I commuted to LA either by plane or by car to record my role as Firestar—sometimes I think I can relate the life of every scrub bush on the very fast but boring Highway 5 that is the corridor from San Francisco to LA. Firestar is a great character "with legs," and animation fans heralded her arrival on the Marvel scene as one of their preeminent heroines. She helped set the stage for other animated superwomen heroines to enact their derring-do, and indeed, I voiced the character of Storm/Ororo Munroe in a Marvel short to further the tales of women superheroes. Dan as Spiderman and Frank Welker as Ice Man proved their mettle as strong voice characters. We would read the Spiderman scripts and then record as if our relationship had been ongoing for many years—which, by now, it has!

I later was cast in other *Spiderman* variations. I played Ms. America and the Gila Monster in *The Amazing Spiderman*. As I have said, you can play any character with your voice—it doesn't matter how you look. A Gila monster, a lanky giraffe—bring 'em on!

I created voices for several roles in *Superfriends* and *Happy Days* for Hanna

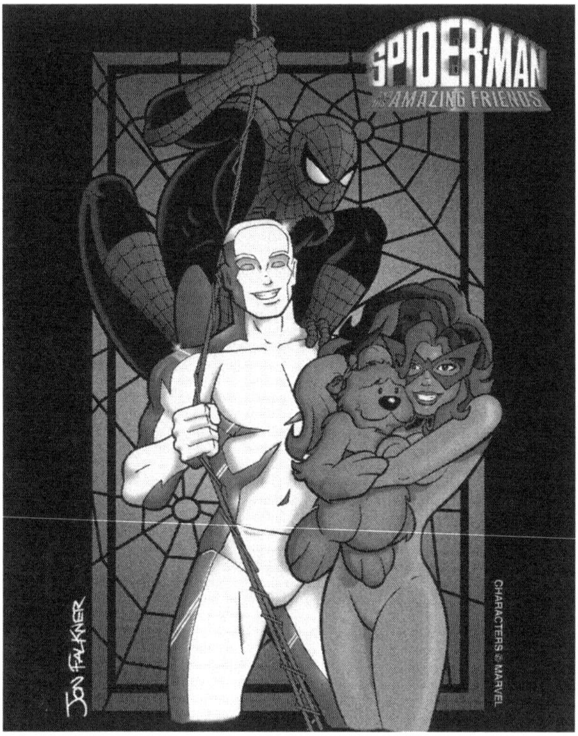


My alter ego in *Spiderman and His Amazing Friends* as the voice of Firestar with Dan Gilvezan and Frank Welker. © Marvel

Barbera and played the title voice role in *Dixie's Diner* for Tyco during this time. As Dennis the Menace's mother in *Mayday for Mothers*, a special for TV, I worked with DePatie-Freleng. I reconvened with Chuck Norris and essayed the role of Pepper, an automotive whiz, in his animated series *Chuck Norris Karate Kommandos*. I had originally met Chuck on a PR photo shoot, and he taught me with one chop how to break a balsa wood board in half. It sure does make one feel powerful! Recently my friend Ray Normandin sent me the four Kommando comic books from Marvel and a plastic figure of Chuck from the series, and I relived that fun show—now, of course, on DVD—with a great deal of delight.

I enjoyed recording voices for animation augmented with commercial and industrial projects, and my career was going fine, but I found myself still missing something . . .

With some of the animated characters for which I've created voices.

# 48

# Weaving a New Swatch

I have always loved children and was taught by my mother how to care for and treat them. I coddled and cuddled my dolls, dressed them with glee, and tended to their toy needs. I had a Tiny Tears doll that shed winsome watery trickles after she was fed from her fake milk bottles, and in the second grade in a contest, my entry of a baby doll won the "most realistic" title. I had a Little Ricky doll, which I cherished. The first time I met Keith Thibodeaux, who played Little Ricky on the *I Love Lucy* show, I shared that my mother and I would go to the Broadway department store in Hollywood and buy my life-sized infant Little Ricky doll real baby clothes. Keith loved the anecdotes. Even though I thought I was getting a little old for dolls at age eleven, my parents presented me with a gorgeous gray perambulator one Christmas that I proudly took onto our neighborhood sidewalk to parade my pretend babies.

As a young woman I would often go into the infant department and look longingly at the soft, comfy clothes and fantasize about the baby I would have. But now I realized I was approaching forty, and no baby! "Where is my baby?" I cried to myself. David and I had been busy with our careers, and we had just purchased a home in a lovely suburb of San Francisco and were in the throes of decorating it. I told him: "Tick, tick, tick, where is my baby?" His answer: "If it happens, it happens." As I have related, he was in no hurry; he had already fathered a son when he was just a lad of twenty-one. That son, Scott, looks very much like David, with beautiful turquoise eyes and sandy hair. But whereas David is six-foot-three, his son grew to be six-foot-seven. It was a little disconcerting when I was with Scott in his twenties and he would peer down to my five feet and say, "I love you, Mom!"

But I wanted my own baby and was not at all happy about David's *laissez-faire* attitude. However, when I was forty-four I purchased that little pregnancy test, and it turned pink. "Hooray!" I thought. "But here I am, forty-four years old.

Hmm. Isn't pregnancy a little risky for a first-time mother at my age?" I read, I consulted, and then I took a chorionic villus sampling test (CVS), which my friend Julie Corman had explained to me; one can take this test earlier than amniocentesis. It shows the sex of the baby and whether there are any defects. The test would certainly quell a lot of anxiety. I don't know what I would have done if there had been something wrong with my baby. But the diagnosis proved that all was fine up to this stage, and I was able to look at my growing fetus on the sonogram. Even at that embryonic age, the picture showed the baby with a very strong resemblance to David. However, when our little bundle was born, the politic nurse said, "I have never seen a baby that looks more like both its parents." Maybe that was standard fare, but it made me feel good, especially since I felt I had done most of the work and I was probably going to opt for just one child.

I was very excited to be pregnant, and I took my unborn baby on walks, patted my stomach, cooed to him, and played him classical music. On a routine exam it was found that I had gestational diabetes, a form of diabetes one gets only when pregnant and which usually appears with older mothers. After the baby is born, insulin readings return to normal.

I surmise that my mother may have had this condition when she was pregnant with my brother Lance, who weighed over ten pounds at birth. Usually women with gestational diabetes gain a great deal of weight and have larger than normal babies. My friend Susan, who is five-foot-five and about 108 pounds, gained 70 pounds when pregnant because of gestational diabetes. My diabetes could be controlled with diet, and I remember having a turkey sandwich with milk every day for lunch—I had to still my cravings for ice cream and pickles, but I only gained twenty-two pounds.

David had to fly to New York two weeks before the baby was due, and we still hadn't decided on a name. I was reluctant and nervous to have him go on the trip since it was so close to my due date, but it was important for business and he was expected to return in just four days. Turned out he was back the next day. The night he left, my water broke, and that baby wanted to see the light of day. I left a frantic message for David at his hotel to return immediately. My good friend and neighbor Lynn, who lived one house away, was not exactly happy when I awakened her at 3:00 a.m. that morning, but she dutifully walked up the hill of our private road with a smile on her face to tend to me and take me to the hospital. Thankfully, Vera, my then sister-in-law, who lives in Hermosa Beach, Southern California, had gone to some of the Lamaze birthing classes with me. David had attended just one, not really enjoying this part of the process at all. My flight attendant sister-in-law immediately boarded a plane to San Francisco, an hour's flight. David picked up Vera at the airport, stopped for breakfast for some inexplicable reason, missed the turnoff, and then finally arrived at the hospital. But there was no reason to rush. That baby decided to stay inside, where it was warm and cozy, for a while. The doctor had a different idea and started to prepare for a C-section. My dear friend Carolyn says that's the way all babies should be delivered.

So there we were in the delivery room, and I thought the anesthesiologist was very nice as he stood next to me, gently wiping my brow. At one point, both the baby's and my heartbeat dropped precipitously; the doctor thought it was time to get that baby no matter what and acted quickly. He did what he had to do and then cut the cord. David proclaimed, "He looks like an alien," and handed the newborn, squalling baby to Vera. We welcomed our six-pound perfect baby boy into the world, Reid Garver Travis.

I had a bit of postpartum depression, but my friend Margory brought some brown beer to me in the hospital, claiming that it was good for all types of things. Indeed it was, and I felt better in two days.

As David and I sat in the hospital room enjoying our beautiful baby boy, I said to him, "Everyone is so helpful here, all the doctors, the staff."

"Yes," David agreed. Chatting further, I said, "I especially liked the anesthesiologist who was so nice to stay beside me. He was so kind. And he kept gently stroking my forehead."

"What do you mean the anesthesiologist?" my husband hurtfully exclaimed. "That was me!"

And indeed it was my kind husband comforting me and helping to welcome new life into our world.

My parents had passed away, my father in 1980 of emphysema and bladder cancer. My mother died ten years later, in 1990. She had been suffering from Alzheimer's disease and living at St. John's Hospital in Los Angeles. She died two months before Reid was born. I don't know what I would have done if my cherished child had not come to me at that time. My mother and I were very close, and her loss affected me greatly, but God in his infinite wisdom had given me a new treasured soul to love. I used to have dreams where I would fly. It was easy for me. I would put out my arms, ascend and glide smoothly over towns and countries. Sometimes I would just hover. Since the night I became pregnant, I never again had that recurring dream. Books, friends, and I agree that I was looking for a soul. I found Reid's, and he is adored.

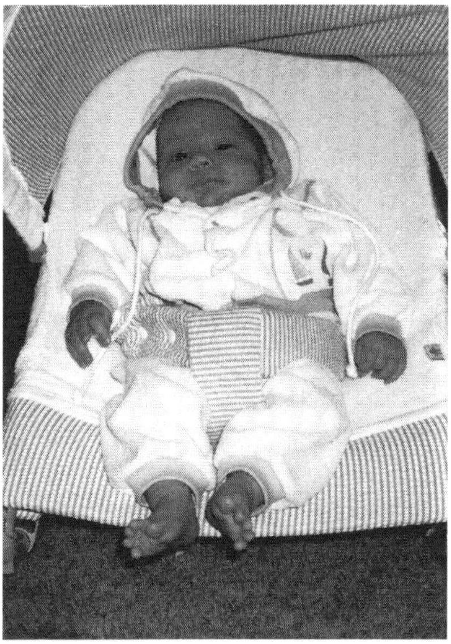

My beautiful son, Reid Garver Travis, was born in 1991.

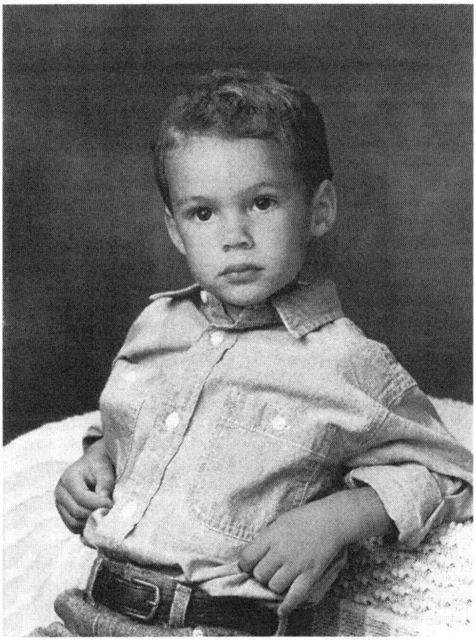

Reid's foray into show business.

# 49

# Playing with Kiddy Threads

I was very happy with my life: I had a faithful husband, a beautiful child, and a lovely home. Acting had been my priority, but now family was. And I was tired of waiting for jobs to come to me, waiting for my agent to call, keeping on with selling myself. That's when work started pouring in. I became more confident than ever to pursue my profession. The entertainment market is wide, and I embraced many of its aspects: voice-over, writing lyrics, and narrating and producing audio books, such as Beatrix Potter CDs and Mother Goose rhymes and songs for the Smarty Pants Company. I joined my friend Lanette's company, Edutainment for Kids. We licensed, created, and manufactured toys for the worldwide market. Some of the products we released were Richard Scarry's Busy Town Talker and the plush Huckle and Lowly Worm—that cuddly plush toy worm lit up as well as talked. Our plush talking Huckle Cat could say 250 concatenated phrases.

After Reid was born, I gravitated toward this children's market. Everything I created or worked on was family oriented, and that kept me amazingly busy. I was producing and making things happen instead of waiting for the phone to ring. And that was very important and crucial to a former child actress. I ventured forth and produced things for myself. Too many times child actors are catered to, depriving them of important life skills. There are parents and agents who set up auditions, sign the contracts. All the young actor has to do is show up with lines learned, face scrubbed, and teeth brushed.

Then somehow the youngster is supposed to make the transition from child actor to adult smoothly and seamlessly. This rarely happens. Most minors have not been taught how to handle transition nor how to cope in a very competitive, cutthroat, and underhanded business. Most "tweeners" are not prepared for the difficulties. I had thankfully jumped the hurdle, and now I further had taken on the professional mantle of an adult who could find my own work. Settling into family life, I took Reid to Cub Scouts and then Boy Scouts, piano lessons, and karate class. I kept up my career in the children's interactive market as David continued his work with a new company, Attorney Recovery Services. We would go to Palm Springs and relax at the condo.

My brother Lance, ever the caretaker and overseer of my career, thought his little sister should have a star on the Walk of Fame in Palm Springs. He had added a second location to his Motel Brokers real estate business and traveled to the desert often. Starting a campaign, he enlisted his partner, Lee Permut (father of the successful movie producer David Permut—*Dragnet*, *Face/Off*), and others he knew to approach the Palm Springs Chamber of Commerce and Bob Anderson and fill out the paperwork. I was approved. My star was to be placed between Michael Dante, my former boyfriend, and Connie Stevens, Michael's former girlfriend as well. We were all right down the walk from Frank Sinatra. A good placement I thought, although ironic with the girlfriends. With the help of my publicist at the time, the winsome Donna Linn, who is an organizer extraordinaire, we planned a star ceremony and party for the laying of the star. Many came down to celebrate, including my friends Ellen Weisser and Paul Petersen. We had a great time, but to quote Ruta Lee, as she so aptly put it when she received her star, "I never thought I'd be laid on Palm Canyon!"

Happily showing my star at the ceremony on the Palm Springs Walk of Fame.

My husband, David, son, Reid, and I when I received my star on the Palm Springs Walk of Fame.

## Dropping Stitches

At about this time, there was a yearning for nostalgia and good programming so Gavin Polone and Pariah Entertainment thought it would be a good idea to do a remake of *Family Affair*—after all, it had been over thirty-five years, enough time so that audiences were ready for a new family. So in 2002 the new *Family Affair* debuted with Gary Cole as Uncle Bill, Sasha Pieterse as Buffy, Jimmy "Jax" Pinchak as Jody, and Caitlin Wachs as Sissy, not Cissy—Sissy as in Sigourney, not Cissy as in Catherine—go figure. Besides the short skirts Caitlin wore on the new *Family Affair*, Sissy also played the guitar and visited questionable nightclubs for a fifteen-year-old. My politically moderate son, Reid, who watched the remade show when he was eleven, proclaimed loudly to the TV set, "Cissy would never do that!"

Cissy would not have done that in the 1960s and 1970s. Even in the 2000s, the behavior was questionable for the family-oriented television show, as were the relationships between the new cast members. They didn't seem to like each other no matter what decade. The remake missed the point. One element that made the original *Family Affair* so successful was the chemistry between the cast members and their individual outpouring of warmth and connectivity.

Fifteen episodes of the new series were shot; only nine were broadcast. Johnny Whitaker played a part in the episode "Holiday Fever" in the new series—that of a portly Santa Claus. I played a character named Beverly in the same show who becomes enamored with a gentleman's gentleman named Mr. French. Despite the guest appearances of Johnny and me on the last show that aired, it was too late to save the ratings. In their eagerness to bring the show up to date, the producers left out one of the most important factors that made the original show such a hit and a classic—the endearing quality of a perfectly cast show and the love that was demonstrated warmly among the characters.

While filming my episode of the remake I felt the ghosts of *Family Affair*'s past spinning around me. Photographed at the same studio on the same stage 10 at CBS Studio Center where the original *Family Affair* was filmed, the faux family didn't stand a chance.

Joining the cast of the remake of the new *Family Affair* (left to right back row) are Caitlin Wachs, Gary Cole, Tim Curry, myself, Johnny Whitaker. Front row are faux twins (left to right) Sasha Pieterse and Jimmy "Jax" Pinchak.

# 50

# Breaking Threads

It was the day of my son's eighth birthday. Reid and I were both very excited. We had been planning his birthday party for a month. His friends had been invited. The cake had been ordered, the favors bought. The roller-skating rink was to handle the entertainment. I dropped Reid off at school the Friday morning of his birthday and decided I would take a run before I picked up the cake for the afternoon's festivities. I parked on one of the sloped streets in Hillsborough and started slowly walking, then picked up a little speed as I jogged down the semi-sidewalk. All of a sudden, swash, I slipped on some ooze slithering from an open drain across the path, fell, and then heard a loud crack. "Owwww!" I howled—sure to be heard from SF to LA. The owner of the house above the street where I had fallen heard the onerous scream. She came running out of her home to see what had happened. A gardener halted his truck and ran up to me as I writhed on the stony pavement. Then a car stopped, and I heard a door slam. I learned later that the second driver who tried to rescue me was a psychologist. The gardener reached me first. Grateful that he had come to help, I began to thank him profusely in Spanish: "Muchas gracias, señor, muchas gracias!" Then I heard the psychologist talking into his phone, frantically explaining, "No, I can't ask her any questions, she only speaks Spanish!"

I cried, "Wait!" However, by that time, the lady of the house had come bearing blankets. She was a nurse, her husband an anesthesiologist. She said to the men, "Gently bring her out of the street and onto my drive."

Soon I heard the alarming noise of the sirens. A big, burly man was trying to find my vein. My teeth were chattering as I kept trying to tell him, "I have to pick up the cake. My son's birthday cake; I have to pick up the cake!"

"It'll be all right," he tried to tell me soothingly.

He couldn't find a vein. I have very tiny veins. Even on a good day it's hard to find one large enough to stick in a needle to draw blood.

The EMT finally found a needle small enough, and as the morphine oozed into my bloodstream, my teeth stopped chattering and my hands stopped shaking a bit. The technicians quickly wheeled the stretcher into the ambulance and zoomed me over to Mills Hospital, which was ten minutes away. The EMT recognized me and started asking questions about *Family Affair* and Brian Keith. Shaking, I tried to be cordial to my new fan but stuttered out answers.

When we arrived at the emergency clinic, I gave the attendant my friends' numbers. My neighbor Kathleen and two of my friends from my mother's club, Leslie and Robin, soon appeared at the hospital. I entreated them to pick up the cake and make sure the birthday party at the roller rink went on. They assured me they would take care of everything and not to worry.

I had broken my tibia and fibula, and the doctor wanted to do surgery in two hours. We discussed putting a pin in my leg. The healing process would be a lot faster. But then Dr. Cohen said, "If it were my leg, I wouldn't want a big scar on it." He convinced me that the extra time spent in a cast would be worth it.

David was finally located and was there when I came out of the recovery room. I was feeling all right as they had given me more doses of morphine. I had a chalky white cast from the top of my thigh to the tip of my toe. I asked how the birthday party had gone, and everyone who visited me told me it was great—only one fight among the second-grade boys.

When I was able to return to my home, my good friend Leslie came to visit bearing lasagna, the DVD of *There's Something about Mary*, and a stuffed dog with a cast. She helped restore my spirits. I have never laughed so hard. I don't know whether it was the painkillers, Leslie's good humor, or the bandaged dog like the one in the movie who had hurtled through the faux window, but the levity certainly cheered me. I am so grateful to my friends!

The good thing about breaking my leg was that it gave me time to learn how to operate a computer. Given my very active lifestyle, sitting down to learn something quietly would not usually be in my nature. Since I was restricted to bed and then to my home for two months and then to physical therapy, it provided me the time.

The bad news was trying to deal with a broken leg given my very active nature. Never to let an interview go unauditioned, I eventually was able to travel to LA on a plane with my removable cast, rise on the lift that Southwest provided, and gently be brought in and out of the 737. I had a red disabled-parking placard that I used with great glee. I hate trying to find parking places, and as I hobbled from my spaces, I at least stumbled along on a happy note, enjoying that I had found such convenient places to park. I was a little clumsy with the crutches, and once I put the heavy wooden stick down on my right little toe and broke it. There I was, tottering along with a broken leg and a broken toe, and then I put the crutch on my other little toe and broke it. Kathy's handy hint: wrap a broken toe with the adjacent one. The unharmed toe acts as a splint, and it will heal. And . . . be careful where you put your crutch.

The toes healed a lot faster than my leg, which took six months. And I don't even have brittle bones or osteoporosis. It was just a very bad fracture.

The cast was eventually replaced with a removable brace, and I would go on an interview, hobble up to the audition office, take off the plastic support, ditch the crutches out front in the bushes, and slowly enter the few steps into the casting office. I was relentless. But I got jobs!

One of the unfortunate outcomes of injuring my leg was that I couldn't exercise as fully as I had been and gained fifteen pounds that not even Marie Osmond and her Nutrisystem could take off for a while.

When my leg was finally healed, I was able to start doing more on-camera work. Both Reid and I appeared in the movie *Black August* and in *Princess Diaries*.

# 51

# The Garment Lengthens

For the *Princess Diaries* film, Reid had been hired as an extra. I thought it would be good experience and enable him to work with the stars Julie Andrews and Anne Hathaway as well as the excellent comedic director Garry Marshall. Reid's scene took place during the cable-car episode of the movie. Anne Hathaway is in her jalopy, driving her royal grandmother, Julie Andrews, up one of San Francisco's notoriously steep hills. Suddenly, the brakes give way and the car speeds backwards down the hill, her rusty heap gaining momentum. The old car then crashes into a waiting iconic cable car. Due to great editing, no one is hurt.

Like a good stage mother, I was standing on the sidelines of the set, watching my budding actor with pride as he stood attentively by the side of the cable car, when a good-looking young man approached and asked, "Are you 'Cissy' from *Family Affair*?" My cover blown, I replied with a noncommittal, "Yes?"

He told me he was very happy to meet me and that he was with *The Nob Hill Gazette*—a tony San Francisco newspaper that chronicles the activities of the rich and famous. He was the *Gazette*'s photo editor. He had come to interview Ms. Andrews, but at the time, she was in her trailer and he was waiting, so he approached me to introduce himself.

During the course of the ensuing conversation, he asked, "Do you know Garry Marshall, the director of this film?"

I said, "No." And Barry Barsamian, outgoing, personable person that he is, said, "You must meet him!"

Barry escorted me to meet the assistant director, Heather, who was also duly impressed with my *Family Affair* status, and she enthusiastically said, "Garry would love to meet you!"

She took me to meet the famous producer/director who has family in San Francisco. Garry told me how much he liked Brian Keith and how he had worked with him on a film. The director then stopped midsentence, paused, looked at me, and then said, "Would you like to be in this movie?"

When anyone offers me a part in a movie, especially a Disney film, I am loath to say no, and here was a great movie, with a stellar cast, being shot in close proximity to my own home. I stemmed my enthusiasm and decorously replied, "Yes, I think it can be arranged." *Ten Commandments*, déjà vu.

After the filming was completed for the day, Reid and I went home. We showed up on the set the next day to see what Garry had created: I was to play Cable Tourist Cissy.

As the *Princess Diaries* story unfolds, Anne's jalopy crashes into the cable car Reid and I occupy. Actually, some strong-armed crew rocked the car back and forth to simulate the crash. The cable-car operator jumps down from his steel perch and is joined by a San Francisco police officer as they try to understand the situation. Queen Renaldi (Julie Andrews) and princess-in-waiting Mia (Anne Hathaway) try to talk their way out of jail and a ticket; the queen has an idea. The ever-intelligent royal flatters the two awestuck men as she dubs them knights of her country, Genovia, by the order of the Rose—an invented name the queen picks by looking up at a street sign near her, Rose Avenue. The crisis averted, Queen Renaldi grandly sweeps away with Mia in tow.

Reid and I had been reacting throughout the scenes with close-ups and medium shots as we stood rapt inside the cable car. There were some lines that did not make the final cut, but there is a big close up at the end of the scene, as I turn to Reid and urge him: "Wave good-bye; that's a queen!" The San Francisco film audiences really loved it, although Reid had a hard time living it down in junior high school.

Barry and I continued our warm friendship. We created a talk show in San Francisco, *Backstage with Barry and Kathy*, where each week we led audiences "on a colorful journey to meet new people, visit interesting places, and attend exciting events." Barry and I have gone backstage with Claude Jarman, Jr. (recipient of an Academy Juvenile Award for the film *The Yearling*), Brian Foster (*The Partridge Family*), and Sidney Mobell, legendary jewelry laureate of San Francisco whose amazing one of a kind collections of bejeweled masterpieces can be seen in the Smithsonian. We hosted Jon Provost, Timmy on TV's *Lassie*, and his wife, Laurie Jacobson, Hollywood historian and author of such books as *Hollywood Haunted* and *Dishing Hollywood*. They are a wonderful couple. We have shared such adventures as dining with our dear friends Bill and Claudia Gruber in Napa Valley, dining in fabulous restaurants and wine tasting in luscious vineyards—a laughingly good time always had by all.

As mentioned previously, Jane Russell was the subject of another show Barry and I hosted. Barry and Jane had become friends because of his association with a charitable organization in Northern California, Peninsula Volunteers. He had sung at one of the events, and the organization was enchanted by his voice and personality. When they were putting on another one of their annual fund-raisers, Barry volunteered to drive four hours south to pick up Ms. Russell and take her to the event, where she was being honored. Jane and Barry became good friends. Barry

My son Reid and I with Julie Andrews in *The Princess Diaries.*

had again driven to her home in Santa Maria the night before we were to do our interview with her for our *Backstage* show. I was enchanted to enter her home and partake of the feeling of nostalgia by looking at the many pieces of wonderful memorabilia that graced her surrounds. There were photos and souvenirs from Howard Hughes to Clark Gable. Displayed were grand mementos of her lustrous show-business career starring with handsome leading men and gorgeous actress friends such as Marilyn Monroe from *Gentlemen Prefer Blondes*. Ms. Russell was vibrant and feisty. Even at the age of eighty-eight she was singing happily with a group at a venue in Santa Maria and attending charity and autograph events. She unfortunately passed away a few months after our show, but we have her spirit on tape and in our hearts to remember.

Barry has an extensive collection of celebrity Hollywood costumes, and he structured a beautiful and successful exhibit of them in 2009. At his venue at the Metreon in San Francisco, Barry showed gowns owned by Elizabeth Taylor, Judy Garland, and Carol Channing, among others. For one of our *Backstage* shows, Tippi Hedren (*The Birds*) came to San Francisco and presented Barry with one of the gowns that Edith Head had created for her. We created a terrific episode with Tippi, and she is as beautiful and gracious as ever.

My cohost, Barry Barsamian of *Backstage with Barry and Kathy*, and I interviewing Jane Russell at her home in Santa Maria, California.

Barry and I also interviewed Paul Petersen for our show. Paul, star of *The Donna Reed Show*, as I stated earlier, became a tireless advocate for child actors. His work on A Minor Consideration, the nonprofit to help child actors, is being carried on by other supporters, but Paul is still a consultant for the organization. Paul has now put many of his incredible talents to work for senior citizens and hosts a show on aging in Los Angeles. We interviewed Paul at an event in Stockton created by ex-pro baseball player Dave Oliver. Dave played for the Cleveland Indians, but his excellent teaching skills and managerial abilities made him a favorite of many teams. Hired by Hall of Famer Nolan Ryan, Dave is now with the Texas Rangers as special assistant for player development. But every year he puts on a celebrity bowling event for his GO Foundation and the United Way. I bowl once a year, and it is at this well-attended event. In 2014 Dave contracted esophageal cancer, but like his attitude for baseball in the past, he fought the disease with great determination and is now in remission. And he still puts on his successful charity bowling tournament in November, where he received a standing ovation for his courage in 2014.

Paul and I have roles in the movie *Executive Ranks*, released in 2015 and shot

Between actor Paul Petersen and Dave Oliver of the Texas Rangers at a GO Foundation celebrity bowling event.

in one of my favorite cities, Chicago. The Grubers' beautiful manse was used as one of the locales, so I felt right at home! Off set, Paul and I joyously regaled each other with showbiz stories from our long careers and were treated to the humorous and Tony Award–winning musical *Kinky Boots* by the prolific and erudite lawyer, host, and raconteur Paul Lisnek.

One of my favorite interviews was that with Patty Duke, which I have mentioned. She, her husband, and their puppy were staying in a beautiful apartment off Lombard Street in San Francisco while she starred in the musical *Wicked*. She was as down to earth, bright, and personable as when we first met on the set of *The Patty Duke Show*. Barry, collector that he is, had bought one of her first albums, and he brought it to the shoot, where Patty graciously signed it. During the show, Barry asked her to sing the intro to *The Patty Duke Show*. She started and then I joined in warbling as her faux twin. It was a fun show with the singing, even if the music was off one-quarter of a step by one member of the duo.

Barry also makes costumes and had created an exact replica of Judy Garland's red-sequined magical shoes worn in *The Wizard of Oz*. I bought a special pair Barry had cobbled for a silent auction at his charitable costume exhibit for the Academy of Fine Arts in San Francisco. I wore them to Patty's interview. I deemed it apropos as she was starring in *Wicked.* Patty was so taken with my sparkling, magical shoes that Barry crafted a pair for her tiny feet and sent them to her at her ranch in Idaho—he's such a generous guy!

Speaking of magical, it was as if glimmering red shoes had flown us to Los Angeles to record one of our most charming shows—that of the installation of the Munchkins' star on the Hollywood Walk of Fame on Hollywood Boulevard. I just heard an anecdote today about *The Wizard of Oz* being the ultimate chick flick with the wicked witch and doleful Dorothy. "Why so?" one asks. Because it's about two women killing each other over a pair of shoes. I know, low groan. But I was delighted to wear my red sparkling shoes, and they were quite a highlight.

When Barry and I flew down for the show and the installation of the Munchkins' star, we watched the screening of the original *The Wizard of Oz* film at Mann's Chinese Theatre. My good friend Robert Nudelman had obtained a special restored movie print, and the color was fabulous. Stan Taffel conducted an interview before the screening with the remaining four Munchkins, a couple of whom were having difficulty hearing. Stan asked one of the aging actors whether he enjoyed playing the Lollipop Kid.

The Munchkin, leaning in to hear, queried, "What?"

Stan repeated the question.

"Lollipop?" the Munchkin asked.

"Yes," Stan replied, "Lollipop."

"Oh," the actor replied, smiling and finally getting it. "Lollipop!"

Jerry Maren, the Munchkin, then burst into a rousing rendition of the song "Lollipop Guild," to the delight of the audience and a confused Stan. It was a charming moment.

After the screening of the restored film, the next day it was time for the installation of the Munchkins' star and the big celebration. Press and fans had gathered to help cheer on the little people who had added so much to the enduring success of *The Wizard of Oz*. The Munchkins' assemblage made a grand entrance in a white carriage drawn by horses whose hair had been dyed in a rainbow of pastel colors with Jell-O. The ceremony was conducted, the Munchkins' star installed, and then it was time for lunch across the street at the legendary Roosevelt Hotel on Hollywood Boulevard. Robert was my escort for the lunch, and the room had been transformed with a colorful arch of balloons decorating the stage into a magical place. As I am writing these lines, I look on my desk and see the charming wicker basket with a stuffed replica of Toto on one side and faux flowers on the other: the basket had been one of the centerpieces of the gaily decorated tables. Ted Bulthaup from the Hollywood Palms Cinema complex in Naperville, Illinois, had worked long and hard with petitions and finance to gain the star for these well-deserving little actors. Each year, Ted and his assistant Angelique had arranged for the Munchkins to travel to Illinois from wherever they lived and sign autographs for their many fans after *The Wizard of Oz* was shown in one of Ted's Hollywood-themed theaters in the complex.

I had made an appearance at one of his theaters, arranged by Robert, to sign autographs when the DVDs of *Family Affair* were released. It gave me an opportunity to see my TV series on a giant screen—in my humble estimation, the show looks great magnified!

Back at the Roosevelt hotel, a delightful luncheon was served. A green transparent screen provided an enchanting backdrop onstage, and a few short and heartfelt speeches were given. It was a fitting finish to a great day for the little stars of the big screen.

Barry Barsamian and I at the installation of the Munchkins' star on the Walk of Fame in Hollywood.

# 52

# Exotic Threads

One guest star I really enjoyed working with on *Family Affair* was the handsome and engaging Michael Blodgett. He was smart and appealing. I had no trouble acting when my character, Cissy, developed a crush on this charming actor. Michael later became a successful novelist/screenwriter who married Meredith Baxter. Michael died at just sixty-seven of a heart attack in 2007. In a two-part episode, "Family in Paradise," Mr. French, Buffy, Jody, and I meet Uncle Bill in the alluring islands of Tahiti, built with realistic aplomb on the set at CBS Studio Center. Drums vibrating and palms swaying, I attempt an exuberant, fast-paced Tahitian dance on the imported sands. Dressed in a colorful native *pareo*, I attempted to imitate the dancers as the family urged me on. At the end of my fervent and rhythmic hula, Buffy says, "You shook real good, Cissy."

I eventually was able to go to the real islands of French Polynesia, not just the fake sandy ones built at CBS. I took my son, Reid, and then realized, "What am I doing here in the most romantic place in the world with my ten-year-old son?"

One reason is that my sister had kindly offered me her time-share in Moorea plus the phone number of a wonderful travel agent who could arrange the exotic trip. My husband wasn't able to join Reid and me because of his work, but he had already visited the isles with a former girlfriend, and we both thought it not a particularly good idea to bring back any unsettling memories. Besides, someone had to feed the dog and water the plants.

If you ask Reid what is the best experience he has ever had, he will describe to you lying on the balmy, sandy beach in Bora Bora, half in and half out of the foamy water, with the gentle waves of the azure seas washing over him.

We loved strolling along the inviting sands and wiggling our toes in their intriguing layers. Reid enjoyed the toasty grittiness of the beach and the warmth of the glowing sun. He is quite a sensitive and aware young man.

For the first week of our trip, before we went to my sister's time-share in Moorea, I rented one of those alluring thatched huts set right in the water on the shore's edge in Bora Bora. It was beautifully decorated in French Tahitian style and included fresh native flowers in vases; rose petals had been leisurely dropped in colorful array in the bath area.

In the next hut, coincidentally, a family with a ten-year-old girl was vacationing from Marin, Northern California. It was surprising to encounter a neighbor so far from home. Marin is forty minutes from our town yet miles from this enchanted paradise. The children became friends and one afternoon decided to don their flippers and snorkeling masks and descend the wooden steps to the inviting waters below our bungalow. In five minutes they were both flopping back up as fast as their large rubber fins permitted.

"What happened?" I called.

Sputtering, my shaking son pointed to the lapping water. I looked down, and there, hiding in the rocky shoals, was the biggest, ugliest sea creature I had ever seen. His large, wrinkled head totally filled a hole in the craggy rocks. I yelled, "Shoo!" I was hoping to scare him more than he scared us. The creature stared at me with bulging eyes. Louder I shouted, "Shoo, shoo!"

The monster then slowly backed out of its peering hole and started swimming away, and swimming, and swimming. It was the longest as well as the ugliest sea creature I had ever seen. I later found out it was a menacing moray eel, more lethal than a shark if you get in a tussle with one of them. If the monster gets its sharp teeth into you, it does not let go! The kids had been right to hurriedly scuttle out of the portentous waters.

The experience did not dampen my son's enthusiasm for the isles, however. He delighted in sailing on the catamarans while watching as sharks were fed not far from our hut and swimming with the dolphins in a special area. One of his favorite experiences was swimming, not with the sharks but with the affable dolphins—the friendly sea mammals and my son both had engaging smiles for each other.

The trip to beautiful Tahiti had definitely made an impression on Reid: in December of that year, it was my birthday. Reid and I had returned from the relaxing island journey and gotten back into the busy swing of school and work. On the day of my birthday at about 6:00 p.m., Reid requested that I go into my home office and wait for fifteen minutes; he then came to the room and told me to close my eyes. He quietly took my hand and led me into the master bath. When we arrived there, he excitedly told me, "Open your eyes, mom!" Strewn before me was a path of rose petals. The fragrant flowers led to a luxuriant bath filled with foaming bubbles. A chilled glass of Chardonnay awaited on the marble ledge of the tub, my book and glasses by its side. Reid had bought a rhinestone tiara with a good friend of mine and had placed it on a small terrycloth pillow on a

My son, Reid, and his dolphin friend in Bora Bora.

corner of the tub. He then proudly exclaimed, "Happy Birthday, Mom!" My son, like his father, a true romantic.

Back to the romantic *Family Affair* faux Tahiti.

I loved the flowery clothes I wore in these island episodes. I had discovered the designer Holly Harp, who owned a chic boutique off Sunset Boulevard in Hollywood. She selected charming antique fabrics and fashioned them into wonderfully unique minidresses, purses, and accessories. The *Family Affair* production company had finally started buying clothes for the cast, and the wardrobe mistress, Thelma Strahm, and I would go shopping at the beginning of each new season. Most of the time, our shopping was limited to Bullocks Wilshire and their beautiful, but conservative, selection of appropriate clothes for the urban Cissy. One season, I was able to steer Thelma to Holly's store for an extra shopping excursion and convince her to buy me some stylish and hip clothes for the Davis family's trip to the islands of Tahiti and other locales. The best part was that I got to keep the clothes after the season was finished. I then had a nice wardrobe for publicity appearances and to go on dates with newfound appealing escorts.

I was certain Holly's fabulous and charming outfits would steal the heart of handsome Michael Blodgett. I flirted, I cajoled, I shimmied the tantalizing Tahitian

Reid and I on our sumptuous Crystal cruise to Alaska.

hula. All to no avail. As life imitates art, just like in the episodes we shot for the Tahitian *Family Affair* adventure, Michael seemed to have eyes only for another. My fanciful budding romance ended when his acting job on the episodes was over. I regrouped my romantic illusions and survived my infatuation and went on to find true love with my husband and son.

# 53

# Burning Threads

It was the day after my birthday, December 14, 2003. I was enjoying a lazy Sunday, drinking coffee in my small home office and answering e-mail after I had put my second load in the clothes washer in the garage. I was peaceful as I looked out my paned window and admired the green ivy and heather that decorate the hillside across the drive from my workroom. David had taken Reid to Sunday school at St. Bartholomew's Church down the street from our home and then was going to sip coffee at Starbucks and read the Sunday paper, relaxing until it was time to pick up our son.

Working on my computer, I again glanced out the window and then saw a strange, luminous striation. "What is *that*?" I said to myself. I went back to work and then heard a thump in our attached garage. Hmm. I guessed that David had dropped off Reid at home and then gone on to his gym. Reid must have raced into the garage to grab his skateboard; he was almost thirteen and loved to ride. "I'll take a break from my work and go see how he is," I thought, "and what noisy mischief he is up to." I pattered to the kitchen in bare feet, still in pajamas, and was shocked to see enormous crackling flames licking hungrily at the supposed fireproof door to the garage.

"Oh no!" I screamed into the flaring space. "The house is on fire!"

I quickly stumbled back to my office and tried to call 911 on my home phone. I had no cell phone. Being wired, the computer was hooked up to the phone, and I couldn't get a dial tone. I frantically pulled the plug on the computer and dialed again. My instinct told me I had to get out of the house. I ran out the front door and, climbing our steep driveway, scraped my feet while talking to the arrogant 911 operator. I was trying to escape as the roof spewed flames behind me; I gave her the address and shrieked, "My house is on fire, my house is on fire!"

"Calm down," she said.

Don't you just love it when all hell is breaking loose and someone tells you to calm down? Anyway, I finally got through to her that the fire trucks were needed immediately!

Our closest firehouse is five minutes from my wooded neighborhood in the hills, but it took the fire engines thirteen minutes to get to my house. It was a three-alarm blaze.

David had picked up Reid from Sunday school and had started back to our house when he saw fire trucks screaming up Crystal Springs, our closest thoroughfare. He reported that his heart beat more rapidly when he saw them turn up our twisty, winding street. "I wonder where they are going?" he thought nervously. He soon found out as he trailed the fire trucks and then had to park five houses down from our home. He ran up the street with Reid closely at his heels. David found me at the top of the drive, sitting on the ground, crying inconsolably. He grabbed and then hugged me.

"What's happening?" he said.

"I don't know," I croaked out. "There's fire everywhere."

Our little family then stood and watched as the firefighters hosed the blazing house. The flames were finally doused, with just remnants groveling in their final throes. The firemen had gotten the best of the fiercest flames, and they were now humiliated and lying abjectly in an ashen heap.

The fire had started in the garage. I had purchased a new dryer two weeks before the conflagration. It was the same type of dryer that I had previously bought from a large department store chain—their own brand of dryer. When the deliveryman appeared in the outfit of the store to connect and install the dryer, it was discovered that the new dryer cord wouldn't reach the outlet. I was surprised, as it was the same dryer I had purchased before. I was also disappointed that I wouldn't be able to get my dryer installed—so close to Christmas—and so many things still to be done.

The installer queried, "Do you have an extension cord?"

I scouted the house and came up with one. "But it doesn't have three prongs," I told the deliveryman.

"That's okay," he said, "it'll work."

It worked, but not well, as the next week the cord sparked and caught fire.

The flames instantly ran up the corner of our garage and caught the wooden shingles on fire. The entire roof burned quickly and hotly. Everything in the garage caught, as did the interior of the house. The firefighters sprayed the powerful water to quell the flames, but the fire was strong competition. They were able to finally put out the blaze and save some of the furniture, but there was a significant amount of water damage throughout the house.

My car, a Lexus SUV only six months old, looked like a sad-faced Mini Cooper, and my tires were melted into rubbery gum. The culprit metal dryer was caved in, and everything else in the garage was in ashes. The family room and dinette were completely burned. All of the other rooms sustained damage.

So how am I going to survive *this*!?

First, my neighbor loaned me a jacket and some shoes since I was still barefoot and in my pajamas. Then, the fire chief led me through the burned-down remains of my home, Reid stayed next door with the neighbors, and David paced up and down the street. I was able to recover some soggy checks and my purse. I found my jewelry and grabbed some clothes and water-soaked important papers from my drenched office.

A restoration company had already put plywood over some burned remaining frames, such as the garage, without my consent. Even though there were other restoration purveyors walking back and forth on the street above our private road, employees from a particular company had descended uninvited and started working. Their centurion stood by with a clipboard in his hand.

I asked the fire chief, "Who are these people?"

He confidently said, "Oh, they're the fire and water restoration company that will help you. I've worked with them before."

I asked him whether he thought it was all right to sign the papers the uniformed man held on his clipboard.

The fire chief said, "Oh, yes, as I said, I work with them all the time."

I shakily took the clipboard from the company's soldier and tried to read what I could without my glasses. He showed me the place on the three-page document to sign my name, which I could barely see through my tear-stained eyes. Then the social worker that had been sent by the Red Cross gave us some vouchers for a hotel and encouraged David, Reid, and me to get some rest and come back to our house in the morning. We took his advice, and David drove us in his car to a nearby hotel.

During the initial cleanup of the fire, David had been pacing back and forth on the street. Of course he was depressed, but I sensed there was something else bothering him.

"What's wrong?" I queried.

"I don't think we have insurance on the house," he said.

"What?" I screamed.

In the Travis family, we are very independent. Each one of us has his or her own checkbook, and each of us is responsible for certain things. I was responsible for all of Reid's care; David was to pay the mortgage insurance, taxes, utilities, and all of his expenses. I paid for everything else and my expenses.

He disconsolately whispered, "I don't think I paid the insurance the last couple of months."

I was flabbergasted. I paled. I called my brother Lance and told him of our tragedy and about the insurance. In his most professional real-estate voice, he told me, "Kathy, you have to have insurance. The mortgage company won't continue your loan unless you have insurance on the house." That was good and bad news. I had to get in touch with the mortgage company. The good news was that they had applied a surcharge to our monthly mortgage payment to cover home insurance. I actually remember David saying the month before that he was surprised that our mortgage payment had gone up since the interest rates were going down on our adjustable loan. We found later that the mortgage company had added an insurance surcharge. The bad thing was, the insurance covered only the exterior of the home's structure, nothing else. Hotel, furnishings, landscaping, and so on were not covered. The bank wanted to cover only its interest: the house. Furnishings, no. "We'll manage," I thought. "We have to survive."

# 54

# Putting Together the Pieces

The next day I went back to our burned-down wreckage. There were people there packing and carting out anything that was salvageable. I found the supervisor and asked him, "What are all these people doing?"

He eagerly responded, "Oh, we're packing and we'll take the things to our warehouse for safekeeping." He smiled.

"Oh," I thought. "How much is this costing?"

He said, "We're up to about $30,000."

Losing my temper, I shouted, "What? Get out! Get out right now!"

He started to stutter, "Bu . . . but you signed."

"I don't care what I signed, get out of here!" I yelled.

They did. I contacted a lawyer. There are many of them in the Bay Area. The attorney and the company reached an agreement. I would pay for what the restoration company had already done and put the costs on a monthly payment plan. The insurance company the mortgage firm had contracted did not cover their "service." I don't know why I have always felt *so* obligated to pay all my bills. They reduced the amount and Reid, some workers, and I packed up our salvage and rented a storage facility while David continued working on his job. Our kind and good friend Chuck arranged for us to stay at the Hotel Sofitel in Redwood City for a month while we tried to figure out what to do. One of David's friends had a vacant furnished condo that we could live in by paying the homeowners association dues each month. We were extremely grateful and spent a year and a half there. I became the general contractor for the restoration, Reid became the interior designer, and David continued his work. My husband told us to do whatever we wanted; his only request was that we install a spray water massage in the master shower.

I had kept the plans from the original house in a plastic garbage barrel in our basement and was able to use them. The city, understanding our plight, was very helpful in expediting approvals. As I had grown up with architecture and contracting, I had a smattering of knowledge about the building process, but a little knowledge is a dangerous thing, as many of my subcontractors will tell you.

The house was rebuilt. I had wanted to sell the whole burnt-out mess, but Reid plaintively groaned, "But, Mom, you can't—this was where I was born and grew up!"

I found it difficult to still his pleas, and so I gave in and spent the next year of 2004 on the verge of a nervous breakdown every other day. I would don my face mask, venture into the ruined house with its smoky residue, and try to redeem any of the recoverable items that were left behind by the fire restoration company. I hired some workers from the resource center to help me; Reid put in his labor as well. David was busy going to work every day and then drowning his depression in Napa red wine. I must admit that I would certainly have a couple glasses of Chardonnay after I had spent all day trying to salvage some waterlogged items and viewing, day after day, the detritus of our home and breathing in the ashy fumes. Clearing the property and overseeing the rebuild and furnishing was quite a harrowing experience. I had read that Stacy Keach had taken a year off work to remodel his home. At the time, I thought, how could he take so much valuable time off his career just to oversee the remodel? I later learned how very important it is to supervise every part of work done.

For instance, I had asked for a certain pattern of tile for our entryway. When I returned from an out-of-town autograph convention assignment, I saw that the entry looked like a bad deck of cards with black fours of diamonds laid out. Large black marble geometric figures glared out from a creamy limestone base. The entry was to have been classic and discreet with small diamond-shaped pieces connecting the squares of limestone—now it was gaudy and blatant. I was distraught, but Reid came to the rescue and said, "Why don't you put a smaller diamond in the center to break it up?" It wasn't the perfect solution, but it looked 86 percent better and we didn't have to tear the whole thing out.

The rebuild was costing a tremendous amount of money, even with my scrimping. And we had no funds for the interior. That's when I decided to sue the department store where we bought the dryer. I cojoined with the insurance company: they could redeem the money they had put out for the exterior rebuild. It was our believable and true assertion that the fire started because of the incompetent installation of the dryer.

We believed the department store would settle. No, they were determined. And they were a big corporation with a slew of lawyers. But I retained the lawyer who had sued the school where my precious child had been injured as a toddler. Reid was going to a Montessori school in San Mateo. I wanted my only child to have every opportunity and not miss out on any experiences. I enrolled him in a toddler class when he was but three years old from 9:00 am. until noon three days a week so he could socialize with other children. One day after he had been going to school there for a month, I came to pick him up and heard him screaming.

What is wrong? I panicked and ran to the classroom, which was located in a little house behind the main house.

"He fell," the teacher exclaimed.

I looked at him. He had fallen on their open radiator, which had the heat on. Can you imagine a classroom dedicated to toddlers that has an open radiator with a little ledge eight inches above the floor next to the heater so that the kids can look out the window? I can't either. Reid had fallen from the small, slippery wooden step, and his beautiful pure face, without a mark on it, hit the searing arms of the radiator. I immediately snatched him up and raced to the emergency room.

My gorgeous child was left with a third-degree burn across his previously unmarked face. He spent the next two years with a hat on his head and sun lotion slathered on his face whenever he went outside. The scar has now almost completely disappeared because of creams, protective lotions, and the natural growth of tissue. A plastic surgeon said it would do more harm to Reid for him to try and eradicate the scar. He suggested that the burn should be allowed to heal itself as best it could. There is now just a faint remembrance of the accident on his face. As a teenager he put up posters all around his room of his favorite movie, *Scarface*. Reid survived by dealing with the burn and developing a great liking for Al Pacino and cigars.

Terry Anderlini, the lawyer who helped us with Reid, is well educated and erudite and has dealt with numerous personal injury cases. He is past president of the State Bar of California. David and I decided to hire him again to help us with our fire and our suit against the large department store chain. Because the corporation would not settle, we went to trial—one month of nerve-racking testimony. Even though the days of the trial numbered only nine, it was sporadic. So there would be two days on and then a break and then another day of testimonies, a break and then another two days of presentations. A murder trial has taken less time. One day, the attorney for the corporation, having looked at the long list of burned and destroyed items, asked me what the most valuable thing I had lost was. I paused and then ruefully and emotionally said, "Our sense of security."

Finally, the verdict was in. The jury had voted in our favor. The insurance company was paid back all its money, and we were recompensed for the items we had lost in the fire. We were not reimbursed for our hotel, landscaping, or storage. And we had to give Terry a large percentage of the funds because the case went to trial instead of settling. Even so, there were some monies left to restore our damaged three-hundred-year-old antique door (which was later stolen as it rested in a friend's garage for "safekeeping") and for some of the waterlogged items. I did lose a lot of memorabilia and the prototypes of the toys I helped to create for Edutainment for Kids, which had been stored in the garage—irreplaceable.

My dear and good friend Robert Nudelman flew up from LA and single-handedly erected a plastic storage unit on our property to protect the few things we were able to save while the house was being restored. Robert, as a Hollywood historian and expert eBay purveyor, was also able to replace some of the photos that had been lost. He unfortunately died too young in 2008, but his legacy and his fight to save historic Hollywood and its classic buildings is memorialized in plaques placed on buildings throughout Hollywood. He is now interred in the Hollywoodland Forever Cemetery, along with such notables as Mel Blanc, Mickey Rooney, Rudolph Valentino, and even Cecil B. DeMille. On his grave marker is engraved:

> ROBERT W. NUDELMAN
> HOLLYWOOD'S GREATEST ARCHITECTURAL
> PRESERVATIONIST, PROTECTOR AND HERO
> 1952–2008
> YOUR MEMORY LIVES ON AND ALL WHO KNEW
> YOU AND UNDERSTOOD THE IMPORTANCE
> OF YOUR WORK WILL CONTINUE TO STRIVE
> FORWARD WITH PASSION AND YOUR MISSION

Other friends and family came to our aid; my brother Bud provided a small loan, which I quickly paid back after the trial. A church member I knew gifted us with a monetary donation, one of my high school friends helped me with a very generous cash gift, and friends in my mom's club gave me clothes and comfort. One of my other friends, Carolyn, totally outfitted me from pajamas and slippers to dress gowns

Robert Nudelman proved to be a good and true friend as he singlehandedly built a shed to store some of my waterlogged but saved belongings.

with matching shoes that she had worn slightly. I am so blessed to have such good and true friends.

Reid wanted to be back in the restored house when he started his first year of high school for the ninth grade in 2005, so even though our home was not ready and the electricity had not been turned on, we moved back with our candles and thanked God for our survival.

# 55

# Nostalgic Threads

Ray Courts, as I mentioned earlier, was the one of the first purveyors of autograph conventions highlighting entertainment stars. Folks were hungry for nostalgia and the "good old days," so Ray and his wife, Sharon, created shows where dealers could bring collectible movie posters, previously signed photos, and other film and TV memorabilia to display and sell. Ray thought he would sweeten the conventions and increase the draw by adding celebrities to the mix; the spectators and fans could meet the stars, and the stars would be able to sign photos, greet the fans, and chat. The concept proved to be very popular, viable, and financially successful. The shows were a win-win situation, as the classic-show actors who had not been given additional residual money when their shows hit the cable and DVD markets were able to add to their income by signing and selling their ephemera, and fans and dealers were able to purchase memorabilia for investment and enjoyment.

Then the *Star Wars* phenomenon began, and sci-fi conventions and costume-wearing fans flocked to burgeoning festivals to further their obsessions with *Star Wars* and other science-fiction films and TV shows. Even if an actor had only one line on a *Star Trek* show, he or she became fodder for a collector's album.

My dear friends Dr. Fred Eichelman and his wife, Carolyn, are also fans of the sci-fi genre. Dr. Fred has been credited with starting the first sci-fi conventions in western and southwestern Virginia. The inaugural show began in 1976 and for sixteen years was under the name of RoVaCon, for Roanoke Valley Nostalgia Convention. The first show garnered 300 people and the last, 1,500. It was mainly science fiction, but not completely. The initial media guest was Elizabeth Taylor, who then appeared for two more years and created the Roanoke Valley Drama Scholarship. Dr. Fred had met and become friends with Ms. Taylor when he worked on her husband's (John Warner's) campaign for the US Senate. Dr. Fred is quite personable as well as a "get-things-done" type of person.

The group broke up, but in 2000 Dr. Fred created Starz 2000, and that was the first festival I attended in Roanoke. After that, there were four Point North Media conventions. Point North concentrated on family-friendly and inspiring films, TV, and media and now has an online and print newsletter that is published four times yearly. I am proud to be on the advisory board of Point North, whose mission it is to reach beyond ourselves for the highest star and create quality and excellent entertainment on an inspirational plane.

I continue to travel to the beautiful Roanoke Valley and have conducted workshops at the Burton Center for the Performing Arts and the high school where Dr. Fred and his wife Carolyn's daughter, Carol Webster, is a superb instructor. Carol was recently selected as regional teacher of the year. For state teacher of the year she was honored in the second position. Also in Roanoke I have appeared at their fairs, spoken at Rotary Club, and starred in a rendition of the play *Love Letters*.

Nostalgia and western conventions continue, as does my participation in these oldie-but-goodie shows, and as the vibrant actress Ruta Lee states, "I'm not an antique, I'm a collectible!" The venue provides stars and fans an opportunity to get to know one another in a fun and active setting. Some of those fans are ardent friends of mine today.

The different types of people who attend the conventions always fascinate me. I met John Semper, an animation writer and story editor, at one of Ray Courts's early shows in Hollywood, and we became fast friends. John cast me in two of the animated projects he was overseeing: *Spiderman* and *The Amazing Spiderman*. John had written episodes of *Spiderman and His Amazing Friends*, but I hadn't known him then—it took a fan show to cement our relationship. And then there are my wonderful friends, the Grubers. I met Bill and Claudia at one of Ray Courts's shows in Chicago. We became great friends and have enjoyed unforgettable times laughing in Napa, Chicago, and LA. They are fun, generous, and dear, dear people.

Bill is a successful businessman, loves collecting signed guitars, photos, and memorabilia, and enjoys meeting some of his favorite stars. He had an idea simmering for a time, and one day Bill and I met at Scoma's Restaurant in San Francisco and he asked whether I would like to help him put together a special Christmas party for his employees, friends, and business acquaintances in Chicago. The idea immediately grabbed my attention: I love to help produce events, and working with good people is always a plus.

Bill is an ally of Jim Lovell, the astronaut. Bill went on an expedition to the South Pole with Jim and also American astronaut Owen Garriott. They had an exciting time slipping and sliding on the ice but managed to return with wonderful memories and photos. They found actual pieces of meteors that had crashed into our planet eons ago, but most of those valuable pieces are protected in the Chicago Field Museum. Bill also went to the North Pole with leading astrophysicist Eugene Parker, who proved the existence of solar winds, if not Santa Claus. Of course we now call Bill "bi-polar."

Jim's son and daughter-in-law, Jay and Darice Lovell, own a fabulous and

My good friends Bill and Claudia Gruber, and I at the "Starry Night" Celestial Ball for the Adler Planetarium in Chicago, 2012.

successful restaurant in Lake Forest, Illinois, called . . . Lovell's of Lake Forest. Tom Hanks, who played the character of astronaut Jim Lovell in the Oscar-winning film *Apollo 13*, presented Captain Lovell and the restaurant with an incredible frieze of horses that presides grandly over the well-appointed and exquisite bar. Downstairs at the fabulous restaurant is an intimate and well-stocked wine cellar with a dining table and great ambiance, perfect for small dinners, which I have been happy to enjoy with Bill, Claudia, and some of their friends. The downstairs area also houses a cozy cigar room with fireplace and displays Captain Lovell's fascinating memorabilia from his Apollo mission as well as other interesting paraphernalia. The main floor is for dining and upstairs, a terrific place for a party.

So Bill and I worked together on a celebrity list of guests to invite for a lively holiday soiree. The gala was a grand success. My friends Paul Petersen, Jon Provost and his wife, Laurie, and Ruth Buzzi and her husband, Kent Perkins, among others, attended that first year. Bill and Claudia are big *Seinfeld* fans, so Larry Thomas (the Soup Nazi) invited some of his friends, Richard Herd (Wilhelm), Liz Sheridan (Helen Seinfeld), Ian Abercrombie (Mr. Justin Pitt), Steve Hytner (Kenny Bania), and Brian George (Babu Bhatt). We had such a good time that we produced three more "Dine with the Celebrities" events at Lovell's at Christmas. One of my favorites was when Davy Jones and Martha Reeves attended. To understand, the celebrities were not asked to do anything per se, just show up and have fun. But when the band started playing—an entertainer is an entertainer, and Davy popped out of his chair, sprightly jumped on the band's stage, and began to warble wonderful renditions of his hits, and then Martha, stirred by the compelling music, also got up and sang her songs. It was a resounding and memorable evening.

I still go to autograph conventions and now bring my *Family Affair Cookbook* to sign, along with other memorabilia from my career. I recently saw the spirited Ruta Lee at the Western Legends Round Up in Kanab, Utah, where I accepted a bronze plaque on behalf of Brian Keith, who had starred in two films that were shot in Kanab—*Fort Dobbs* and *Ten Who Dared.* The plaque is secured to a hitching post placed on the streets of Kanab for their Little Hollywood Walk of Fame. I gladly made an acceptance speech on Brian's behalf and contributed to a panel on westerns in Hollywood with James Drury, Peter Brown, Dan Haggerty, and Wyatt McCrea. Western film fairs are great, and I enjoyed the Williamsburg Festival put on by Bill Sasser and his great posse. The year I was there, the sterling Anne Jeffreys appeared along with other western and media stars. Most recently I appeared at the Western Film Fair in Winston-Salem, North Carolina, in July 8–12, 2015, produced by a great group, including Fred Jones, Tommy Hildreth, Bill Loving, and, of course, Dr. Fred. I took orders for my new book, signed photos and memorabilia, and sat on a panel telling tales from the Old West and answering questions about the films and TV shows that survived it. Always a delight to see old friends and meet and greet new ones. Yee haw!

Work continues for me and I starred in the stage adaptation of the movie *Tom Sawyer—River Song: The Adventures of Tom Sawyer*—at the beautiful Niswonger Performing Arts Center in Greeneville, Tennessee, in January 2015. Playing the role of Aunt Polly was a real treat, but the best part was that I was able to work again with the talented Gerald Maloy, who had originally cast me as Amanda in *The Glass Menagerie* and Margaret Carey in the musical *Summer Magic.* For this outing, the talented Mr. Maloy adapted music by the Sherman brothers from the Academy Award–nominated original score and songs used in the movie *Tom Sawyer.* The script is based on the original Mark Twain novel. Jeff East, who starred as Huckleberry Finn in the original Disney movie *Tom Sawyer* and then as the eponymous Huckleberry Finn, was to have played the role of Muff Potter in our production, but a week before the performance, surgery he had on his knee the month before had serious repercussions and his doctor advised against him singing and dancing in the strenuous role. The multi-talented Jerry Maloy, who had been rehearsing his cast (without me or Jeff—we were to come in two weeks before the performance) for four months prior to opening and knew all the lines, songs, and dance routines of the character of Muff Potter, was able to jump in and save the day. And he was great! We enjoyed standing ovations every night, and at closing the audience reaction to Mr. Maloy's

Group photo from the wonderful Williamsburg Film Festival.

personal bow was loud and sustained. Kudos to our illustrious producer, composer, director, actor, singer, dancer, and all around great guy! *River Song: The Adventures of Tom Sawyer* was a hit. The audiences loved the show and were transported by the songs, words, and emotions to a time of fantastic freedom and heartfelt Americana. Tours of the successful show are now planned for Owensboro, St. Louis, and, of course, Hannibal, Missouri, Mark Twain's birthplace.

My special friend director Gerald Maloy and I.

Poster from the premier of the new musical *River Song: The Adventures of Tom Sawyer*, where I starred as Aunt Polly.

# 56

# Audio Swatches

Audio narration has played a large part in my professional life for over twenty years. I have always loved to read, and as I had already started a voice-over career, I wanted to investigate another aspect of the audio-entertainment field. I had experience narrating, casting, and producing children's audiobooks for the Smarty Pants Company. The Beatrix Potter and Mother Goose CD renditions I created had sold over three million copies a few years back, but I wanted to narrate longer projects. After I broke my leg, I decided it would be a good time to start. There was a book convention in LA, so I flew down with my cast and wheelchair, determined to find out about audiobook narration. My stepson, Scott, graciously met me at the Los Angeles Convention Center and pushed my wheelchair from book publisher to book publisher. I made some good contacts. The most meaningful audio publishing group I met was the crew from Brilliance Audio, and then I met a person who was to become a business contact and good friend. I had wanted to go to the dinner event, but Scott had other plans, so I was sitting alone in a corner of the lobby in my wheelchair with my cast-leg hoisted on a pillow. A very nice man came up and introduced himself as Carl Amari. He was very kind and offered to wheel me into the dinner to sit at his table; we got along famously.

Carl lives in Chicago, but we kept in contact, and when I was in the Windy City at an autograph convention, we had lunch together. We chatted about many things. Carl Amari is a radio enthusiast but had recently sold his company, Radio Spirits, which had a library of classic radio shows and other audio theater. At the time, he was producing a movie, *Madison County*, for his new company, Falcon Pictures. Carl was the one who also had secured the rights to adapt the classic *Twilight Zone* television shows to radio. I have starred in five of these wonderful productions for him, including "The Long Morrow," "The Invaders," and "The Fever."

Carl had always been a fan of *Family Affair* and had connections with MPI

Media Group, an excellent home video company in Illinois. We talked about putting *Family Affair* on DVD. We discussed how I would create bonus features for each season. I put Carl in contact with the lawyer handling the Fedderson affairs, they worked out a deal, and now all five seasons are out on DVD with wonderful extras.

On the first DVD released, I exhibited memorabilia from *Family Affair* and explained how the show was created and then became such a hit. Robert Nudelman offered Cecil B. DeMille's original barn studio, now the Hollywood Museum, situated across from the Hollywood Bowl, to film the featurettes. I loved presenting the story of *Family Affair* in the surrounds of the historic moviemaker's studio home, which contained such a large part of my own theatrical history.

For one of the extra features, I contacted the original story editors and writers, Austin and Irma Kalish. On set and on video they regaled us with stories, as did Sherry Alberoni, my friend Sharon in the series, with remembrances of *Family Affair.* John Stephens was our moderator and with his wry humor and intelligence made for a great panel leader. He also led a group of my peers on another bonus feature: Jerry Mathers, Veronica Cartwright, Kym Karath, and Pamelyn Ferdin—all child actors when they appeared as guests on *Family Affair*—a fun group! On one of the other features, I guided the audience on a tour of CBS Studio Center in Studio City where we filmed four years of *Family Affair* and on to stage 10, where the ghosts of *Family Affair*'s past still roam.

Carl also produced audio recordings of the New and Old Testaments with an extremely talented cast—I was honored to be among them. For *The Word of Promise Audio Bible*, the cast included James Caviezel as Jesus, Marisa Tomei, Richard Dreyfuss, Michael York, and me. The book won the Audie Award—the Oscar for spoken-word productions—as Best Multicast Production the year it was released, among other awards.

I thoroughly enjoyed directing Amy Tan as she recorded the audio version of her successful novel *Saving Fish from Drowning*. I got to know her as the fascinating and accomplished talent she is. When we recorded her novel, Amy was unfortunately suffering from a debilitating bout of Lyme disease, and her energy was low—not her usual vibrant self. The volume had to be cranked all the way up to record her soft voice. Also, because of some death threats due to her activism, she carried with her a small Yorkshire terrier that had been designated as a service dog. The animal was trained when brought into a room to sniff and ferret out any suspicious persons or potential evildoers. When Amy first walked into the recording facilities at Voice One Studios in San Francisco, the dog performed her sniffing duties and then was scooped up by Amy and taken into the recording booth. She kept the small dog on her lap while she recorded. Later, the engineer and owner of Voice One, Elaine Clark, listened to the recording and heard loud sounds and gulps of air in the background.

As I listened with her, Elaine said, "What's that noise?"

We heard, "Nahhh, cahhh, nahh, cahh."

"Oh no," I said. "That's the Yorkie snoring!"

And indeed the dog had been so relaxed that it had gone into a deep sleep and did what dogs and my husband do in their REM sleep—snore very loudly. It is very difficult to remove extraneous sounds that are woven into a recording, but Elaine in her creative research found a product called Sound Soap and was able to erase most of the errant audio.

Notwithstanding technical difficulties, Amy and I were nominated and then won the Audie Award for the book. When I found out about the honor, I called Amy and delightedly exclaimed, "Amy, isn't it great that we won the Audie?"

"Yes," she said, "but when they first called, I thought I had won a car."

I have recorded many other audiobooks for which I have won Audie Awards. Among them are *Even Now*, by Karen Kingsbury, a very successful Christian fiction writer, published by Zondervan, and *The World's Shortest Stories*, published by Listen and Live Audio.

Audiobook recording, like many technologically oriented endeavors, is constantly changing. I used to travel to the audio publishing companies like Brilliance Audio in Grand Haven, Michigan, or to Zondervan Publishing, which is located in Grand Rapids, Michigan. The companies supplied a director and engineer for the narrations. Now, home recording studios are *de rigueur* for the industry. With advances in technology, it is not difficult to sustain a career if one has even the basics of a quiet, dedicated room, good microphone, and laptop.

With owner Elaine Cark and author Amy Tan at Voice One Studios, where I teach many VO classes.

Collecting my nomination ribbon before winning an Audie Award for narrating an audiobook.

I teach audio narration at Voice One Studios in San Francisco, and I explain to my students why it is a good idea to develop skills in all genres of audiobook narration: fiction, nonfiction, and children's books. The more skills you have, the more work you will do. Because of the computer, much of the marketing is accomplished from home, as is the recording. It is a self-motivating business, so besides developing skills for performance, one must also be able to sell one's audio wares. It is also possible to create one's own publishing company, as Scott Brick, a very successful narrator, and now publisher, has done. The audio narration industry is growing, and books such as this one are recorded and marketed. Listened to a good book lately?

# 57

# Helping Others to Sew Their Own Piece

I never thought I would teach, but I am finding it quite fulfilling and have now been conducting classes and workshops for over ten years. I specialize in voice-over, teaching classes in speech and diction, creating characters for toys, audio narration, and ADR, or automated digital replacement (ADR), which is utilized for postproduction in film, TV, animation and multimedia.

My students at Voice One especially like the classes I teach on automated dialogue replacement. ADR was originally called looping, as film was contained on large reels that looped around a spool. As an explanation of looping/ADR, imagine a scene being filmed in a restaurant. The camera may be recording the dialogue of two main characters. The duo may be sitting in a crowded eatery. The diner may be filled with extras—or actors who have been hired for background and who are not allowed to speak. It would seem odd if one were watching the scene in a movie and only the two main characters were talking and the rest of the people were mute. So after the film has been assembled, before sound effects, music, and Foley (effects generated by Foley walkers use various items such as broken glass, leaves, pebbles, and so on to create desired sounds), the rough cut or working print is brought to a sound studio. A group is hired, or specific people, to voice background actors. It is quite a skill and also lots of fun to replace one's voice. I call it the Zen of postproduction character acting.

For a time, I was part of the Loop du Jour group, which voiced Ron Howard's movies. There are some catchy names for loop groups, for instance, LA Mad Dogs, Loopers, Loop Troup, 3 Beeps Looping ("three beeps" refer to the sounds that an ADR talent hears right before starting to voice a part), and Groupers. Through the loop group, I worked on such excellent films as *Apollo 13*, which won the Academy Award for Best Sound Mixing, *Backdraft*, *Jingle all the Way*, and *Parenthood*, to name a few.

ADR also includes dubbing in the digital replacement of voices. I had watched versions of *Family Affair* dubbed in various languages. I loved that "Cissy" could speak Japanese, German, and Spanish so fluently. But it was a challenge and a delight for me to dub non-English versions of foreign films, TV, and multimedia into English. I dubbed an entire series, *The Monkey King* (which is a classic fable in China about the Monkey King and his disciples, the Pig Demon and the River Demon, plus the Buddha) from Chinese into English. It is quite an adventure to make sure that the English fits the Chinese characters' original voices. One must begin speaking when the character being dubbed opens his/her mouth and end when the lips close. One also has to be certain that the emotion, tone, and tenor match the situation in the scene. And it takes quite a bit of skill to deliver an excellent rendition that enhances rather than detracts from the emotion and direction of the film, TV, cartoon, or other media.

Japanese anime is quite popular and another situation where one endeavors to match an English voice to the original foreign version with realism and verisimilitude. The challenge is that Japanese words often are much longer than their English translations. For instance, the Japanese *Domo arigato gozaimasu* means "thank you" in English. There are a lot more syllables in *Domo arigato gozaimasu* than in "thank you." I teach how to make the translated words fit the original language through elongation of vowels, subtle pauses, and sighs or added breaths. It's satisfying to view the outcome and observe that the dubbed words actually match the movements of the mouth, look natural, and seem like they originated from the character. It's fun and fulfilling.

Besides conducting voice-over workshops, I give speeches and interviews at colleges and universities to students and guests. I recently had the pleasure of appearing at BYU, hosted by the erudite Scott Boyter, where I was interviewed and then did a Q and A with the theater and film students. Many inquiries came my way, and I delighted in the enthusiasm of young creators. I was surprised when I spoke of *The Night of the Hunter* that there was such interest and knowledge. I told the story of my son and how he had written L-O-V-E and H-A-T-E on his knuckles after he had seen the movie, and the anecdote received a great deal of laughter. After the Q and A, students came up to me, and I asked why they knew so much about *The Night of the Hunter.* It was revealed that the film is one of the movies that must be analyzed and reviewed as a requisite for entering the department. I smiled to myself, knowing that Charles Laughton, in his directorial debut, had been vindicated by the reviewers and that his film was rightfully installed in the annals of moviemaking history.

# 58

# Still Sewing

I also sound off now, by giving speeches—to women's clubs, on cruise ships, for charities and special events. I give speeches on the power of perseverance, growing up in Hollywood, or specific speeches for special events. I have been honored to emcee the Leukemia and Lymphoma Society Man and Woman of the Year Awards at their annual dinner at the beautiful Ritz-Carlton in St. Louis. Mary Pillsbury Wainwright not only won the honor of Woman of the Year on the local level but through her grace and humanitarianism also won on the prestigious national level. Mary is also involved in the Missouri Baptist Children's Home, whose fund-raisers I have emceed.

I have been happy to make several thank-you speeches for awards I have won, such as the Lifetime Achievement Award given by the Young Artists Group, the Golden Halo Award, and in 2013 the prestigious Lifetime Achievement Award presented by the Southern California Motion Picture Council—even though my son proclaimed, "But mom, you're not dead yet." No, son, I'm not, and I still "got a lot of livin' to do."

I host *Family Tree Recipe* for Drew International Concepts. Drew Brewer has an incredible amount of creativity as well as the ability to set new ideas and shows into motion. On the *Family Tree* show, a recipe which has been handed down through generations is presented and cooked by my guest. The series appears on the web and also in the new e-magazines Drew is producing. I have also hosted *Celebrity Gives* and edited the eponymous magazine, which heralds the generous nature of our actors. I conducted interviews with some of my child star pals, including Angela Cartwright, Darby Hinton, Jeanne Russell, Tony Dow, and Stanley and Barry Livingston, among others.

The delightful comedy/mystery film *Mom, Murder and Me* in which I starred as Mom was released in 2014 and is continuing to gain momentum. We shot entirely on location in the beautiful city of San Francisco and surrounding area.

Interviewing Angela Cartwright for my show *Celebrity Gives*.

The multifaceted Heather Donnell, who wrote and directed the film, did a superb job. The delightful film has been greeted with excellent reviews and shown at the California Independent Film Festival in Northern California under the guidance of Derek Zemrack as well as at the Idylwild Film Festival in Southern California and the Bahamas International Film Festival. Sorry I missed the azure waters of the Caribbean for that one. The movie will be broadcast soon on television and then be released for DVD.

By joining the incredible group the Family Media Angels through my friends Ken Waters and Frank Pollifrone, helmed by the ever personable and inviting Brad Zielinski, I help to define, discover, and fund family-oriented projects for new movies, TV, and multimedia as one of the board members. The investment group also funds start-up companies from our talent-rich pool from Silicon Valley, the Bay Area, and other Northern California locales. It is an energized and exciting group. FMA is also the place where I met Gordon Granger, a wonderful family-oriented producer with whom I am working on a slate of delicious projects, such as *SOLD*, the movie and *SOLD, Back on the Market*, as well as the intriguing film *Medusa*, among others. I have many projects to look forward to and accomplish. But there are always challenges to survive . . .

With Heather Donnell, director and producer of *Mom, Murder and Me*, in front of the movie's poster at the Orinda Theatre.

# 59

# Unraveled

My husband and I were invited to cruise with my generous friend Mike Schrimmer and his friends and family to celebrate Mike's sixtieth birthday in 2013. I had met Mike at the Hollywood Collector's Show when he and his wife visited from Chicago, where he owns Windy City Novelties. Windy City has more than ten thousand different types of party accessories; Mike was instrumental in creating glow sticks and glow necklaces that are worn at sports games and elsewhere. Besides being an astute businessman, he also is an inveterate collector, with many fabulous pieces of movie and TV memorabilia and costumes displayed at his showroom and warehouse in Illinois. The idea of a relaxing vacation to the Caribbean seemed like a lovely adventure and a time for a much-needed rest for all. However, David could not get off work, but since I am a freelance actor, I was able to escape the entertainment realm for a few days. Besides hosting forty guests for the cruise, Mike brought aboard plenty of lighted delights such as flickering hats and glowing wands to add to the festivities. Snorkeling in the beautiful waters of the Caribbean on St. Martin, St. Croix, and the Bahamas added to the enjoyment.

It was a wonderful cruise and then time to return to reality. The plane back to San Francisco arrived early, but I went to baggage claim expecting to see my husband. Instead, I was greeted by my son and his girlfriend, Megan. Reid explained that dad wasn't feeling well and so they had come to the airport to pick me up.

Arriving home, we unloaded the heavy luggage, and then I greeted Coco, my whirling dervish Cocker Spaniel, quickly looked at the accumulated mail, and went to check on David. He was freezing cold and ashen, and he had been violently vomiting. He looked deathly ill. I told him we had to call the doctor. "No," he emphatically proclaimed. Reid and I worriedly discussed what to do. I gave David some water and then I finally decided to call our family physician. As it was a Saturday night, the service answered. The operator put me through to the nurse on duty. After I explained David's symptoms, she immediately connected me to 911. The wailing fire engine landed in front of our house in five minutes. After their examination of David, one of the EMTs took me aside and said that he thought David was having a heart attack. They whisked him onto the waiting stretcher, quickly strapped him in, and then hurriedly pushed him into the waiting ambulance. Inside, they attached a bag to his arm. I was close on their heels, peering anxiously, standing by with a robe and slippers for him. I was not allowed in the ambulance so Reid, Megan, and I quickly jumped into Reid's car and followed them to the emergency room at Mills-Peninsula hospital, ten minutes from our home.

David was quickly removed from the ambulance and taken into emergency while my small family entered the greeting area of the emergency room. The receptionist told me someone would come out to let us know what was happening in fifteen minutes. Fifteen minutes became a long forty-five minutes until a doctor finally appeared with grave news. David was in cardiac arrest. His potassium level was over nine—a lethal amount. The doctor explained that when David had arrived at emergency his heart stopped; the team did CPR. The cardiologist and nephrologist (kidney doctor) plus a vascular surgeon were called in.

We heard, "Code Blue, Code Blue," and our hearts almost stopped. Our family trio then sat around consoling one another, trying to divert our attention via the television in the brightly lit waiting room, and waiting some more. Then the hospitalist came out to advise us, shook his head, and told us that it didn't look good. David had literally died twice from cardiac arrest. With my most commanding and emotional look, I stared straight into his eyes and said, "Save him." The doctor went back to tend to David, and then Reid, Megan, and I waited two more fitful hours and were then told we would be led to the consultation room. What did that mean? The three of us clanged through the emergency room doors and then found ourselves in a puke-green room with no windows and the smell of death. I told my family, "We are not going to stay in this room." I found a door and it led to the well-lit waiting room. "We'll stay here," I told Reid and Megan.

Another hospitalist came forth and told us again it did not look good but that David's heart was beating and why were we in the waiting room and not the consultation room? I told her that we wanted to be here, not there. She barely overlooked our disobedience to inform us that a blood clot had been dislodged and had traveled to David's arm. She left, and the vascular surgeon then came out and asked permission to do surgery to remove the clot with the admonition that he may not be able to remove the clot entirely and a question: "Has David's arm ever been blue?" "Blue?" I queried. I emphatically declared, "No, never," and with that, Reid shook his head and emphatically agreed. "All right," the surgeon said, "I'll do the best I can."

We waited some more on our plastic seats, and at about 3:00 a.m. the vascular surgeon clanged the door and announced that we could go see David. He was a mess. He was gulping deep breaths from a loud machine, and his entire right arm was a startling shade of bright blue, but the surgeon declared that he had been able to remove all of the clot.

David was admitted to intensive care. The next day the team was still trying to find the reason for his cardiac arrests. Another hospitalist explained to us that David would begin a long road to recovery as they explored kidney, heart, and other organs to find why the potassium level had risen so deathly high and so abruptly.

Reid was the one who discovered the answer. The night after we had heard about the extent of David's recovery period, Reid examined our vitamin cabinet. He found a bottle of previously unused potassium chloride minerals. I had bought these for David for occasional cramping in his hands, but he had never opened the bottle. Now we saw that it had been opened and some of the potassium was missing. I reached for my glasses and read the very tiny print on the label. The instructions called for a pinch with water after food. I had obtained these crystals online from a company located in Vietnam. David was poisoned by potassium.

After three rounds of dialysis to clear his blood of the lethal mineral, David was transferred to a semi-intensive care unit. On the fourth day of his hospitalization, the physical therapist greeted him with a walker to help him get out of bed and start the restorative ambulatory procedures. David threw aside the walker, got up, and gingerly walked the periphery of the hospital on his own. The hospital staff dubbed him "Miracle Man."

Indeed it was a miracle. Few survive a potassium level over nine. He was spirited away to the hospital just in time—he had only a ten-minute time frame according to his team of doctors. My husband has a strong will to live. I sent out a prayer request to all my faithful Facebook friends. They shared the request and forwarded it to their friends and churches. I called on God to help save my husband and then there he was, breathing, walking, and on a stable road to recovery.

I am, along with the help of two of the doctors who tended David, now investigating the selling of online drugs and their lack of regulation by the FDA. It will be a long haul to get some remedies for the dispersal of these seemingly innocuous minerals, but I am ready for the fight so that others will not suffer as did my husband. He survived and I survived, albeit with new gray hairs and some additional wrinkles. They are a small price to pay.

Our family became much closer after this harrowing incident in November 2013. We treasure our time together. Reid's girlfriend, Megan, is a member of our household and the comfort, support, and sentiment she showed during this emotional time endeared her to us even more than we had previously cared for her. Reid shouldered responsibility, drove us every day to the hospital, and engaged in heartfelt talks with his dad. They have an especially close bond now. Thank you to my many friends for the good wishes for David's recovery, and thank you, God.

Megan, Reid, David, and I celebrating Reid's twenty-second birthday in San Francisco.

# 60

# Completing the Garment

How did I survive the stigma of child actors and my stereotypical role as Cissy? I not only survived but thrived with a strong understanding of self, a beautiful family, and the impetus to keep the creative juices flowing. I survived jealous slings and conniving bullets. I relied on my higher spirit and a strong foundation. A fan recently told me that having read of the tragedies that befell the other members of the *Family Affair* cast, she wondered how I had escaped. She said it seemed that I was the stability of the show. I thanked her but told her that we all had had our trials, but we also had the courage to overcome and to share our jubilations.

That higher spirit gets one through it. I survived because of the support of my family. I survived because of my God-given intelligence and my determination to keep my head above the most shark-infested theatrical waters. I survived because I have a love affair with life and I greet each new day with optimism, faith, and hope.

Fire, flood, cardiac arrest, child-actor syndrome, loneliness. Whatever the challenges, I believe one can meet them through faith, perseverance, and determination. As Winston Churchill so admirably put it in his address to the students of Harrow School in 1941, "Never give in, never give in, never, never, never—in nothing, great or small, large or petty—never give in except to convictions of honor and good sense."

I take his words to mean never, never, never give up! When times seem the darkest, when you want to throw in the proverbial towel, I believe if you look to a higher good and to that inner light that shines in each of us, you gain momentum and the ability to face whatever challenge there is.

Not all days are great. Sometimes you might say, "I just can't get through this." But as Scarlett O'Hara so aptly proclaimed in the film *Gone with the Wind*, "After all, tomorrow is another day."

Life runs in cycles. Remember those good days, surge forward, advance from where you are, and life can be enjoyed fully every day, even though one must overcome obstacles and fears. We can all not just survive but learn from those obstacles that we have conquered, bathe in the glory of a job well done, and look with hope to a new day.

I survived. I not only survived Cissy but growing up Hollywood. I persevered and prospered. I am happy and hopeful, sustaining just a few "tics" along life's path. I have a few more threads to gather, some loose ends to tie together as the fabric of my life continues to be joyfully woven.

# FILMOGRAPHY

2016 *Love's Last Chance* — Mrs. Johannsen
2016 *The Lovaganza Convoy: Part 1 — Follow Your Sunshine* — Mother Superior
2016 *Sold* — Helen
2105 *Surge of Power: Revenge of the Sequel* — Firestar
2015 *Executive Ranks* — Ms. Jones
2014 *Gabriel Knight: Sins of the Fathers 20th Anniversary Edition* (Video Game) (voice)
2014 *1954 Alcatraz* (Video Game) — Mrs. Mason
2014 *A Blank Slate* (Short) — Diva Left
2014 *Mom, Murder & Me* — Joan
2014 *The Comeback Kids* (TV Series) — CeCe Foster, Agent
— *The Sun Will Come Out Tomorrow* (2014) — CeCe Foster, Agent
2013 *Building a Character* (Short) — Diva
2012 *Hercules Saves Christmas* — Sister Augustus
2012 *Technicolour Llama* — Mrs. Black
2011 *Horrorween* — Zombie
2010 *I (Almost) Got Away with It* (TV Series documentary) — Susan Burnside
— *Got the Wrong Four People Killed* (2010) — Susan Burnside
— *Got Remarried* (2010) — Susan Burnside
2010 *Soupernatural* — Donna
2007 *Black August* — Mary
2005 *Race You to the Bottom* — Spa Owner
2002 *Family Affair* (TV Series) — Beverly
— *Holiday Fever* (2002) — Beverly
2001 *Family Secrets* — Jessica Talmadge
2001 *The Princess Diaries* — Cissy, the Cable Tourist
2001 *Sweet November* — Nurse Amy
2000 *Nash Bridges* (TV Series) — Helen Richards
— *Jump Start* (2000) — Helen Richards
2000 *The Trial of Old Drum* (TV Movie) — Aunt Katey
1999 *Invisible Mom II* (Video) — Ms. Mason
1998 *Where in the World Is Carmen Sandiego* (Video Game) (voice)
1998 *Closer Than the Boy Next Door* — Mrs. Gilliam
1997 *Spider-Man* (TV Series) — Miss America / Madeline Joyce / Gila
— *Six Forgotten Warriors Chapter 5: The Price of Heroism* (1997) — Miss America / Madeline Joyce (voice)

— *Six Forgotten Warriors Chapter 4: The Six Fight Again* (1997) — Miss America / Madeline Joyce (voice)
— *Six Forgotten Warriors Chapter 3: Secrets of the Six* (1997) — Miss America / Madeline Joyce (voice)
— *Partners in Danger Chapter 10: Lizard King* (1997) — Gila (voice)
1996 *The Siege at Ruby Ridge* (TV Movie) — Real Estate Lady
1996 *Invisible Mom* (Video) 1994
1995 *Inherit the Earth: Quest for the Orb* (Video Game) (voice)
1993 *Gabriel Knight: Sins of the Fathers* (Video Game) — Madame Deveraux (voice)
1993 *Tom & Jerry Kids Show* (TV Series)
— *Penthouse Mouse/Twelve Angry Sheep/The Ant Attack* (1993)
1993 *Jojo's Bizarre Adventure* (TV Mini-Series) — School Girl, Enyah (English version, voice)
1989 *Matlock* (TV Series) — Carolyn
— *The Best Seller* (1989) — Carolyn
1989 *Marvin: Baby of the Year* (TV Short) — Jenny Miller (voice)
1983–1988 *Simon & Simon* (TV Series) — Karen Davidson / Joanie
— *Ain't Gonna Get It from Me, Jack* (1988) — Karen Davidson
— *Room 3502* (1983) — Joanie
1988 *The New Yogi Bear Show* (TV Series) — Attendant (voice)
1987 *Superior Court* (TV Series) — Jane
— *Yes, Mother* (1987) — Jane
1986 *New Love, American Style* (TV Series) — Mary
— *Love and the Acting Class* (1986) — Mary
1986 *Chuck Norris: Karate Kommandos* (TV Series) — Pepper
— *Terror Train* (1986) — Pepper (voice)
— *Target: Chuck Norris* (1986) — Pepper (voice)
— *Menace from Space* (1986) — Pepper (voice)
— *Island of the Walking Dead* (1986) — Pepper (voice)
— *Deadly Dolphin* (1986) — Pepper (voice)
1965–1984 *This Is the Life* (TV Series) — Carol / Joyce / Molly /
— *Little Boy Lost* (1984) — Carol
— *Man Adrift* (1966) — Joyce
— *Are You Chicken?* (1965) — Molly
— *Crisis in Hearts* (1965) — Alice
1981–1983 *Spider-Man and His Amazing Friends* (TV Series; 24 episodes) — Firestar / Angelica Jones / Storm
— *Mission: Save the Guardstar* (1983) — Firestar / Angelica Jones (voice)
— *The X-Men Adventure* (1983) — Firestar / Angelica Jones / Storm (voice)
— *Spidey Meets the Girl from Tomorrow* (1983) — Firestar / Angelica Jones (voice)
— *Origin of the Spider-Friends* (1983) — Firestar / Angelica Jones (voice)
— *Attack of the Arachnoid* (1983) — Firestar / Angelica Jones (voice)
1981 *Dennis the Menace in Mayday for Mother* (TV Short) — Alice Mitchell (voice)
1980–1981 *The Fonz and the Happy Days Gang* (TV Series) — Additional Voices
— *Give Me a Hand: Something's Afoot* (1981) — Additional Voices (voice)
— *All This and Timbuktu* (1981) — Additional Voices (voice)

— *Around the World in 80 Ways* (1981) — Additional Voices (voice)
— *Perilous Pauline* (1981) — Additional Voices (voice)
— *There's No Place Like Rome* (1981) — Additional Voices (voice)
1977 *The All-New Super Friends Hour* (TV Series) (voice)
1975 *The Ghost Busters* (TV Series) — Carola de Canterville
— *The Canterville Ghost* (1975) — Carola de Canterville
1971 *Adam-12* (TV Series) — Paula Jessup
— *Pick-up* (1971) — Paula Jessup
1966–1971 *Family Affair* (TV Series; 138 episodes) — Catherine "Cissy" Patterson-Davis
— *You Can't Fight City Hall* (1971) — Catherine "Cissy" Patterson-Davis
— *Buffy's Fair Lady* (1971) — Catherine "Cissy" Patterson-Davis
— *Goodbye, Mrs. Beasley* (1971) — Catherine "Cissy" Patterson-Davis
— *Cinder-Emily* (1971) — Catherine "Cissy" Patterson-Davis
— *The Joiners* (1971) — Catherine "Cissy" Patterson-Davis
1969 *The Big Valley* (TV Series) — Laura Hayden
— *The Royal Road* (1969) — Laura Hayden
1966–1968 *Insight* (TV Series) — Andrea / Hold up victim / Joan
— *Mr. Johnson's Had the Course* (1968) — Andrea
— *A Reason to Live* (1966) — Hold up victim
— *The Oleander Years* (1966) — Joan
1965–1966 *Death Valley Days* (TV Series) — Peggy Conway / Dorita Duncan
— *Lady of the Plains* (1966) — Peggy Conway
— *Magic Locket* (1965) — Dorita Duncan
1966 *The Patty Duke Show* (TV Series) — Monica Robinson
— *Patty, the Psychic* (1966) — Monica Robinson
— *A Visit from Uncle Jed* (1966) — Monica Robinson
— *Patty the Diplomat* (1966) — Monica Robinson
1966 *Ben Casey* (TV Series)
— *In Case of Emergency, Cry Havoc* (1966)
1965 *Dr. Kildare* (TV Series) — Tracey Richards
— *Going Home* (1965) — Tracey Richards
— *The Tent Dwellers* (1965) — Tracey Richards
— *A Gift of Love* (1965) — Tracey Richards
— *Fathers and Daughters* (1965) — Tracey Richards
1965 *Daniel Boone* (TV Series)
— *The Reunion* (1965) — 1965
*The Bing Crosby Show* (TV Series) — Mary Benson
— *The Keefers Come Calling* (1965) — Mary Benson
1965 *Branded* (TV Series) — Ginny Pollard
— *Rules of the Game* (1965) — Ginny Pollard
1964 *Kiss Me, Stupid* — Autograph Seeker
1964 *Mr. Novak* (TV Series)
— *Sparrow on the Wire* (1964)
1963 *The Travels of Jaimie McPheeters* (TV Series) — Pretty Walker
— *The Day of the Pawnees: Part 1* (1963) — Pretty Walker
1961 *The Rifleman* (TV Series) — Amy — Waitress

— *The Queue* (1961) — Amy — Waitress
1958 *This Is Alice* (TV Series; 8 episodes) — Sally
— *Rags to Riches* (1958) — Sally
— *Pig in a Poke* (1958) — Sally
— *Paper Drive* (1958) — Sally
— *Hypnotist* (1958) — Sally
— *Freedom of the Press* (1958) — Sally
1957 *Father Knows Best* (TV Series) — Autograph Seeker
— *Kathy's Big Chance* (1957) — Autograph Seeker
1957 *Panic!* (TV Series) — Charlene
— *Mayday* (1957) — Charlene
1957 *Monkey on My Back* — Noreen
1957 *The Adventures of Jim Bowie* (TV Series) — Simone De Lannes
— *German George* (1957) — Simone De Lannes
1957 *Telephone Time* (TV Series) — Carol Wallace
— *Parents of a Stranger* (1957) — Carol Wallace
1956 *Fury* (TV Series)
— *Joey and the Little League* (1956)
1956 *The Ten Commandments* — Rachel
1956 *The Sheriff of Cochise* (TV Series) — Anita
— *Con Man* — Anita
1956 *The Bad Seed* — Rhoda's Classmate
1956 *Crusader* (TV Series) — Waif
— *The Waif* (1956) — Waif
1955–1956 *The Millionaire* (TV Series) — Betty Murdock / Annabell
— *The Ed Murdock Story* (1956) — Betty Murdock
— *The Mildred Milliken Story* (1955) — Annabell (uncredited)
1955–1956 *Matinee Theatre* (TV Series) — Sally
— *One of the Family* (1956) — Sally
— *See You on Sunday* (1955) — Sally
1955 *My Favorite Husband* (TV Series) — Carolyn
— *The Statue* (1955) — Carolyn
1955 *The Night of the Hunter* — Child
1953 *Our Miss Brooks* (TV Series) — Gina
— *Spare the Rod* (1953) — Gina
1953 *Private Secretary* (TV Series) — Angela
— *Child Labor* (1953) — Angela
1953 *Dave and Charley* (TV Series) — Marlene
— *Uncle Charley* (1953) — Marlene

# *FAMILY AFFAIR* EPISODE GUIDE

## Season 1

| | | | |
|---|---|---|---|
| 1 | 1-01 | 12/Sep/66 | Buffy |
| 2 | 1-02 | 19/Sep/66 | Jody and Cissy |
| 3 | 1-03 | 26/Sep/66 | The Gift Horse |
| 4 | 1-04 | 03/Oct/66 | The Matter of School |
| 5 | 1-05 | 10/Oct/66 | Marmalade |
| 6 | 1-06 | 17/Oct/66 | Room with a Viewpoint |
| 7 | 1-07 | 24/Oct/66 | Mrs. Beasley, Where Are You? |
| 8 | 1-08 | 07/Nov/66 | Who's Afraid of Nural Shpeni? |
| 9 | 1-09 | 14/Nov/66 | A Matter for Experts |
| 10 | 1-10 | 21/Nov/66 | Beware: The Other Woman |
| 11 | 1-11 | 28/Nov/66 | Take Two Aspirin |
| 12 | 1-12 | 05/Dec/66 | Love Me, Love Me Not |
| 13 | 1-13 | 12/Dec/66 | The Thursday Man |
| 14 | 1-14 | 26/Dec/66 | Thick Deep |
| 15 | 1-15 | 02/Jan/67 | Hard Hat Jody |
| 16 | 1-16 | 09/Jan/67 | That Was the Dinner That Wasn't |
| 17 | 1-17 | 16/Jan/67 | All Around the Town |
| 18 | 1-18 | 23/Jan/67 | One for the Little Boy |
| 19 | 1-19 | 30/Jan/67 | Fancy Free |
| 20 | 1-20 | 06/Feb/67 | A Helping Hand |
| 21 | 1-21 | 13/Feb/67 | Once in Love with Buffy |
| 22 | 1-22 | 20/Feb/67 | Ballerina Buffy |
| 23 | 1-23 | 27/Feb/67 | The Mother Tongue |
| 24 | 1-24 | 13/Mar/67 | Everybody Needs Somebody |
| 25 | 1-25 | 20/Mar/67 | The Way It Was |
| 26 | 1-26 | 27/Mar/67 | All Nephews Are Created Equal |
| 27 | 1-27 | 10/Apr/67 | The Prize |
| 28 | 1-28 | 17/Apr/67 | What Did You Do in the West, Uncle? |
| 29 | 1-29 | 01/May/67 | The Award |
| 30 | 1-30 | 15/May/67 | The Butler Method |

## Season 2

| | | | |
|---|---|---|---|
| 31 | 2-01 | 11/Sep/67 | Birds, Bees and Buffy |
| 32 | 2-02 | 18/Sep/67 | First Love |
| 33 | 2-03 | 25/Sep/67 | Go Home, Mr. French |
| 34 | 2-04 | 02/Oct/67 | Arthur, the Invisible Bear |
| 35 | 2-05 | 09/Oct/67 | The Other Cheek |
| 36 | 2-06 | 16/Oct/67 | The Candy Striper |
| 37 | 2-07 | 23/Oct/67 | Fat, Fat, The Water Rat |
| 38 | 2-08 | 06/Nov/67 | The Toy Box |
| 39 | 2-09 | 13/Nov/67 | Take Me Out of the Ball Game |
| 40 | 2-10 | 20/Nov/67 | You Like Buffy Better |
| 41 | 2-11 | 27/Nov/67 | Freddie |
| 42 | 2-12 | 04/Dec/67 | Our Friend Stanley |
| 43 | 2-13 | 11/Dec/67 | Somebody Upstairs |
| 44 | 2-14 | 18/Dec/67 | Star Dust |
| 45 | 2-15 | 25/Dec/67 | Best of the Breed |
| 46 | 2-16 | 01/Jan/68 | Family Reunion |
| 47 | 2-170 | 8/Jan/68 | A Man's Place |
| 48 | 2-18 | 15/Jan/68 | The Great Kow-Tow |
| 49 | 2-19 | 22/Jan/68 | The Fish Watchers |
| 50 | 2-20 | 29/Jan/68 | The Day Nothing Happened |
| 51 | 2-21 | 05/Feb/68 | A House in the Country |
| 52 | 2-22 | 12/Feb/68 | A Matter of Tonsils |
| 53 | 2-23 | 19/Feb/68 | Member of the Family |
| 54 | 2-24 | 26/Feb/68 | His and Hers |
| 55 | 2-25 | 04/Mar/68 | The New Cissy |
| 56 | 2-26 | 11/Mar/68 | The Family Outing |
| 57 | 2-27 | 18/Mar/68 | Mr. French's Holiday |
| 58 | 2-28 | 25/Mar/68 | The Mrs. Beasley Story |
| 59 | 2-29 | 01/Apr/68 | The Baby Sitters |
| 60 | 2-30 | 08/Apr/68 | Family Portrait |

## Season 3

| | | | |
|---|---|---|---|
| 61 | 3-01 | 23/Sep/68 | The Latch Key Kid |
| 62 | 3-02 | 30/Sep/68 | By a Whisker |
| 63 | 3-03 | 07/Oct/68 | A Waltz from Vienna |
| 64 | 3-04 | 14/Oct/68 | Your Friend, Jody |
| 65 | 3-05 | 21/Oct/68 | The Substitute Teacher |
| 66 | 3-06 | 04/Nov/68 | Oliver |
| 67 | 3-07 | 11/Nov/68 | Christmas Came a Little Early |
| 68 | 3-08 | 18/Nov/68 | The Unsound of Music |
| 69 | 3-09 | 02/Dec/68 | Albertine |
| 70 | 3-10 | 09/Dec/68 | A Matter of Choice |
| 71 | 3-11 | 16/Dec/68 | Ciao, Uncle Bill |

| | | | |
|---|---|---|---|
| 72 | 3-12 | 23/Dec/68 | A Nanny for All Seasons |
| 73 | 3-13 | 30/Dec/68 | Family Plan |
| 74 | 3-14 | 06/Jan/69 | To Love with Buffy |
| 75 | 3-15 | 13/Jan/69 | A Family Group |
| 76 | 3-16 | 20/Jan/69 | A Lesson for Grown-Ups |
| 77 | 3-17 | 27/Jan/69 | Oh, To Be in England |
| 78 | 3-18 | 03/Feb/69 | A Matter of Privacy |
| 79 | 3-19 | 10/Feb/69 | Lost in Spain (1) |
| 80 | 3-20 | 17/Feb/69 | Lost in Spain (2) |
| 81 | 3-21 | 24/Feb/69 | Lost in Spain (3) |
| 82 | 3-22 | 03/Mar/69 | A Diller, A Dollar |
| 83 | 3-23 | 10/Mar/69 | The Young Man from Bolivia |
| 84 | 3-24 | 17/Mar/69 | Speak for Yourself, Mr. French |
| 85 | 3-25 | 24/Mar/69 | The Flip Side |
| 86 | 3-26 | 31/Mar/69 | The Matter of Dignity |
| 87 | 3-27 | 07/Apr/69 | Flower Power |
| 88 | 3-28 | 14/Apr/69 | My Man, the Star |

## Season 4

| | | | |
|---|---|---|---|
| 89 | 4-01 | 25/Sep/69 | No Uncle Is an Island |
| 90 | 4-02 | 02/Oct/69 | The Wings of an Angel |
| 91 | 4-03 | 09/Oct/69 | Uncle Prince Charming |
| 92 | 4-04 | 16/Oct/69 | Cissy's Apartment |
| 93 | 4-05 | 23/Oct/69 | The Jody Affair |
| 94 | 4-06 | 30/Oct/69 | With This Ring |
| 95 | 4-07 | 06/Nov/69 | What's Funny About a Broken Leg |
| 96 | 4-08 | 13/Nov/69 | The Birthday Boy |
| 97 | 4-09 | 20/Nov/69 | The Stowaway |
| 98 | 4-10 | 04/Dec/69 | Number One Boy |
| 99 | 4-11 | 11/Dec/69 | A Tale of Two Travels |
| 100 | 4-12 | 18/Dec/69 | Maudie |
| 101 | 4-13 | 25/Dec/69 | Goodbye Harold |
| 102 | 4-14 | 01/Jan/70 | The Girl Graduate |
| 103 | 4-15 | 08/Jan/70 | Grandpa, Sir |
| 104 | 4-16 | 15/Jan/70 | Marooned |
| 105 | 4-17 | 22/Jan/70 | Mr. Osaki's Tree |
| 106 | 4-18 | 29/Jan/70 | The Language of Love |
| 107 | 4-19 | 05/Feb/70 | The Inheritance |
| 108 | 4-20 | 12/Feb/70 | There Goes New York |
| 109 | 4-21 | 19/Feb/70 | Wouldn't It Be Loverly |
| 110 | 4-22 | 26/Feb/70 | The Boys Against the Girls |
| 111 | 4-23 | 05/Mar/70 | The Old Cowhand |
| 112 | 4-24 | 12/Mar/70 | Angel in the Family |
| 113 | 4-25 | 26/Mar/70 | Family in Paradise (1) |
| 114 | 4-26 | 02/Apr/70 | Family in Paradise (2) |

## Season 5

| | | | |
|---|---|---|---|
| 115 | 5-01 | 17/Sep/70 | The Good Neighbors |
| 116 | 5-02 | 24/Sep/70 | Desert Isle, Manhattan Style |
| 117 | 5-03 | 01/Oct/70 | Eastward, Ho! |
| 118 | 5-04 | 08/Oct/70 | Meet Emily |
| 119 | 5-05 | 15/Oct/70 | The Return of Maudie |
| 120 | 5-06 | 22/Oct/70 | It Can't Be Five Years? |
| 121 | 5-07 | 29/Oct/70 | Travels with Cissy |
| 122 | 5-08 | 05/Nov/70 | Stamp of Approval |
| 123 | 5-09 | 12/Nov/70 | And Baby Makes Eight |
| 124 | 5-10 | 19/Nov/70 | Say Uncle |
| 125 | 5-11 | 26/Nov/70 | Class Clown |
| 126 | 5-12 | 03/Dec/70 | The Unsinkable Mr. French |
| 127 | 5-13 | 10/Dec/70 | Wish You Were Here |
| 128 | 5-14 | 17/Dec/70 | Feat of Clay |
| 129 | 5-15 | 31/Dec/70 | Heroes Are Born |
| 130 | 5-16 | 07/Jan/71 | Nobody Here but Us Uncles |
| 131 | 5-17 | 14/Jan/71 | Too Late, Too Soon |
| 132 | 5-18 | 21/Jan/71 | The Littlest Exile |
| 133 | 5-19 | 28/Jan/71 | Put Your Dreams Away |
| 134 | 5-20 | 04/Feb/71 | The Joiners |
| 135 | 5-21 | 11/Feb/71 | Cinder-Emily |
| 136 | 5-22 | 18/Feb/71 | Goodbye, Mrs. Beasley |
| 137 | 5-23 | 25/Feb/71 | Buffy's Fair Lady |
| 138 | 5-24 | 04/Mar/71 | You Can Fight City Hall |

# ACKNOWLEDGMENTS

Where would we be without friends and family!

Many thanks to Fred Anderson, who began my first edit and gave excellent advice on publishing. Kudos to Gerald Maloy, who spent much valuable time in reading the manuscript and then correcting my use of commas and my habit of omitting hyphens for adjectives. Thanks to my writing class who listened with attention, criticism, and laughter to the anecdotes I would bring them. The ever-talented Rick Stasi provided the idea and expertise to make the book cover come alive. Thank you, Rick. Kudos also to the untiring energy and talents of Fred Ascher and Manny Cabachunga for their help and technical guidance in getting photos to the editors on time.

Cary Kozlov, David Shelton, Megan Stafford, and Carolyn Daly were at the ready with words of encouragement for the process as was my brother Lance, who reminded me of some of the adventures I had undertaken and admonished me to be sure and include them in my memoir. My nephew Gregory Garver was firm in his support as were Ken and Marci Kalbfell, Bill and Claudia Gruber, Herbie J Pilato, Dennis and Sheryl Madison Lancaster, Helen Darras, Dr. Fred and Carol Eichelman, and Paul Lisnek. Taylor Trade was wonderful in organizing deadlines and appearances and in supplying me with wonderful editors and support. Thank you Rick Rinehart and your team!

To my agent, Melissa McComas, who guided me through the literary process with humor, aplomb, and sage and invigorating advice, many thanks. Melissa always has the answer to a question at the tip of her tongue or perchance failing that will find it at the tip of a finger click.

And finally to my family, husband David and son Reid, who put up with photos scattered on the floor and my back turned as I clacked on the computer. I love them so very much.